TRANSFORMATIONS AND THEIR USE
IN THE RESOLUTION OF SYNTACTIC HOMOMORPHY

JANUA LINGUARUM

STUDIA MEMORIAE NICOLAI VAN WIJK DEDICATA

edenda curat

SERIES PRACTICA

95

1970

MOUTON

THE HAGUE · PARIS

TRANSFORMATIONS AND THEIR USE IN THE RESOLUTION OF SYNTACTIC HOMOMORPHY

PREPOSITIONAL *OT* CONSTRUCTIONS IN CONTEMPORARY STANDARD RUSSIAN

by

D. BARTON JOHNSON

UNIVERSITY OF CALIFORNIA
SANTA BARBARA

1970
MOUTON
THE HAGUE · PARIS

LIBRARY OF CONGRESS CATALOG CARD NUMBER: 79—118278

PRINTED IN HUNGARY

To Jan

PREFACE

The present work is an investigation of the use of analytic transforms for the resolution of syntactic homomorphy of the sort commonly found in Russian (and English) prepositional constructions. Very briefly, the problem may be posed thusly: the Russian phrases *ključ ot biblioteki* 'key to the library' and *setka ot komarov* 'netting against mosquitoes' are identical in terms of their formal grammatical structure (N *ot* N), but the relational meaning between the two nouns is clearly quite different in the two cases. In the absence of overt formal features paralleling the intuitively obvious differences in relational meaning, structural linguistics relegated such problems to the field of semantics. Transform analysis affords the linguist with a new tool for attacking this problem.

Much of the previous work utilizing analytic transforms on Russian materials has suffered from two serious defects: 1) the absence of a rigorous definition of basic concepts and analytic procedures and 2) the use of an overly diverse body of linguistic data as a corpus. One consequence of the latter is that in cases where transform analysis fails to resolve cases of constructional homomorphy it is often difficult to determine whether the technique itself is inadequate or whether the failure is due to some unrealized qualitative difference in the data under analysis.

The present study tries to eschew both of these shortcomings by carefully defining the basic concepts and procedures and by an exhaustive analysis of a highly restricted body of data. The study focuses on the resolution of the numerous structural homomorphs existing within each of the constructional types N *ot* N, A *ot* N, and V *ot* N. By thus circumscribing the range of material under analysis it is hoped that a clearer picture of the strengths and weaknesses of the analytic technique itself may be obtained.

English glosses have been provided for Russian words and phrases. In some cases, the glosses succeed in giving the reader some approximation of the structural and semantic differences between two or more Russian phrases. For example, the semantic and structural differences of the phrases *utomlen-*

nost' ot žizni and *žizn' utomljaet X* are reflected with reasonable accuracy by the English glosses 'weariness because of life' and 'life wearies X'. Unfortunately, there are a great many cases, probably a majority, where a normal English translation either badly distorts or completely fails to reflect the differences existing between the Russian phrases. For example, the phrases *ključ škafa, ključ ot škafa,* and *škafnyj ključ* would normally all be rendered into English as 'the cupboard key'. Cases of this sort present the alternatives of either ignoring the structural distinctions inherent in the Russian or of using nonstandard and/or highly artificial English in the phrase glosses. Since our interest is structural rather than literary, the latter course is taken. Consequently the above examples are translated as 'the cupboard's key' *(ključ škafa)*, 'key to the cupboard' *(ključ ot škafa)*, and 'cupboard key' *(škafnyj ključ)*. For the convenience of the reader, an attempt has been made, where possible, to oppose Russian homomorphs by means of distinctive English translations. Thus most Russian examples of the type *ključ ot biblioteki* 'key to the library' are translated as 'X *to* Y'; those of the type *butylka ot vina* 'bottle for wine' as 'X *for* Y', *etc.*, although non-contrasting translations such as 'library key' and 'wine bottle' are equally possible. There are, however, many cases where such a neat opposition in terms of translation is, unfortunately, not possible.

The present work is a somewhat revised version of the writer's doctoral dissertation which was submitted in the Department of Slavic Languages and Literatures at the University of California, Los Angeles. The writer wishes to express his appreciation to the members of his doctoral committee for their suggestions and comments on the work in its earlier form. Particular thanks are the due of D. S. Worth, who was chairman of the doctoral committee. Needless to say, any deficiencies are the sole responsibility of the author. Finally, the writer owes a major debt of gratitude to his wife, Jan, who typed the manuscript four times and performed the myriad of clerical and editorial chores associated with such an undertaking.

TABLE OF CONTENTS

LIST OF TABLES

LIST OF ABBREVIATIONS

A	Adjective
CS	Common Slavic
CSR	Contemporary Standard Russian
N	Noun
Nn, g, d, a, i, p	N in nominative, genitive, dative, accusative, instrumental, or prepositional case
Nsb, ob, dp	Subject noun, object noun, dependent noun
OR	Old Russian
P	Preposition
Q	Adverb
T	Transformation or transform
TA	Transformation Analysis
TG	Transformational Grammar
V	Verb
Vø, sja, t	1) ø—unmarked intransitive *begat'*, 2) *sja*—marked intransitive *kolebat'sja*, 3) t—transitive *bit'*
Vpa, pp, ppp	1) pa — active participle, 2) pp — passive participle, 3) ppp —past passive participle
X, Y	Any syntactic elements occurring in the transform but not in the source phrase, *e.g.*, T: *osvoboždenie ot gneta* → *X osvoboždaet Y ot gneta*
( )	Optional (deletable) elements
→	Transforms to
←	Transforms from
↔	Are transforms of each other
$\sqrt{}$	Root
	Superscript numbers indicate the same lexeme on both sides of the arrow.
	Superscript letters indicate the part of speech of the word from which the indicated item is derived.
	Both of these usages are illustrated in the following example:

$$N^1 \text{ ot } N^2 \rightarrow N^2_{sb} \quad V^{n1}$$

svet ot fonarja → *fonar' svetit*

1

INTRODUCTION

In Russian the burden of the expression of syntactic relationships falls upon the highly developed inflectional system. Within this inflectional framework, however, an increasing proportion of syntactic relationships is expressed by analytic prepositional constructions.[1] That is, the rather gross spectrum of meanings expressed by the morphological devices of the language is segmented and refined by the use of prepositions.

This latter situation is particularly clearly illustrated by the genitive case, which bears a very heavy functional load — both semantically and grammatically. The immense semantic load of the genitive is reflected by R. O. Jakobson's definition of it as the case that " . . . indicates the limit of the participation of a designated object in the substantive content of the utterance."[2] The grammatical load borne by the genitive case is indicated in part by the fact that it accounts for over 36 per cent of oblique noun usages in CSR.[3]

The proportion of these occurrences of the genitive case that involve prepositions is not known but is doubtless quite substantial. According to a recent frequency count, 10 of the 40 most common words in the written language were prepositions; of these, 4 *(s, u, iz, ot)* are followed by the genitive case.[4] The work load of primary prepositions in Russian is also very great. As the preceding statistics indicate, their frequency is extremely high and, like that

[1] V. V. Vinogradov, *Russkij jazyk: grammatičeskoe učenie o slove* (Moscow—Leningrad, 1947), 167–8 and 695–700.

[2] Roman O. Jakobson, "Beitrag zur allgemeinen Kasuslehre: Gesamtbedeutungen der russischen Kasus", *Travaux du Cercle Linguistique du Prague*, VI (1936), 240. The Russian genitive, in addition to the semantic load inherited from the IE genitive, has also taken over the meanings of the IE ablative; André Vaillant, *Grammaire comparée des langues slaves: Morphologie, II*, Part 1, "Flexion nominale" (Paris, 1958), 22.

[3] E. A. Štejnfel'dt, *Častotnyj slovar' sovremennogo russkogo literaturnogo jazyka* (Tallin, 1963), 52. The distribution of the cases in CSR exclusive of proper names is: N — 28.3%, G — 26.0%, D — 5.0%, A — 21.8%, I — 8.6%, and P — 10.3%.

[4] *Ibid.*, 95. Of the next 25 prepositions (in terms of their relative frequency), 16 occur in conjunction with the genitive case (pp. 217–8).

of the case suffixes, their grammatical meaning is very general. Vinogradov in his *Russkij jazyk* gives an incomplete list of 21 types of grammatical relations expressed by prepositions.[5] No less than 13 of these relational groupings involve the genitive case: 1) spatial — *ot;* 2) temporal — *ot;* 3) comitative — *promeždu;* 4) ablative — *ot;* 5) transgressive — *iz;* 6) possessive — *u;* 7) genetic — *ot;* 8) contrastive — *protiv;* 9) modal — *s;* 10) goal — *dlja;* 11) causal — *ot;* 12) instrumental — *do;* 13) deliberative — *naščet.* Thus it can be seen that the spectrum of meaning expressed by prepositions 'taking' the genitive case is scarcely less wide than that of the case itself.[6]

Taken together, the wide range of grammatical meaning displayed by the genitive case and by prepositions associated with it results in a very high degree of ambiguity in Russian constructions of the type N, A or V plus PN_g. Even within the limits imposed by a single P, the inherent ambiguity is still very great. The extent of this grammatical ambiguity is reflected in the following examples:

N	ot N		
1. *židkost'*	*ot klopov*	—	'liquid against bedbugs'
2. *ključ*	*ot škafa*	—	'key to the cupboard'
3. *utomlennost'*	*ot žizni*	—	'weariness because of life'
4. *osvoboždenie*	*ot gneta*	—	'liberation from oppression'

A	ot N		
1. *mokryj*	*ot slez*	—	'wet because of tears'
2. *dalekij*	*ot goroda*	—	'far from town'
3. *zavisimyj*	*ot druzej*	—	'dependent on friends'
4. *slepoj*	*ot detstva*	—	'blind since childhood'

V	ot N		
1. *otplyvat'*	*ot berega*	—	'to swim out from the shore'
2. *otvyknut'*	*ot kurenija*	—	'to get out of the habit of smoking'
3. *nabuxnut'*	*ot syrosti*	—	'to swell because of dampness'
4. *isxodit'*	*ot morja*	—	'to issue from the sea'

From the formal point of view, each of the four examples in the above three sets is identical with the remaining three. Each unit consists of a head word (N, A, or V) plus the preposition *ot* plus a dependent noun in the genitive case. On the semantic level, however, the relationship between the head word and

[5] Vinogradov, 685–9.

[6] The complicated question of the relationship between the preposition and the case ending of the dependent noun will not be discussed here. The interested reader can find a survey of this matter in A. V. Isačenko, *Die Russische Sprache der Gegenwart*, Part 1, "Formenlehre" (Halle, 1962), 549–54. Also see H. C. Sørenson, *Studies on Case in Russian* (Copenhagen, 1957), 84–96.

the dependent noun of each of the four examples within each set is understood quite differently from that of the remaining three. This is quite independent of the lexical meaning of the particular words involved.[7]

The type of grammatical ambiguity represented in the above sets of examples falls within the context of the more general linguistic problem of constructional homonymity. The term *constructional homonymity* is used in the present work in a somewhat broader sense than is usually the case. According to Chomsky "... we have a case of *constructional homonymity* when a given phoneme sequence is analyzed in more than one way on one level."[8] The most striking examples of this phenomenon are those referred to as absolute constructional homonyms, *e.g.*, "the shooting of the hunters".[9] In cases of this sort the homonymy is both syntactic and semantic. A second type of ambiguity is represented by pairs of the type: 1) "the growling of lions", 2) "the raising of flowers".[10] On the level of phrase structure, both of these share a single representation *(the — V — ing — of NP)*, but they are none the less understood quite differently. In order to account for this difference, we must move from the phrase structure level to the transformational level. At this new, higher level the homonymy is automatically explained in terms of the differing derivational histories of the two phrases. The first, "the growling of lions" derives from an underlying kernel "lions growl"; the second, "the raising of flowers" derives from "X raises flowers". For our purpose, pairs of this type, which share the same morphological pattern but which are differently understood, will also be considered as constructional homonyms of each other.

The homomorphic examples given within each of the above three Russian constructional types display the same type of constructional homonymity as we observe in the case of Chomsky's 1) "the growling of lions" and 2) "the raising of flowers". Compare, for example, the Russian phrase *utomlennost' ot žizni* 'weariness because of life' and *osvoboždenie ot gneta* 'liberation from oppression'. Here too, on the phrase structure level the examples have the same representation (N^1 *ot* N^2). It is only by going into the derivational histories of the two units that we can account for the intuitively felt differences between them. Transformationally, the first of these examples *(utomlennost' ot žizni)* derives from an underlying *žizn' utomljaet X* 'life wearies somebody' while the second *(osvoboždenie ot gneta)* stems from *X osvoboždaet Y ot gneta* 'some one frees somebody from oppression'.

[7] This assertion can be easily demonstrated by the fact that a great many lexical items can be substituted for the head word and the dependent noun with full preservation of the original relationship between the two units, *cf. židkost' ot klopov* 'liquid against bedbugs' and *poroški ot nervov* 'powders against nerves' or *otvyknut' ot kurenija* 'to get out of the habit of smoking' and *otdyxat' ot raboty* 'to rest from work'.

[8] Noam Chomsky, *Syntactic Structures* (The Hague, 1957), 86.

[9] *Ibid.*, p. 88.

[10] *Loc. cit.*

The present study constitutes an investigation of the utility of analytic transformations in the resolution of syntactic homomorphy. The analytic technique is examined in its application to multiply ambiguous homomorphic *ot* constructions in contemporary standard Russian.

The term transformation has been used in various ways by various linguists. Before proceeding to a description of the organization of the analysis, it is necessary to make a distinction between the transformational method or transformational analysis and generative grammar.

The concept of linguistic transformation was first evolved by Zellig Harris, who describes it as follows: "If two or more constructions (or sequences of constructions) which contain the same n classes (whatever else they may contain) occur with the same n-tuples of members of these classes in the same sentence environment . . . , we say that the constructions are transforms of each other, and that each may be derived from any other of them by a particular transformation."[11] The definition is illustrated by the constructions N V v N (a sentence) and N*s* V*ing* N (a noun phrase) which share the same *triples* of N, V, N *(he, meet, we; foreman, put up, list)*. Thus any choice of members found in the sentence may also be found in the corresponding phrase: *he met us — his meeting us; the foreman put the list up — the foreman's putting the list up.*[12] In spite of a certain amount of leeway in the degree of equivalence which two constructions must satisfy to qualify as transforms of each other, Harris has a very narrow interpretation of the requirement that their sentence environments be the same.[13] Such pairs as N V*ed* *(the cliff crumbled)* and N *will* V *(the cliff will crumble)* are excluded on the grounds that while the two may be transformationally related in the cited form, they will differ in their more distant co-occurrents, *e.g.*, *the cliff crumbled yesterday* but *the cliff will crumble tomorrow*. A second reason for excluding such pairs is that *-ed/will* seems to display a greater differential in meaning than is usual for transformations. This last brings us to Harris' rather tentatively expressed requirement that two constructions that are transforms of each other " . . . seem to hold invariant what might be interpreted as the information content".[14]

Noam Chomsky has adopted the concept of transformation and set it within the context of a generative grammar. In this setting the term *transformation* is assigned a much more specialized meaning. In Chomsky's system a transformation is a particular type of re-write rule that operates on the terminal strings generated by the phrase structure part of the grammar.[15]

[11] Zellig S. Harris, "Co-occurrence and Transformation in Linguistic Structure", *Language*, XXXIII, (1957), 288.

[12] *Loc. cit.*

[13] *Ibid.*, p. 289.

[14] *Ibid.*, p. 290.

[15] Chomsky, p. 44.

Robert B. Lees, although utilizing transformations in the realm of word formation rather than sentence structure, has adopted the Chomskian formulation. In addition, he has specifically dealt with the provenience of the elements in the transform. In his view, the elements of the transform must represent symbols specified in the source phrase, that is, new elements cannot be arbitrarily introduced. A partial exception is reluctantly allowed to this rule in that there are "... unfortunately ... cases where new structures appear to be created by the transformation de novo and are thus of unspecified provenience".[16] This last is illustrated by the occurrence of the preposition *by* in the passive transform *(John was taken by Mary ← Mary takes John)*.[17]

Both Harris and Chomsky see transformation as a type of process that operates upon a limited number of kernel sentences and that permits the enumeration of all of the more complex utterances of the language in question. The grammar is synthetic and hence speaker-oriented. It has been pointed out by Lees that one of the weaknesses of transformational grammar is that it is a purely synthetic process and does not provide for the analysis of utterances, *i.e.*, it does not account for grammar from the hearer's point of view.[18]

This gap has been filled in part by a number of studies by linguists who have used transformations as purely analytic devices.[19] One of the major claims of generative grammar is that it provides a rigorous explanation for cases of constructional homonymity. It is precisely this feature of generative grammar that has been drawn upon by linguists in their efforts to describe intuitively understood relational differences existing in a single morphological framework, *i.e.*, just the sort of problem as that posed above in connection with Russian *ot* constructions.

[16] Robert B. Lees, *The Grammar of English Nominalizations* (Bloomington, Indiana, Research Center in Anthropology, Folklore, and Linguistics, 1960), 31.

[17] *Ibid.*, 31–2.

[18] Robert B. Lees, review of Noam Chomsky, *Syntactic Structures* (The Hague, 1957), *Language*, XXXIII (1957), 404.

[19] The most important of these in regard to Slavic are: A. V. Isačenko, "Transformacionnyj analiz kratkix i polnyx prilagatel'nyx", *Issledovanija po strukturnoj tipologii*, ed. T. N. Mološnaja (Moscow, 1963), 61–93; M. Ivič, "Jedan problem slovenske sintagmatike osvetljen transformacionim metodom (grammatička uloga morfeme *se* u serbskoxrvatskom jeziku)", *Južnoslovenski filolog*, XXV (1961/62), 137–51; F. Papp, "Transformacionnyj analiz russkix prisubstantivnyx konstrukcij s zavisimoj čast'ju — suščestvitel'nym", *Slavica*, I, ed. B. Sulan (1961), 55–83; R. Ružička, "O transformacionnom opisanii tak nazyvaemyx bezličnyx predloženij v sovremennom russkom literaturnom jazyke", *Voprosy jazykoznanija* (1963), 3, 22–31; H. Walter, "Die Struktur der Reflexiven Verben in der modernen bulgarischen Literatursprache", *Zeitschrift für Slawistik*, VIII (1963), 793–806; Dean S. Worth, "Transform Analysis of Russian Instrumental Constructions", *Word*, XIV (1958), 247–90.

It is of particular importance to stress that transform analysis is a procedure that is entirely independent of transformational or generative grammar.[20] Hence, the validity (or invalidity) of TA as an investigative technique is in no way contingent upon the well-foundedness of generative grammar. This independence of TA from TG has another important consequence. The rigid restraints that are necessarily imposed upon transformations in generative grammars do not necessarily apply to analytic transformations used outside of the generative context.[21] It might be noted, however, that the independence of the two procedures does not preclude the borrowing of certain concepts from the generative realm for use in connection with analytic transformations. Indeed, their insightfulness in the generative context is precisely what makes these ideas of interest for analytic use. One of the most striking claims that has been made for transformational grammar is that it may provide a key to formal semantic analysis through the explication of syntax.[22] This assertion assumes particular importance in connection with the use of analytic transformations to resolve constructional homonymity.

The use of analytic transformations to resolve the multiple ambiguity of constructions of the type X *ot* N (where X stands for any N, A, or V heading the construction) represents a formal effort to explicate the intuitively understood semantic relations within a single constructional framework in terms of the syntactic properties of the particular lexemes involved. In the case of Russian, this use of syntactic analysis to formalize semantic relational groupings draws upon still another linguistic level — that of derivational morphology. This arises from the fact that many of the transformations used in our investigation involve changes in the derivational structures of the lexemes as well as the inflectional and syntactic changes. Thus, in the case of the two homomorphs already cited, *utomlennost' ot žizni* 'weariness because of life' and *osvoboždenie ot gneta* 'liberation from oppression', their transforms, *žizn' utomljaet X* 'life wearies someone' and *X osvoboždaet Y ot gneta* 'someone frees somebody from oppression', involve not only alterations of syntactic patterns and inflectional endings but also changes of certain words from one part of speech to another. The possibility or impossibility of such interclass derivational

[20] In spite of the almost synonymous use of the terms *transformational* and *generative* grammar, it is quite possible to construct a generative grammar without transformations and conversely to have a grammar using transformation, but which is not generative in its orientation. See Dean S. Worth, "Ob otobraženii linejnyx otnošenij v poroždajuščix modeljax jazyka", *Voprosy jazykoznanija*, 5 (1964), 46–58.

[21] This is not to say that analytic transforms should not be subject to rigid constraints, but rather that these constraints are not necessarily the same as those imposed within TG.

[22] This point is given particular emphasis by Harris, Chomsky, and Lees. See, for example: Harris, 339–40; Chomsky, 102; and particularly Lees, *The Grammar of English Nominalizations*, xvi.

transformations proves to be of prime importance to the analysis. Our investigation shows that for X *ot* N units there is a close-knit tie between the formal features of derivational constituency, syntactic co-occurrence privileges, and the different semantic classes within morphologically identical constructions. Thus, the study falls into a border area where three linguistic levels converge — syntax, derivational morphology, and semantics.

The interdependence of analytic transformations and derivational morphology at the constructional level is most strikingly demonstrated by the fact that the limits of their utility as analytic classificatory devices are largely coterminous. In the analysis of nominal units (N *ot* N, A *ot* N), the close relationship between overt derivational features and transform potential is readily apparent. Thus the fact that *otklonenie ot zakona* 'deviation from the law' and *utomlennost' ot truda* 'weariness because of labor' are identical in their grammatical form while different in the type of semantic relation prevailing between N^1 and N^2 may be accounted for both on the lower level of derivational morphology and on the higher transformational level. On the derivational level it is obvious that the relational differences between N^1 and N^2 in the two examples are, in some way, correlated with the fact that *otklonenie* is directly derived from the transitive verb *otklonit* 'to deviate'; whereas *utomlennost'*, also a deverbal, is a step further removed from the transitive verb *utomit'* 'to weary' in that an intermediate stage in the derivational chain must be posited, *i.e.*, the passive participle *utomlennyj* 'wearied'. On the transformational level these static derivational acts are utilized in a much more insightful and dynamic way: *otklonenie ot zakona* differs from *utomlennost' ot truda* in that the former may be viewed as a transform of *otklonit' ot zakona* 'to deviate from the law', whereas the latter stems from the very different construction *trud utomit X* 'labor wearies X'. Thus the transformational process is intimately connected with the derivational constituency of the lexemes. The cases in which analytic transforms successfully discriminate among homomorphs are those in which the derivational constituency of the lexemes is discernible. Generally speaking, the constituency of Russian nominal constructions is reasonably transparent, at least in gross outline.

In the verbal construction (V *ot* N), on the other hand, it is not infrequently the case that neither derivational nor transformational features can be found that will formally oppose homomorphs. Thus in the examples *drožat' ot otca* 'to tremble because of father' and *slyšat' ot otca* 'to hear from father' the intuitively obvious semantic difference in the relationship between V and N does not appear to be correlated with any formal differences on either the derivational or the transformational levels. In sum, interclass transformations are usually possible where overt derivational features are present and conversely where such features are lacking, the transforms are usually not possible. This correlation finds support in the situation just described, *i.e.*, analytic transforms are highly effective in discriminating among nominal homomorphs where the derivational structure lies relatively close to the surface; the transforms are considerably less effective for verbal constructions where the derivational structure in most cases lies much deeper below the surface.

The study has the following organizational framework. Russian constructions involving the preposition *ot* occur with three major types of grammatical heads: nouns, adjectives, and verbs. The three following chapters treat these three constructional types. The analytic sections of each chapter are prefaced by a list of the transformations used therein together with examples of their operation. There is also a schematic listing of the homomorphic semantic groups that are formally isolated and characterized by means of the transformations. The major portion of each chapter presents and discusses the transformationally defined semantic groups contained within the construction type being treated. The discussion of each semantic group commences with a table listing all of the examples of the group in question along with their transformational specifications. The accompanying discussion generally falls into three parts: 1) a discussion of the transformations that specify the group, 2) a description of the derivational features that characterize the examples, and 3) a brief statement of the semantic features that unite the examples of the group. Basic definitions and procedures are set forth in the course of the first chapter and in particular in the initial part of the 'analysis' section thereof.

It is hoped that this detailed mapping of the underlying syntactic and derivational correlates of the various semantic relations subsumed within the constructions N^1 *ot* N^2, A *ot* N, and V *ot* N will prove to be of value in the analysis of Russian prepositional constructions in general. In a wider context, it is hoped that the analysis presented herein may not be without value as a contribution toward the solution of the general linguistic problem of syntactic homomorphy.

2

TRANSFORM ANALYSIS OF N^1 *ot* N^2 CONSTRUCTIONS

2.1. INTRODUCTION

This chapter examines the problem of formally isolating and characterizing the several semantic subgroups to be found within the construction N^1 *ot* N^2. The first part of the chapter is devoted to an examination of the treatment of the problem by three representatives of what may be termed the traditional school. This includes brief surveys of the views of A. A. Šaxmatov, A. M. Peškovskij, and of the scholars who contributed to the recent grammar put out by the Soviet Academy of Sciences.[1] Also examined are two more specialized traditional studies of the *causal* use of the preposition *ot*.

The second part consists of a discussion of two transformationally oriented studies that have been made of Russian word-combinations including the N^1 *ot* N^2 construction. Following this, the views of Zellig S. Harris, the only American transformationalist who has treated prepositional constructions, are examined from the point of view of their theoretical and practical implications for the analysis of Russian prepositional constructions.

The final and major portion of the chapter presents an original transform analysis of the N^1 *ot* N^2 construction. The results of this investigation are set forth and discussed in ten sections. A survey of the results concludes the chapter.

2.2. SURVEY OF LITERATURE

2.2.1. *Traditional treatments*

The problem of homonymy within the morphological structure N^1 *ot* N^2 is treated only implicitly by traditional Russian grammars. The existence of widely differing types of relational meanings within the construction is tacitly

[1] Akademija Nauk SSSR, Institut jazykoznanija, *Grammatika russkogo jazyka*, 2 vols. (Moscow, 1954; 2nd ed. 1960). The work on nominal word-combinations is credited to V. A. Belošapkova, II, 1, 3. Henceforth referred to as the *Academy Grammar* in the text and as *AG* in footnote citations.

recognized by listing the various semantic categories (spatial, temporal, causal, *etc.)* into which different examples are thought to fall. No definition is given either of the semantic categories or of the procedure whereby an example is assigned to them. Few of the older Russian grammarians even speculate about formal reasons for the intuitively felt differences in meaning among examples of the N^1 *ot* N^2 construction.

Šaxmatov, in his monumental but uncompleted *Sintaksis russkogo jazyka,*[2] offers a typical analysis of the N^1 *ot* N^2 construction. Prepositional constructions, which are treated under the heading of relative complementation *(reljativnoe dopolnenie)* in the section on "Word-Combinations", are examined on the basis of the part of speech of the head word and then alphabetically by the preposition. The classification for N^1 *ot* N^2 is as follows:[3]

1. a) *Nu-s, a na drugoj že den' . . . k večeru, ja xitrym obmanom, kak tat' v nošči, poxitil u Kateriny Ivanovny ot sunduka ee ključ.*
'Well, but on the very next day . . . toward evening, I with cunning deception, like a thief in the night, stole from Katerina Ivanovna the key to her trunk'.

 b) *Dlinnye kosye luči ot okon, samaja temnota sten i svodov — vse govorilo ego serdcu.*
'The long slanting rays from the windows, the very darkness of the walls and arches — all spoke to his heart'.

 c) *Gde-to upala na kamen' čajnaja ložka, i zvuk polučilsja čistyj, kak by ot kolokol'čika.*
'Somewhere a teaspoon fell on stone and the sound was pure as if from a little bell'.

2. *V čisle ètix pisem bylo pis'mo ot Nikolaja Rostova k otcu.*
'Among these letters was a letter from Nikolaj Rostov to his father'.

3. a) *Vot tol'ko i rečej ot orla ot moego — tae tae, a čto tae — sam ne znaeš'.*
'Here there are only speeches from my eagle — tae, tae, but what tae [means] — nobody knows'.

 b) *Anatol' Kuragin totčas polučil naznačenie ot voennogo ministra i uexal v Moldavskuju armiju.*
'Anatol' Kuragin immediately received an appointment from the war minister and went to the Moldavian army'.

 c) *Už ne ždut li napadenija ot kirgizcev?*
'Don't they really expect an attack from the Kirghiz?'

[2] A. A. Šaxmatov, *Sintaksis russkogo jazyka,* 2nd ed. (Leningrad, 1941). Photomechanic reprint (The Hague, 1963).

[3] *Ibid.*, 361–2. Number and letter divisions supplied by the writer. The numbers correspond to Šaxmatov's paragraph divisions and the letters to the number of the examples in the paragraph.

4. *Bab doroga — ot peči do poroga.*
'Womens' road — from the stove to the threshold'.
5. *Ja predpočel prosit' o uvol'nenii menja ot ministerstva.*
'I preferred to ask about my release from the Ministry'.
6. a) *Ober-kamerger graf F. V. Rostopčin zastupil mesto Fel'dmaršala grafa Gudoviča i pereimenovan ot armii generalom.*
'Ober Kamerherr Graf F. V. Rostopčin replaced Field Marshal Graf Gudovič and was renamed General of the Army'.
b) *Mesto ego zastupil Aleksandr Andreevič Beklešov, byvšij dejstvitel'nyj tajnyj sovetnik i senator, potom ot armii general i kievskij voennyj gubernator.*
'A. A. Beklešov, former active Privy Counselor and Senator, later General of the Army and Kiev military governor, took his place'.

There seems to be a good deal of diversity of relational meanings within the groups. Note, for example, 1a) *(ključ ot sunduka* 'key to the trunk') versus b) *(luči ot okon* 'rays from the windows') and c) *(zvuk ot kolokol'čika* 'sound from a little bell'). A more unified semantic grouping is found in the first edition of the work which lists 1b) and c) together with 2 *(pis'mo ot Nikolaja* 'letter from Nikolaj') as a single group.[4] Examples 3b) *(naznačenie of ministra* 'appointment from the minister') and c) *(napadenie ot kirgizcev* 'attack from the Kirghiz') are also listed as a separate group. This earlier set of groupings yields a set of semantic categories much more in harmony with the usual classification system.

Šaxmatov himself realized the inadequacy of his treatment of prepositions and in an extended comment appended to the section on relative complementation observed that the analysis of the prepositions should have been placed under the general heading of the "Syntax of the Parts of Speech" rather than that of "Word-Combinations".[5] The new plan called for studying them in conjunction with the part of speech which serves as the head word and then in terms of a priori relational categories. That is, all NPN constructions expressing causal relations would be treated, then those expressing ablative relations and so on. The revised analytic procedure is essentially the one adopted by V. V.

[4] A. A. Šaxmatov, *Sintaksis russkogo jazyka: učenie o predloženii i o slovosočetanijax*, Vypusk pervyj (Leningrad, 1925), 359. Both this and the 1941 edition were edited by E. S. Istrina from Šaxmatov's incomplete manuscript. In her postscript (435–437) to the first edition, Istrina notes that the manuscript contained many incorrectly placed examples. Where these mistakes were of a formal nature, Istrina reassigned the examples to the proper subheading. In cases where formal grounds were lacking, questionable examples were left in place. In her foreword to the second edition, Istrina reports that small changes in the ordering of examples were made (16).

[5] Šaxmatov, 2nd ed., 552–3.

Vinogradov in his treatment of prepositions in his *Russkij jazyk*.[6] Since classification in terms of semantic categories is the basis of both systems, they are equally unsatisfactory from the formal point of view.

The most striking feature of Šaxmatov's treatment is that the problem of the multiple ambiguity displayed by examples of the N^1 *ot* N^2 group is never explicitly noted. Its existence is noted only implicitly in that he subdivides the examples into *appropriate* semantic categories which are taken as given. No attention is directed to why a given example falls into a particular category.

A. M. Peškovskij gives only a very cursory survey of nominal prepositional constructions which he treats together with N^1 N_{dp} combinations.[7] These are treated under the general heading of "Secondary Members of the Sentence". N N_{dp} and NPN constructions are divided into two categories.[8] The first category consists of examples in which the head noun governs either the same case or preposition plus case as 1) its cognate verb: *mščen'e vragu* 'vengeance on the enemy' = *mšču vragu* '[I] take vengeance on the enemy', or 2) a verb similar in meaning to the head noun: *nastojčivost' v trebovanijax* 'insistence in [one's] demands' = *uporstvovat' v trebovanijax* 'to persist in [one's] demands', or 3) a verb frequently found in word-combinations with the same head word: *bereza na kraju ovraga zavjala* 'the birch withered at the edge of the ravine' = *bereza rastet na kraju ovraga* 'the birch grows at the edge of the ravine'. It is noted that these types are not basically nominal, but transfers from verbal constructions and should be studied from the point of view of their degree of relatedness to verbal constructions. The second category consists of those cases not covered by the three subcategories above, *i.e.*, which are not in any way parallel to verbal constructions.

It is clear that Peškovskij anticipates that most of the NPN constructions will fall in the above category, especially in view of the very vague non-formal nature of its second and third subdivisions. According to these, if it is possible to find a verbal paraphrase for a NPN construction, the latter is reclassified as an example of a VPN construction. Since almost any nominal construction can be loosely paraphrased by a verbal expression, Peškovskij, in effect, simply transfers the problem of classifying the different semantic groups of N^1 *ot* N^2 to the V *ot* N constructional type. Under this new heading, however, the classification is largely semantic and intuitive. Again, no explicit awareness of the problem of structural ambiguity in prepositional constructions is manifested. This is somewhat surprising in view of the fact that Peškovskij makes relatively heavy use of formal, semi-formal, and even transformational criteria in the

[6] V. V. Vinogradov, *Russkij jazyk: grammatičeskoe učenie o slove* (Moscow–Leningrad, 1947), 685–91.

[7] A. M. Peškovskij, *Russkij sintaksis v naučnom osveščenii*, 7th ed. (Moscow, 1956), 321–6.

[8] *Ibid.*, 321–2.

similar problem of sorting out the different semantic groups subsumed within the N N_g construction.[9] For example, the possessive genitive of the type *dom otca* 'house of the father' is formally characterized by its equivalence to the possessive adjective form *otcov dom* 'the father's house' and to the periphrastic *u otca dom* 'father has a house'. The attributive genitive *trubka mira* 'pipe of peace' is formally characterized by the attributive adjectival form *mirnaja trubka* 'peace pipe'.

The recent grammar of the Soviet Academy of Sciences[10] provides the fullest description of the N^1 *ot* N^2 construction to be found in any general grammar.[11] Following Peškovskij's model, N^1 *ot* N^2 constructions are divided into two basic categories. The first includes all examples whose head nouns are in no way, either derivationally or semantically, connected with a verb. These examples express attributive relations. The second category consists of those examples wherein N^1 is verb related. These express objective relations. The two major categories with their relational subgroups present the following picture:[12]

I. *Attributive relations*
   1. Separative relations: *skorlupa ot orexov* 'shell from nuts'
   2. Relations of origin: *nasledstvo ot otca* 'inheritance from father'
   3. Causal-consequential relations: *slezy ot vostorga* 'tears because of rapture'
   4. Designational relations: *setka ot komarov* 'netting against mosquitos'
   5. Attributive-temporal relations: *pis'mo ot p'jatogo marta* 'letter of the 5th of March'

II. *Objective relations*
   1. N^1 — derivationally related to a verb: *otkaz ot ošibok* 'repudiation of mistakes'
   2. N^1 — semantically related to a verb: *doroga ot pristani* 'road from the dock'
      (often supplemented by *do* or $k + N^3$)

This semantic-relational description is supplemented by an ontological description stating the kinds of things N^1 or N^2 refer to in each relational category. For example, "In word combinations expressing *separative* relations there is named an object separated from another object with which it is connected or

[9] *Ibid.*, 322–3.

[10] *AG*, II, 1, 250–2.

[11] The most complete enumeration of the different meanings of *ot* constructions is contained in Vol. VIII of the *Slovar' sovremennogo russkogo literaturnogo jazyka*, 17 vols. (Moscow–Leningrad, Akademija Nauk SSSR, Institut russkogo jazyka 1950/65). There are six major categories and twenty-one subdivisions. The criteria of grouping are entirely semantic or relational and disregard the part of speech of the head word. Henceforth cited as *Slovar' sovremennogo russkogo literaturnogo jazyka*.

[12] *AG*, II, 1, 250–1.

of which it previously constitued a part, *e.g.*: *kryška ot čajnika* ['lid to the teapot'], *ručka ot dveri* ['handle to the door']".[13]

Both Peškovskij and the *Academy Grammar* represent advances over Šaxmatov's incomplete sketch in that derivational evidence is used as the basis for a gross subdivision. Both of the former largely vitiate this limited use of formal criteria by the inclusion of semantic criteria which are not subject to objective verification, at least within the framework of traditional grammar. Indeed, neither source appears to feel that such a requirement is either feasible or necessary. The qualification of the derivationally based subdivision by criteria such as "semantically connected with a verb" or "naming a spatial concept" places the classificational system beyond the limits of formal investigation. Apart from these theoretical problems the *Academy Grammar* system is internally contradictory since the verbal derivation of *nasledstvo ot otca* 'inheritance from father' and *pis'mo ot p'jatogo marta* 'letter of the fifth of March', which are in the nonverbal-related first group, is readily apparent *(nasledovat'* 'to inherit' and *pisat'* 'to write').

In addition to the general treatment of *ot* constructions which have appeared in full-scale grammars, such as those discussed above, two more specialized studies have been made of the causal meaning of *ot* constructions.[14]

The better of these studies, that of L. N. Popova, makes a very thorough examination of the causal meaning of *ot*. The following points are considered:[15] 1) the nature of the type of syntactic tie between the nouns linked by the preposition — attributive, objective, or circumstantial;[16] 2) the gross derivational make-up of the head noun, *i.e.*, its relationship to a cognate verb; and 3) the semantic character of both N^1 and N^2 and their interrelations.

[13] *AG*, II, 1, 250. It is interesting to note that A. X. Vostokov's *Russkaja grammatika* of 1831 characterized the head noun of this group as "... designating a part of some object, when it is necessary to show that such a part is separated from the whole ...." Cited in V. V. Vinogradov, *Iz istorii izučenija russkogo sintaksisa* (Moscow, 1958), 185.

[14] L. N. Popova, "O značenii predloga v sovremennom russkom jazyke (Predlog ot + roditel'nyj padež v značenii pričiny)", *Učenye zapiski Leningradskogo gosudarstvennogo universiteta*, 235, Serija filologičeskix nauk, vyp. 38 (1958), 190–208; R. Ja. Kalnberzin', "Vyraženie pričinnyx otnošenij slovosočetanijami s predlogom 'ot' i roditel'nym padežom suščestvitel'nogo v sovremennom russkom jazyke (na materiale polnogo sobranija sočinenij A. M. Gor'kogo)", Latvijas PSR, Zmanu Akademijas, *Vēstis*, 11 (112) (1956), 49–56. Both of these articles grew out of candidates' dissertations dealing with causal relations.

[15] Popova, 204–6.

[16] Traditional Russian grammar describes the interrelations of the secondary members of the sentence *(i.e.*, everything except the so-called *simple* subject and predicate) in terms of these three rubrics. Like most of the traditional syntactic categories, they lack formal specification, but may be said to coincide very approximately with the normal syntactic roles played in the sentence by adjectives, oblique cases of the noun and adverbs respectively.

It is observed that the syntactic relations between nouns are usually attributive or objective whereas circumstantial relations are the most favorable for the expression of causal relations.[17] From the derivational point of view, Popova concludes that N^1 is most often a deverbative *(povreždẹnie ot vyrubki lesov* 'damage because of the cutting down of the forests'), but not obligatorily so.[18]

The most interesting aspect of the study is the semantic description of N^1 and N^2.[19] This discussion, although not presented in such a way as to allow formal verification, sheds a good deal of light on the make-up of nominal *ot* constructions expressing causal relations.[20] Semantically N^1 usually designates an external physical or internal psychic state. The head nouns, in opposition to cognate verbs that represent this state in the form of an action ascribed to the subject, present this state in isolation — outside of any tie with its bearer.

Conditions are most favorable for the expression of causal meaning when N^2 designates an action *(vozbuždenie ot boja* 'agitation because of battle'), although a shade of objective meaning is present in these cases. *Purely* causal relations are best expressed when N^2 designates "... not an action nor an object presupposing an action, but a state or a quality".[21] Another facilitating factor for the expression of 'purely' causal meaning is the existence of a predicative pause between N^1 and *ot* N^2.[22] Compare: "... *u moej sestry ot maljarii — paralič nog* ... [because of malaria my sister has paralysis of the legs]" with "... *u dvux požilyx ženščin — poteki ot slez* ... [the two elderly women have streaks because of tears]". According to the author, only the first example expresses purely causal relations; while in the second, the causal meaning is complicated by an objective nuance. Popova sums up her findings in the following terms: "Thus in substantive constructions the causal meaning of the preposition *ot* depends upon the syntactic function of the modified words (predicative use) and on the meaning of the dependent words (which designate state or quality)."[23]

R. Ja. Kalnberzin''s article on the causal meaning of *ot* adds little new to the results of Popova.[24] Kalnberzin' observes that *ot*+N is the most widespread

[17] Popova, 204.

[18] *Loc. cit.*

[19] Popova, 204–5.

[20] A transformational basis for much of this elucidation, together with some further insights, is presented on pages 61–66. The morphological and transformational key to the isolation and characterization of the causal use of *ot* lies in the formally demonstrable connection of N^1 with adjectives and passive participles, the two grammatical forms most intimately concerned with expressing states, conditions, or qualities.

[21] Popova, 206.

[22] *Ibid.*, 205–6.

[23] *Ibid.*, 206.

[24] See footnote 14 above for full citation.

device in modern Russian for the expression of causal relations.[25] It is also noted that the head nouns of N *ot* N constructions are usually, but not always, deverbal *(zabluždenie ot nevežestva* 'error because of ignorance'). Non-deverbal heads include 1) nouns referring to an action *(panika ot xoloda i grippa* 'panic because of cold and grippe'); 2) nouns referring to agent *(revoljucionner ot ljubvi* 'a revolutionary because of love'); and 3) nouns referring to conditions or states *(udovol'stvie ot operacii* 'satisfaction because of the operation'). Kalnberzin' also reported that with a single exception all of the nouns dependent on *ot* in causal constructions were abstract and that they often referred to a feeling.[26]

The studies of both Popova and Kalnberzin' suffer from the same deficiencies as the *Academy Grammar, i.e.*, undefined semantic classificational categories and unspecified identification and assignment procedures for examples.[27]

2.2.2. *Transformational Treatments*

The Hungarian linguist Ferenc Papp has attempted a transform analysis of Russian nominal constructions of the types $N^1\,N^2_{dp}$ *(dom otca* 'house of the father'), $N^1\,A\,N^2_{dp}$ *(vopros bol'šogo značenija* 'question of great significance'), $N^1\,P\,N^2$ *(otkaz ot ošibok* 'repudiation of mistakes'), and $N^1\,P\,A\,N^2_{dp}$ *(devuška s dlinnymi volosami* 'girl with long hair').[28] Within the $N^1\,P\,N^2$ structure, the division is by the case of the dependent N^2 and then by the preposition. In order to discriminate among the different meanings of the preposition within the N^1 *ot* N^2 framework, the following set of transforms is used:[29]

[25] Kalnberzin', 50.

[26] *Ibid.*, 51–2.

[27] There are several other Soviet studies on causal relations which make similar descriptions of *ot* constructions. See, for example, E. A. Nazikova, "Vyraženie pričinnyx otnošenij v sovremennom russkom literaturnom jazyke" (Leningrad, 1952) (Unpublished candidate's dissertation).

[28] F. Papp, "Transformacionnyj analiz russkix prisubstantivnyx konstrukcij s zavisimoj čast'ju – suščestvitel'nym", 55–83.

[29] The list of transform formulas is from page 66 of Papp's study. The examples may be found on page 63. In addition to the above transforms, which were used for *ot* constructions, four other transforms were also used in the analysis of $N^1\,P\,N^2$ constructions. These are:

1. T: $\rightarrow A^{n_2}\,N^1$:

podsvečnik iz bronzy	→ *bronzovyj podsvečnik*
'candlestick of bronze'	→ 'bronze candlestick'

2. T: $\rightarrow A^{n_1}\,P\,N^2$:

predannost' do samozabvenija	→ *predan do samozabvenija*
'devotion to self-oblivion'	→ 'devoted to self-oblivion'

T1: → $V^{n1}\ P\ N^2_g$:
A. *otkaz ot ošibok* → *otkazat'sja ot ošibok*
'repudiation of mistakes' → 'to repudiate mistakes'
T2: → $N^1\ V_{pa}\ P\ N^2_g$:
B. *maz' ot vesnušek* → *maz', zaščiščajuščaja ot vesnušek*
'ointment against freckles' → 'ointment protecting against freckles'
T3: → $N^1\ V_{pp}\ P\ N^2_g$:
C. *nasledstvo ot otca* → *nasledstvo, polučennoe ot otca*
'inheritance from father' → 'inheritance received from father'
T4: → $N^1\ V_{pp}\ N^2_i$:
D. *slezy ot vostorga* → *slezy, vyzvannye vostorgom*
'tears because of rapture' → 'tears evoked by rapture'
T5: → $N^1\ P^1\ N^2_g\ P^2\ N^3$:
E. *doroga ot sela* → *doroga ot sela k gorodu*
'road from the village' → 'road from the village to town'

These yield the following sets of transform features for the multiply ambiguous N^1 *ot* N^2 construction:

N^1 *ot* N^2	T1	T2	T3	T4	T5
A. *otdyx ot ustalosti* 'a rest from tiredness'	+	–	–	–	–
B. *krem ot zagara* 'cream against sunburn'	–	+	–	–	–
C. *pis'mo ot materi* 'letter from mother'	–	–	+	–	–
D. *svet ot fonarja* 'light from a lantern'	–	–	–	+	–
E. *vremja ot polunoči* 'time from midnight'	–	+	–	–	+

To complete our description of Papp's transform analysis of the N^1 *ot* N^2 structure, we give all of the examples of the groups that are designated by the

3. T: → $V\ N^1\ P\ N^2$:
činovnik do mozga kostej → *javljalsja činovnikom ... do mozga kostej*
'a bureaucrat to the marrow of [his] bones' → '[he] was a bureaucrat ... to the marrow of [his] bones'

4. T: → *u* N^2 *byt'* N^1:
xvost u lošadi → *u lošadi est' xvost*
'tail of the horse' → 'the horse has a tail'

letters A through E[30] in the two listings above. Where transformed expansions are available, the new forms are also given in parentheses.

A. 1) *otkaz ot ošibok* 'repudiation of mistakes' *(otkazat'sja* 'to refuse')
   2) *otdyx ot ustalosti* 'a rest from tiredness' *(otdyxat'* 'to rest')
   3) *uxod ot sem'i* 'departure from family'
   4) *spasenie ot presledovanija* 'salvation from persecution'
   5) *otorvannost' ot žizni* 'detachment from life'
B. 1) *maz' (, zaščiščajuščaja) ot vesnušek* 'ointment (protecting) against freckles'
   2) *krem (, predoxranjajuščij) ot zagara* 'cream (preserving) against sunburn'
   3) *poroški ot kašlja* 'powders against coughing'
   4) *sredstvo ot bessonicy* 'remedy against insomnia'
C. 1) *nasledstvo (, polučennoe) ot otca* 'inheritance (received) from father'
   2) *pis'mo (, polučennoe) ot materi* 'letter (received) from mother'
D. 1) *slezy (, vyzvannye) vostorgom* 'tears (evoked) by rapture'
   2) *svet (, izlučaemyj) fonarjem* 'light (eradiated) by a lantern'
   3) *delegaty (, naznačennye) stanicami* 'delegates appointed by the stanitsas'
E. 1) *doroga ot sela (k gorodu)* 'road from the village (to town)'
   2) *vremja ot polunoči (do utra)* 'time from midnight (to morning)'

Thus Papp indicates five different formal groups of N^1 *ot* N^2 (A–E) and a unique transformational specification for each of them. Several problems, of both a theoretical and a practical nature, present themselves at this point.

The first of these problems concerns the groups A–E. Just what are these supposed to represent? Papp makes no statement about the matter in regard to N^1 *ot* N^2 constructions, but it appears that they represent purely formal classes defined by their respective transforms. Other sections of Papp's analysis, however, suggest that the transformations are assumed to have some, albeit unspecified, correlation with various traditional syntactic categories such as objective *(dopolnenie)* or attributive *(opredelenie)* relations.[31] It is

[30] The letter designations of the example groups and the Arabic numeral designations for the transforms are provided by the writer for ease of reference. They correspond to the following paragraph numbers in the text: A–3.31, B–3.3211, C–3.322, D–3.3232, and E–3.3212. The paragraphs designated by these numbers each list one of the transformations (1–5 above) and two or more examples of the N^1 *ot* N^2 groups under examination together with its transforms.

[31] Papp, 82. It might be noted at this point that the establishment of purely formal classes is not necessarily of linguistic interest. It is only when such groupings can be shown to have some systematic correlation with certain features either on the level of function or content (or better still, on both) that formal classification systems become linguistically interesting.

also unclear whether or not the transformationally defined groups are supposed to have any degree of semantic unity. Only in the case of B *(sredstvo ot bessonicy* 'remedy against insomnia') is there a sharply defined semantic set. All of the other groups show varying degrees of unity — at least in terms of the traditional intuitive semantic categories.

The most serious difficulty with Papp's unique transformation specifications for each group is that they are inaccurate in a very large number of cases. The problem is that a great many of the negatively marked transforms are just as possible as those marked with pluses. Hence many, if not most, of the examples will not be distinctively characterized in terms of class membership.

This will be demonstrated for one example of each group. For class A, in addition to the indicated T1, the following transformations are also possible:

T2: → *uxod, otdeljajuščij ot sem'i* 'departure separating [one] from [one's] family'

T3: → *uxod, soveršaemyj ot sem'i* 'departure accomplished [by one] from [one's] family'

T5: → *uxod ot sem'i k soderžanke* 'departure from [one's] family to [one's] mistress'

For class B, in addition to T2, the following are also possible:

T1: → *mazat'sja ot vesnušek* 'to smear one's self [with ointment] against freckles'

T3: → *maz', prigotovljaemyj ot vesnušek* 'ointment prepared against freckles'

For class C, in addition to T3:

T1: → *nasledovat' ot otca* 'to inherit from father'

T2: → *nasledstvo, perexodjaščee ot otca* 'inheritance passing from father'

T4: → *nasledstvo, peredannoe otcom* 'inheritance handed down by the father'

T5: → *nasledstvo ot otca k synu* 'inheritance from father to son'

For class D, in addition to T4:

T1: → *svetit ot fonarja* '[it] shines from the lantern'

T2: → *svet, padajuščij ot fonarja* 'light falling from the lantern'

T3: → *svet, izlučaemyj ot fonarja* 'light eradiated from the lantern'

T5: → *svet ot fonarja do konca (ulicy)* 'light from the lantern to the end (of the street)'

For class E, in addition to T2:

T3: → *doroga, vidimaja ot sela* 'road visible from the village'

Similar transformations could be adduced for the remaining examples in each class. Almost all of the transformations are possible for most of the examples. Thus, Papp's system collapses completely.

The root of the problem is clear. Transforms 2–4 call for the introduction of participles modifying N^1. These participles, indicated on page 30, were apparently selected by Papp to fit the individual needs of a particular example in conjunction with a given transform. The series of transformations just listed shows that, given the privilege of hand-picking the verb to be inserted in the transform, almost any example can be transformed (or not transformed) according to any desired pattern. These considerations lead to a more general theoretical problem.

Papp cites a number of articles that use transforms for various purposes, but gives no definition of the terms *transformation* or *transform analysis*. The latter is dismissed with the following comment: "In view of the already widespread renown of this method, it seems possible not to speak about its general principles, about its significance for linguistic analysis, [or] about the difficulties which arise in connection with it."[32]

It is clear that Papp is not working within the framework of any carefully formulated definition of the concept of *transformation,* but merely utilizing certain transformation-like devices for analytical purposes. Some of these devices and in particular transforms 2–4 above are simply trappings to give the appearance of system and rigor to a process which in reality is no more than loose paraphrasing. From the point of view of rigorous linguistic analysis, such a procedure is completely useless. The failure of Papp's system of transforms to make interesting distinctions of any kind lies in his unfounded assumption that new lexical units may be inserted at will in the transformational process.

Although the basic sources whom Papp cites (Chomsky, Harris, and Lees) have somewhat different formulations of the term *transformation,* none of hese interpretations permits the arbitrary introduction of new lexical entities.[33]

The technique of transform analysis has also been used by the Russian scholar V. P. Manolova in an attempt to make such an analysis of all Russian syntagms of the types N(P)N and V(P)N.[34] Manolova defines TA in the following way: "On the basis of data from a particular language an analysis is made of the constructions which can be formed from it with the preservation of the general sense of the initial construction and with complete grammatical cor-

[32] *Ibid.*, 57.

[33] See Chapter 1, pages 16–17 for a discussion of these definitions and their differences and particularly page 17 for a statement of Lees' views on the introduction of new elements into transformed units.

[34] V. P. Manolova, *Transformation of Russian Syntagms of the Type $S + S$, $S + P$, $V + S$, $V + P + S$* (Moscow, 1962). This pamphlet is available to the writer in an English translation under the above title and available through the U. S. Joint Publications Research Service, Washington, D. C. *JPRS,* 19.053 (6 May 1963), 28–71. The translation is apparently incomplete.

rectness and meaningfulness of the construction ....' The definition is illustrated with the examples *luga zalivalo vodoj* '[it] flooded the meadows with water' and *voda zalivala luga* 'water flooded the meadows'.[35] It is further noted that the literature in the field indicates that the method is applicable to the study of syntagms. The above definition of TA is accompanied by one very important qualification. Transformations of the type *igra s ognem* 'game with fire' → *igrat' s ognem* 'to play with fire' or *vospominanie o detjax* 'memory about children' → *vospominat' o detjax* 'to remember about children' are not acceptable.[36] The reasons for this are not altogether clear but it appears that these transformations involve a change of the head word, whereas, according to Manolova, usually only the subordinate word and its attached preposition undergo any change. This latter is regarded by the author as natural since "The main pull *[sic]* of the sense relation falls on the element determined."[37]

Within this theoretical framework all of the syntagms of the types studied were broken down into 89 groups on the basis of morphological criteria. Each morphological type was then divided into intuitive semantic groupings used by the *Academy Grammar*. Each of the 375 meaning groups arrived at in this fashion was subjected to all possible transformations which preserved the relational meaning of the source phrase.

The results of this process for N^1 *ot* N^2 units are indicated in the following series of transforms and examples.[38]

T1: → $N^1 N^2_g$: *teni domov* 'houses' shadows': Genetic relations
kran samovara 'samovar's tap': Attributive relations

T2: → N^1 *posle* N^2: *nasledstvo posle otca* 'inheritance after father': Genetic relations

T3: → N^1 *dlja* N^2: *ključ dlja zamka* 'key for the lock': Attributive relations

T4: → N^1 *k* N^2: *kran k samovaru* 'top to the samovar': Attributive relations

T5: → N^1 *iz-za* N^2: *bessonica iz-za pereutomlenija* 'insomnia due to overtiredness': Causal-consequential relations

T6: → N^1 *protiv* N^2: *poroški protiv kašlja* 'powders against coughing': Designation relations

[35] *Ibid.*, 28.

[36] *Ibid.*, 34.

[37] *Loc. cit.* This statement is certainly open to question inasmuch as what words will be transformed is largely a function of the kind of transformation one selects. Furthermore, the importance of interclass transformations of the type *igra* → *igrat'* for syntactic description has long been recognized. See J. Kurylowicz, "Dérivation lexicale et dérivation syntaxique (contribution à la théorie des parties du discours)", *Bulletin de la Société de Linguistique de Paris*, XXXVII (1936), 79–92.

[38] Manolova, 39.

With the exception of T1, which drops the *ot*, all of the transforms simply involve the substitution of other prepositions that express the particular meaning of *ot* occurring in each of the various semantic groups.

The fact that *dlja* 'for' can be substituted for *ot* in *ključ ot zamka* 'key to the lock', but not in *bessonica ot pereutomlenija* 'insomnia from over-tiredness' does discriminate between the two semantic types. The former can also be rewritten as *ključ prinadležaščij zamke* 'key belonging to the lock', whereas the latter cannot. The trouble with both of these oppositions is that they are based upon features of the lexicon rather than the grammar of the language. Compare the insight provided by the following two transformations:

ključ ot zamka →	1) *ključ dlja zamka* 'key for the lock'
'key to the lock'	2) *zamočnyj ključ* 'lock key'

The first transformation tells us only that *ot* and *dlja* overlap in some part of their respective semantic fields. As a corollary to this we know that there are cases where this overlap does not occur *(e.g., nasledstvo ot* 'inheritance from', but not *dlja otca* 'for father') and, consequently, the preposition *dlja* can be used to isolate some part of the semantic field of *ot*. Since the criteria for decision of whether *dlja* can replace *ot* in any given case are largely subjective, the system has severe drawbacks. For example, *ključ ot zamka* 'key to the lock' and *poroški ot kašlja* 'powders against coughing' are clearly different on intuitive semantic grounds, but in both cases *ot* can be replaced by *dlja*.

The second transform not only isolates *ključ ot zamka* 'key to the lock' from *poroški ot kašlja* 'powders against coughing' but does this both formally and more economically. No new unit *(dlja)* is introduced and we need not be concerned about its meaning or at just what point its semantic overlap with *ot* ends.[39] Furthermore, and even more importantly, we now have grounds to assign a syntactic description to the relationship between N^1 *(ključ* 'key') and N^2 *(zamka* 'of the lock'). *Zamka* is functioning as an attributive to *ključ* just as we have shown in the transformational restatement *(zamočnyj ključ* 'lock key'). This relationship is demonstrated by the fact that *zamok* 'lock' possesses an adjective form which may in fact play the syntactic role of an attributive. In other words, it can be shown that the asserted syntactic tie between N^1 and N^2 is deeply rooted in the derivational structure of the language.

In sum, the first type of transformation is a highly subjective procedure which informs us only about certain correspondences on the lexical level. The second type is formal, operates on the grammatical level, and is insightful.

[39] The arguments against the introduction of new lexical elements have been given in connection with Papp's study. See page 32. It should be noted, however, that there is an important difference between Papp's use of this device and Manolova's. Papp introduces the new elements on a completely ad hoc basis, whereas Manolova is introducing a small number of semi-grammatical words from a previously specified list.

Papp and Manolova both make reference to Zellig Harris' ground-breaking article, "Co-occurrence and Transformation in Linguistic Structure".[40] Papp, in particular, makes specific reference to Harris' work on English prepositional constructions.[41] The efforts of neither Papp nor Manolova, however, give much indication of being influenced by Harris' work. Their understanding of the concepts of transformation and transformation analysis is very different from that of Harris. In addition, their own ideas about transformations differ radically from each other.

Since Harris is the only American transformationalist who has dealt with NPN constructions at any length, it is worthwhile to make a cursory examination of his treatment of the problem and to determine what relevance, if any, his ideas might have for the analysis of Russian NPN constructions. Our interest will, of course, be focused on the methodological and theoretical aspects of his work, since Harris is treating English NPN constructions. One further comment is required. Harris is presenting a scheme hopefully valid (as far as it goes) for all English NPN units.[42] The present study is directed toward a much more specific goal, *i.e.*, an examination of the efficacy of transformational analysis for the resolution of homomorphic constructions containing the Russian preposition *ot*.[43]

A schematization of Harris' transformational treatment of English NPN units is presented below.[44]

I. Parallel NPN type: examples of this minority type undergo three transformations.

N^1 P N^2 / I like the *job of sorting* →

1. N^1 , N^2 / This *job* , *sorting*
2. N^1 is N^2 / The job is sorting
3. (Both a and b are obligatory)
   a) N^1 / I like the *job*
   b) N^2 / I like *sorting*

[40] *Language*, XXXIII (1957), 283–340. Also in *The Structure of Language: Readings in the Philosophy of Language*, Jerry A. Fodor and Jerrold J. Katz, eds. (Englewood Cliffs, New Jersey, 1964), 155–210. Subsequent references are to the latter source.

[41] Papp, 58.

[42] Harris clearly does not intend this to be more than a suggestive sketch.

[43] The closest approach to this type of problem in Harris' article is his demonstration of the transformational resolution of the homonymy of the two *by*-constructions in the examples: "the window was broken by the kids" versus "the wreck was seen by the seashore", 160.

[44] Harris, 168–70.

II. PN = A type: this is a majority type where N^1 is head.

N^1 P N^2		N^1
This raised *hopes for* a *settlement.*	→	This raised *hopes.*

III. Predicative type: this applies mainly to examples of type II. Where it is not possible, idiomatic or compound noun status is indicated *(e.g.*, point of departure, time of day).

N^1 P N^2		N^1 is P N^2
This raised *hopes for* a *settlement.*	→	The *hopes are for* a *settlement.*

IV. N^1 P = A type: N^1 is lexically restricted to a unit of measure.

N^1 P N^2		N^2
A *number of boys* were arguing.	→	The *boys* were arguing.

V. Reversible type: N^1 and N^2 are interchangeable.

N^1 of N^2		N^2 P N^1
This *type of bacteria* grows readily.	→	*Bacteria of* this *type* grow readily.

VI. PNP = P type: PNP is a compound preposition.

P^1 N^2 P^2 N^4		P N^4
He telephoned *in regard to* a *job.*	→	He telephoned *in regard to* a *job.*

Only two of the above transforms have any relevance for the analysis of Russian NPN constructions. The majority type where PN = A is useful in both Russian and English in indicating an attributive relationship between the head noun and the prepositional phrase. This may be seen more clearly if the transformation is stated in the form $N^1\,P\,N^2 \rightarrow A^{n2}\,N^1$. The compound PNP type where PNP simply equals P is also applicable in Russian, but what is involved here is not a transformation but a problem in IC analysis. Is $P^1\,N^2\,P^3\,N^4$ to be parsed as $P^1\,N^2 + P^3\,N^4$ or as $P\,N^4$? In the example *V otličie ot deda otec vygljadel xilym, boleznenym* 'in contradistinction to grandfather, father looked puny, sickly', is *V otličie ot deda* 'in contradistinction to grandfather' to be parsed as *V otličie* 'in contradistinction' and *ot deda* 'to grandfather' or as *V otličie ot* 'in contradistinction to' and *deda* 'grandfather'? In the Russian phrase as in Harris' English example, the latter analysis is clearly superior.

The other groups that Harris has isolated by his transforms are all specialized minor types. The fact that they have no parallel in Russian N *ot* N constructions provides the basis for at least one typological comparison between English and Russian prepositions. Harris' three possible transformations for the parallel NPN type (I like the job of sorting → 1) this job, sorting; 2) the job is sorting; and 3a) I like the job, 3b) I like sorting) indicate very clearly that at least in this type of construction the preposition *of* plays the role of a semantically neutral link, such as *to be* or even *and*. Compare *I like the job of sorting* with its two transforms *the job* is *sorting* and a proposed coordinating transform *I like the job* and *the sorting*. In Russian, on the other hand, the preposition always and obligatorily indicates subordination, never simple linkage or coordination. In other words, in Russian the asemantic quality of prepositions has not reached that of English prepositions.

Harris' third transform, the predicative type, is applicable in Russian to almost any N^1 *ot* N^2 unit.[45] This property of Russian NPN constructions, which allows them to be rephrased as NVPN, was used by Peškovskij as a basis to equate the majority of NPN constructions to corresponding constructions of the VPN type.[46] It has also been used by F. Papp as a basis for a transformational attempt to demonstrate this same correspondence.[47]

Most of Harris' transforms involve word order rearrangements. This is a consequence of the fact that most syntactic relations in English are expressed by taxemes of word order. Since word order rearrangement is the primary syntactic device in English, it is perforce the primary tool of analytic transformational investigation. The possible number of reorderings at the lower constructional levels being sharply limited in English, transformational investigation at the lower IC levels has, understandably, not attracted much attention.[48]

In Russian, on the other hand, the complex morphological system, both derivational and inflectional, plays a very important role in the expression of syntactic relations at all levels. One consequence of this is that transformational analysis has a much greater range of factors to work with. Note, for example, that both intraclass inflectional transforms ($N_n \rightarrow N_g$, N_i: *radost'* → *radosti*, *radost'ju* 'joy' and interclass derivational transforms $N \rightarrow V$: *radost'* 'joy' → *radovat'* 'to gladden') are accompanied by distinctive morphological features. Hence the possibilities for analytic transformations at the lower constructional levels are much richer in Russian than in English.

[45] The only notable exception being examples of the Container-Designation group where *butylka ot vina* 'bottle for wine' cannot be transformed to **butylka byla ot vina* 'the bottle was for wine'. This group is discussed on pages 71–72 below.

[46] See pages 24–25 above for a description of Peškovskij's classification system.

[47] See page 28*ff*. for a description of Papp's insertion of participles between N^1 and $P\,N^2$.

[48] Note that R. B. Lees' work on English nominalizations generally involves a much higher level of syntactic analysis than that involved in most NPN constructions. Lees views most nominal compounds as transforms of full sentences. Robert B. Lees, *The Grammar of English Nominalizations* (Bloomington, Indiana, Research Center in Anthropology, Folklore, and Linguistics, 1960).

2.3. ANALYSIS OF N^1 *ot* N^2 UNITS

The studies of both Papp and Manolova suggest that a much tighter formulation of the concept of transform analysis is needed to provide a satisfactory analysis of homomorphic constructions. Papp's study foundered on the ad hoc introduction of new lexical units. Manolova's analysis involved the interchange of a limited number of new elements, thus restricting its value to that of a comparative study of the degrees of the semantic complementarity of various prepositions.

In the current study it is proposed to use analytic transforms in a more rigorous fashion and in a way which draws heavily upon the inflectional and derivational features of Russian morphology.[49] For present purposes, a transformation will be regarded as the statement of certain systematic morphosyntactic relationships between two similar phrases. Following Worth, these transformations will be used only analytically and for the sole purpose of discriminating among and classifying otherwise identical morphological structures.[50] The morphological unit under examination is N^1 *ot* N^2. Both intraclass and interclass transformations are used. For example, the phrase *podarok ot sultana* 'present from the sultan' transforms to *sultan podarit* 'the sultan presents'. The change *sultana* 'sultan's' ← *sultan* 'sultan' is an intraclass transformation, whereas *podarok* 'present' ← *podarit* '[he] presents' is an interclass transformation. The latter is the more important type in the present analysis.

The analytic transformations utilized in the present study differ from those in previous works in one important respect: new lexical items are not introduced into the transformed phrases. One qualification must be appended to this restriction. For the formal specification of examples with spatial meaning, a transformation involving the addition of the unit PN is utilized, *e.g.*, *doroga ot goroda* 'road from town' → *doroga ot goroda do sela* 'road from town to the village'. This procedure may be justified on two grounds: 1) it may be reasonably argued that what is involved here is not so much the introduction of new lexical elements, but a test of the capability of the original PN unit to undergo a certain structural type of complementation, *i.e.*, can NPN → NPN + PN?; 2) the new elements (PN) are simply added on to the original unit and do not result in any structural change within the latter. Compare this with Papp's purely ad hoc formulations of the type *slezy ot vostorga* 'tears because of rapture' → *slezy (vyzvannye) vostorgom* 'tears (evoked) by rapture'.

[49] See pages 33–34 for an example of this type of transform and a discussion of its advantages.

[50] Dean S. Worth, "Transform Analysis of Russian Instrumental Constructions", *Word*, XIV (1958), 253.

Two criteria were utilized in ascertaining whether or not an example could undergo a given transformation. The first of these was the formal possibility or *grammaticalness* of the result of the transformation. For example, **podarit ot sultana* '[he] presents from the sultan' from *podarok ot sultana* 'present from the sultan' is not a grammatical word-combination in Russian. The second criterion concerns a requisite correlation in meaning between the original phrase and its transform.[51] The criterion may be formulated as follows: if a series of examples are to be classed as a transformationally defined group, the semantic relationship prevailing between the source phrases and the corresponding phrases resulting from any one transformation must be the same in all cases. If this semantic invariancy does not prevail for an example under transformation, the example is not a member of the group. For example, in the following cases the meanings of each of the transformed phrases differ from that of their source phrases in exactly the same way: *strelka ot časov* 'hand from the clock' → *strelka časov* 'clock's hand', *ščepka ot kresta* 'sliver from the cross' → *ščepka kresta* 'cross' sliver', *rukojatka ot šila* 'grip from the awl' → *rukojatka šila* 'awl's grip'; but in the formally identical pair *spasenie ot vraga* 'salvation from the enemy' → *spasenie vraga* 'enemy's salvation', this correspondence does not obtain.[52] This sort of shift is quite common in NPN units and provides a useful tool for classifying otherwise identical phrases.

Examples of the N^1 *ot* N^2 construction were gathered from a variety of sources. The basic corpus was selected from the *Academy Grammar* and from K. Paustovskij's autobiography, *Povest' o žizni*.[53] These were supplemented by examples drawn from a variety of Russian grammar books and dictionaries. In each case either the complete sentence containing N^1 *ot* N^2 was extracted or all parts of the sentence having any conceivable grammatical relevance.

The examples were first subjected to a two-part reduction process that eliminated all elements which were not essential to the analysis. The first part of this process consisted of isolating the N^1 *ot* N^2 unit by IC analysis and then discarding the rest of the sentence. The second part consisted of the elimina-

[51] It should be noted that this is not equivalent to saying that the source phrase and the transformed phrases have the same meaning. It merely states that the differences in meaning should be systematic.

[52] This sudden *non-correspondence* illustrates on the NPN constructional level the same phenomenon demonstrated by D. S. Worth for instrumental constructions in Russian. *Cf.*, *komnata napolnjalas' tolpoj* 'the room was filled by the crowd' → *tolpa napolnjala komnatu* 'the crowd filled the room', *zala osveščaetsja fonarikami* 'the room is lighted by lanterns' → *fonariki osveščajut zalu* 'the lanterns light the room'; but *Ivan vernulsja starikom* 'John came back an old man' → *starik vernul Ivana* 'the old man brought John back', 259.

[53] 2 vols. (Moscow, 1962).

tion of irrelevant grammatical categories.[54] The results consisting of a head word, the preposition, and its object were then written on cards. The cards also contained a list of transformations. The phrases were given to a native speaker of Russian[55] to determine whether or not the proposed transforms met the joint criteria of *grammaticalness* and semantic invariancy which were specified above.

All of the examples of the construction N^1 *ot* N^2 were subjected to a uniform set of six transformations and were analyzed and classified on the basis of their response to them.[56] To help orient the reader to the types of operations involved, each of the six transformations is illustrated below:

T1:	N^1 ot N^2 *ščepka ot kresta* 'sliver from the cross'	→	N^1 N^2_g *ščepka kresta* 'cross' sliver'
T2:	N^1 ot N^2 *srez ot lopaty* 'a cut from a spade'	→	A^{n_2} N^1 *lopatočnyj srez* 'spade cut'
T3:	N^1 ot N^2 *svet ot fonarja* 'light from the lantern'	→	A^{n_1} ot N^2 *svetlyj ot fonarja* 'alight from the lantern'
T4:	N^1 ot N^2 *jarost ot bessmyslicy* 'rage because of an absurdity'	→	V^{n_1} ot N^2 *raz"jarit'sja ot bessmyslicy* 'to become enraged because of an absurdity'
T5:	N^1 ot N^2 *pis'mo ot brata* 'letter from [one's] brother'	→	N^2_{sb} V^{n_1} *brat pišet* '[one's] brother writes'
T6:	N^1 ot N^2 *uxod ot doma* 'departure from the house'	→	N^1 ot N^2 do N^3 *uxod ot doma do reki* 'departure from the house to the river'

[54] A formal basis for this procedure has been pointed out by D. S. Worth in his article "Transform Analysis of Russian Instrumental Constructions", 254.

[55] The informant was born in Moscow in 1936 and resided there until 1962. She is a graduate of the Pervyj Moskovskij gosudarstvennyj pedagogičeskij institut inostrannyx jazykov.

[56] Two of the groups, the *Range Function* and the *Spatial*, occur predominantly in the structural format N^1 *ot* N^2 *do/k* N^3 and, consequently, are subjected to another set of transformations. Of the two transformations that are used for these two groups, one is identical with T6 and the other, which simply involves dropping *do/k* N^3, is illustrated in the text.

Examples of the structural type N^1 *ot* N^2 fall into nine groups in terms of their behavior under the above transformations.[57] The following portion of the chapter consists of a detailed examination of the eleven groups which have been isolated in the analysis. These groups are labeled as follows: 0) Range I) Spatial, II) Ablative, III) Phenomenon-Source, IV) Trace-Origin, V) Communication-Originator, VI) State-Cause, VII) Component-Aggregate, VIII) Container-Designation, IX) Countermeasure, and X) Temporal.[58] The discussion of each of these groups is prefaced by a table listing all of the examples of that group together with their transform features.

TABLE 1

Transform Features of 'N^1 ot N^2 do/k N^3' Units of the Range and the Spatial Groups

N^1	*ot*	N^2	*do/k*	N^3	T1: → N^1 *ot* N^2	T2: → V^{n1} *ot* N^2
1. goroda	ot	Kryžopolja	do	Sosnicy	—	—
'towns—	from	Kryžopol'	to	Sosnica		
	ot	Špoly	do	Gluxova	—	—
	from	Špola	to	Gluxov'		
2. smešenie (ljudej)	ot	jurodivogo	do	poèta	—	—
'a mixing (of people)—	from	holy fool	to	poet		
	ot	tolstovcev	do	(zatjanutyx v korsety) dam	—	—
	from	Tolstoyans	to	(tightly corseted) ladies'		
3. golos (čeloveka)	ot	Bokkaččo	do	Lekonta de Lilli	—	—
'voice (of man)—	from	Boccaccio	to	Leconte de Lisle'		
	ot	Veermeera	do	Bloka	—	—
	from	Vermeer	to	Blok'		
4. partii	ot	kadetov	do	bol'ševikov	—	—
'parties—	from	Kadets	to	Bolsheviks'		
5. korrespondenty	ot	kapitanov	do	kočegarov	—	—
'correspondents—	from	captains	to	stokers'		
6. mgnovenie	ot	volny	do	volny	—	—
'instant—	from	wave	to	wave'		

[57] The utility of the various transformations in isolating the different groups is discussed in detail in each section as are the insights afforded by particular transformations.

[58] The *Range group* is not numbered in sequence with the other groups since it differs from them structurally, *i.e.*, N^1 *ot* N^2 *do* N^3 versus N^1 *ot* N^2.

TABLE 1 (*cont.*)

N^1	*ot*	N^2	*do/k*	N^3	T1: → N^1 *ot* N^2	T2: → V^{n1} *ot* N^2
7. alfavit	ot	A	do	Ja	—	—
'alphabet—	from	A	to	Z'		
8. dom	ot	(pervogo) ètaža	do	(poslednego) ètaža	—	—
'house—	from	the (first) floor	to	the (last) floor'		
9. vremja	ot	polnoči	do	rassveta	—	—
'time—	from	midnight	to	dawn'		
10. vremja	ot	dvux	do	desjati	—	—
'time—	from	two	to	ten'		
11. treščina	ot	kryši	do	podvala	+	+
'a crack	from	roof	to	cellar'		
12. razrez	ot	čerdaka	do	podvala	+	+
'a cut	from	garret	to	cellar'		
13. perexod	ot	Meterlinka	k	vožatomu (tramvaja)	+	+
'transition	from	Maeterlinck	to	conductor (of a streetcar)'		
14. tropinka	ot	dači	k	prudu	+	+
'path	from	the dacha	to	the pond'		
15. xod'ba	ot	pereulka	do	sanatorija	+	+
'a walk	from	the alley	to	the sanatorium'		
16. prostranstvo	ot	kaloš	do	konca (gory)	+	+
'space	from	[one's] galoshes	to	the end (of the mountain)'		
17. put'	ot	(prostogo) rabočego	do	zvanija (mastera)	+	+
'journey	from	(simple) workman	to	the title (of master)'		
18. put'	ot	somnenija	k	priznaniju (very)	+	+
'journey	from	doubt	to	declaration (of faith)'		
19. rasstojanie	ot	stancii	do	doma	+	—
'distance	from	the station	to	the house'		
20. doroga	ot	goroda	do	dači	+	—
'road	from	town	to	the dacha'		
21. doroga	ot	peči	do	poroga	+	—
'road	from	stove	to	threshold'		
22. doroga	ot	granicy	do	Nesviža	+	—
'road	from	the border	to	Nesviž'		
23. doroga	ot	Peterburga	do	Sestrorecka	+	—
'road	from	Petersburg	to	Sestroreck'		
24. bilet	ot	Kieva	do	Moskvy	+	—
'ticket	from	Kiev	to	Moscow'		

2.3.1.0. *Range Group*[59] N^1 *ot* N^2 *do* N^3

Transformationally N^1 *ot* N^2 *do* N^3 constructions fall into two groups. The first category, termed the *Range group*, is characterized by the fact that *do* N^3 may not be dropped from the N^1 *ot* N^2 *do* N^3 unit,[60] *i.e.*, N^1 *ot* N^2 *do* $N^3 \not\rightarrow N^1$ *ot* N^2. Thus *partii — ot kadetov do bol'ševikov* 'parties — from Kadets to Bolsheviks' $\not\rightarrow$ **partii ot kadetov* 'parties from Kadets' because the latter is not a viable semantic unit — at least in the meaning displayed in the original phrase. In other words, *do* N^3 is an integral and obligatory part of the larger units.

Other examples of this type are: *goroda — ot Kryžopolja do Sosnicy* 'towns — from Kryžopol' to Sosnica', *dom — ot (pervogo) ètaža do (poslednego) ètaža* 'house — from the (first) floor to the (last) floor', *(v to) mgnovenie — ot volny do volny* '(at that) instant — from wave to wave'. In these, as in all of the other examples numbered between one and ten in Table 1, the *do* N^3 units are obligatory. In each case the prepositional units specify some type of range variation describing the head noun. N^2 and N^3 fulfill an enumerating function with respect to N^1. Transformationally, the group is characterized and isolated from the spatial N^1 *ot* N^2 *do* N^3 units by the fact that neither of the transforms indicated in Table 1 is possible for it. Both are possible for most of the homomorphic spatial examples (11–24).

There is a tendency for examples of the *Range group* to be set off from examples of the second group *(i.e.*, those which admit T: *do* $N^1 \rightarrow \#$) in the regular orthography by the use of a dash between the head noun (N^1) and the dependent nouns (N^2 and N^3). This use of the dash marking comma intonation occurs in six of the ten examples of this group,[61] *e.g.*, (2) *smešenie (ljudej) — ot jurodivogo do poèta i ot tolstovcev do (zatjanutyx v korsety) dam* 'a mixing (of people) — from holy fool to poet and from Tolstoyans to (tightly corseted) ladies'. The function of the dash is to indicate that N^1 is in apposition to $[N^2 + N^3]$. The occurrence of dual *ot/do* complexes, as in examples 1, 2, and 3, is also common. It would appear that examples of this class are equivalent to

[59] Since examples of the *Range group* have the morphological format N^1 *ot* N^2 *do* N^3, whereas the remaining groups have the form N^1 *ot* N^2, the range examples are examined only in terms of the two transforms indicated in Table 1. The remaining types, being all of the structural type N *ot* N, are analyzed in terms of the uniform set of six transforms given above.

[60] For the sake of simplicity, the N^1 *ot* N^2 *do* N^3 designation will also be used to represent N^1 *ot* N^2 *k* N^3 units which constitute only three of the twenty-three examples. For the purpose at hand, there does not appear to be any significant differences between the *do* and the *k* prepositional phrases.

[61] This tendency is even more marked in the numerous examples where the role of the construction head is played by the pronoun *vse* 'all' *(vse — ot soldata do generala* 'all—from soldier to general').

simple predications in structure with the *ot* N^2 *do* N^3 unit playing the role of complex predicate noun.

It is to be noted that N^1 *ot* N^2 *do* N^3 examples of the range type are quite separate, not only from their spatial constructional homonyms, which do allow the dropping of *do* N^3, but also from any of the N^1 *ot* N^2 groups. Examples of the *Range group* are not formed merely by the addition of *do* N^3 to selected N^1 *ot* N^2 constructions, but are independent units that are not reducible to or explicable in terms of the simple N^1 *ot* N^2 types of construction. They constitute a basic category in themselves.

2.3.1.1. *Spatial Group*[62]

The *Spatial Group* occurs in two structural patterns. By far the greater part of the group's membership has the form N^1 *ot* N^2 *do* N^3. Spatial examples with the N^1 *ot* N^2 structure are a minority type.[63] However, in consideration of the fact that in all N^1 *ot* N^2 *do* N^3 units, which express spatial relations, one can delete the *do* N^3, whereas in the range examples one cannot, it was decided to treat all spatial examples as if they were of the form N^1 *ot* N^2.[64]

The *Spatial group* now may be uniquely described in terms of two transformations. The first of these, T6, involves the addition of *do* N^3 to the N^1 *ot* N^2 structure *(put' ot somnenija k priznanija* 'journey from doubt to declaration [of faith]'). This transform is, of course, relevant only for original N^1 *ot* N^2 units, since for the spatial examples derived from the N^1 *ot* N^2 *do* N^3 it merely restores their original format. It is critical, however, for the minority structural type in order to isolate them from other non-spatial N^1 *ot* N^2 units. Compare, for example, *begstvo ot korolja* 'flight from the king', which can add *k sojuznikam* 'to allies', with *otklonenie ot zakona* 'deviation from the law', which cannot be complemented by *do/k* N^3. The second transform, T4, calls for the

[62] Starting with this group all N^1 *ot* N^2 units were subjected to the set of six transformations illustrated on page 40. Since, however, almost all of the spatial examples, from the point of view of their original structure, are identical with the range function units, the two groups are listed together in Table 1 and described in terms of the two transformations applicable to N^1 *ot* N^2 *do* N^3 units. In the present section the spatial examples in their reduced form (N^1 *ot* N^2) are discussed within the framework of the set of six transformations used for all N^1 *ot* N^2 units. Since most of the spatial examples have already been listed in Table 1, however, no new listing is given. Of the six N^1 *ot* N^2 transformations, only T4 and T6 are relevant and these are illustrated in the text.

[63] The spatial examples that occurred in the simple N^1 *ot* N^2 format are: *begstvo ot korolja* 'flight from the king', *perexod ot kommunizma* 'transition from Communism', and *uxod ot raboty* 'departure from work'.

[64] Transformationally, this form is obtained by subjecting the original N^1 *ot* N^2 *do* N^3 units to T: *do* $N^3 \rightarrow \#$. This is the same transformation whereby *Spatial* and *Range group* homonyms were formally separated from each other.

TABLE 2

Transform Features of 'N^1 ot N^2' Units of the Ablative Group

	N^1	*ot*	N^2	T1: → $N^1 N^2_g$	T2: → $A^{n2} N^1$	T3: → A^{n1} *ot* N^2	T4: → V^{n1} *ot* N^2	T5: → $N^2_{sb} V^{n1}$	T6: → N^1 *ot* N^2 *do* N^3
1.	izbavlenie 'salvation	ot from	bed misfortunes'	−	−	−	+	−	−
2.	izbavlenie 'salvation	ot from	smerti death'	−	−	−	+	−	−
3.	isčeznovenie 'disappearance	ot from	člena the member'	−	−	−	+	−	−
4.	otdoxnovenie 'repose	ot from	trudov labors'	−	−	−	+	−	−
5.	otklonenie 'deviation	ot from	zakona the law'	−	−	−	+	−	−
6.	otstranenie 'dismissal	ot from	dolžnosti duty'	−	−	−	+	−	−
7.	otstuplenie 'a retreat	ot from	principov principles'	−	−	−	+	−	−
8.	otorvannost' 'isolation	ot from	beregov the shores'	−	−	−	+	−	−
9.	otorvannost' 'isolation	ot from	strany the country'	−	−	−	+	−	−
10.	otrezannost' 'sunderance	ot from	mira the world'	−	−	−	+	−	−
11.	otkaz 'repudiation	ot of	proryvov delays'	−	−	−	+	−	−
12.	otboj 'a retreat	ot from	perevodčikov translators'	−	−	−	+	−	−
13.	otdyx 'a rest	ot from	ustalosti tiredness'	−	−	−	+	−	−
14.	otdyx 'a rest	ot from	vlasti power'	−	−	−	+	−	−
15.	otdyx 'a rest	ot from	dnej days'	−	−	−	+	−	−
16.	peredyška 'respite	ot from	sveta the world'	−	−	−	+	−	−
17.	uvol'nenie 'discharge	ot from	ministerstva the ministry'	−	−	−	+	−	−
18.	spasenie 'salvation	ot from	vraga the enemy'	−	−	−	+	−	−
19.	vyzdorovlenie 'convalescence	ot from	bolezni illness'	−	−	−	+	−	−

TABLE 2 (*cont.*)

	N^1	*ot*	N^2	T1: → $N^1 N^2_g$	T2: → $A^{n2} N^1$	T3: → A^{n1} *ot* N^2	T4: → V^{n1} *ot* N^2	T5: → $N^2_{sb} V^{n1}$	T6: → N^1 *ot* N^2 *do* N^3
20.	očistka 'clearing [something]	ot of	kisloroda oxygen'	–	–	+	+	–	–
21.	očiščenie 'cleansing [something]	ot of	skverny vileness'	–	–	+	+	–	–
22.	osvoboždenie 'liberation	ot from	belyx the Whites'	–	–	+	+	–	–
23.	osvoboždenie 'the waiving	ot of	platy the fee'	–	–	+	+	–	–
24.	osvoboždenie 'liberation	ot from	gneta oppression'	–	–	+	+	–	–
25.	osvoboždenie 'liberation	ot from	uslovnostej conditionalities'	–	–	+	+	–	–
26.	otdalennost' 'detachment	ot from	žizni life'	–	–	+	+	–	–
27.	otličie 'contrast	ot to	leta summer'	–	–	+	+	–	–
28.	zavisimost' 'dependence	ot on	bogatstva wealth'	–	–	+	+	–	–
29.	zavisimost' 'dependence	ot on	infekcii infection'	–	–	+	+	–	–
30.	zavisimost' 'dependence	ot on	soderžanija the content'	+	–	+	+	–	–
31.	zavisimost' 'dependence	ot on	stoimosti cost'	+	+	+	+	–	–
32.	zavisimost' 'dependence	ot on	sorta the sort [of goods]'	–	+	+	+	–	–
33.	zaščita 'defense	ot against	goloda hunger'	–	–	+	+	–	–
34.	bezopasnost' 'security	ot against	napadenija attack'	–	–	+	+	–	–
35.	pomošč' 'assistance	ot against	ljudej people'	–	–	+	+	–	–
36.	lekarstvo 'medicine	ot against	boleznej illness'	–	–	+	+	–	–
37.	lekarstvo 'medicine	ot against	bed misfortunes'	–	–	+	+	–	–
38.	lekarstvo 'medicine	ot against	ustalosti tiredness'	–	–	+	+	–	–
39.	lekarstvo 'medicine	ot against	ukušenija biting'	–	–	+	+	–	–

change of N^1 to a cognate verb form *(xod'ba ot pereulka* 'a walk from the alley' → *xodit' ot pereulka* 'to walk from the alley').

The majority of heads of the *Spatial group (treščina* 'crack', *razrez* 'cut', *tropinka* 'path', *xod'ba* 'walk', *perexod* 'transition', *uxod* 'departure', *begstvo* 'flight', *prostranstvo* 'space', and *put'* 'journey') admit verbal transformation of the sort demanded by T4. The remaining three head words do not. The first of these, *rasstojanie* 'distance', although clearly deverbal in origin, does not have a cognate verb **rasstojat'* 'to cover a distance'. The second, *doroga*, also lacks a verbal counterpart with an appropriate meaning. Lastly, the word *bilet* 'ticket', an eighteenth-century borrowing from French,[65] fits into the list of head words only in a metaphorical sense *(cf. bilet ot Kieva* 'ticket from Kiev' and *rasstojanie ot Kieva* 'distance from Kiev').

Thus, the group is transformationally characterized by the admissibility of transformations 4 (T: $N^1 \rightarrow V$) and 6 (T: $\# \rightarrow$ *do/k* N^3). Morphologically, its members are distinguished by the fact that N^1 is usually derivationally related to a verb specifying motion. Semantically, the unifying trait is that all of the examples refer to a spatial function.

2.3.1.2. *Ablative Group*

The transformation that most frequently specifies examples of the *Ablative group* is T4 (T: $\rightarrow V^{n1}$ *ot* N^2; *izbavlenie ot smerti* 'salvation from death' → *izbavljat' [kogo-nibud'] ot smerti* 'to save [someone] from death'). This illustrates the deverbal nature of the members of this semantic group. A second transformation, T3 (T: $\rightarrow A^{n1}$ *ot* N^2; *osvoboždenie ot gneta* 'liberation from oppression' → *svobodnyj ot gneta* 'free from oppression'), provides the basis of a major subdivision within the *Ablative group*. The first subdivision will be termed the *verbal subgroup* and the second — the *adjectival subgroup*.[66]

T4, which converts the head noun to a verb while *ot* N^2 remains unchanged, in most cases, simply restates the phrases in the original verbal form from which they are derived. This transform, which marks the derivational source of the examples of the group, is the most basic in the characterization of the *Ablative group*. Taken together with the impossibility of T5 (T: $\rightarrow N^2_{sb}\, V$), it indicates that the role of N^2 is that of an object. It can never play the subject role as it does in the *Causal* (pp. 61—66) and *Source* (pp. 50—53) *groups*, which also permit T4. Compare, for example, the following cases:

[65] M. Vasmer, *Russisches Etymologisches Wörterbuch, I* (Heidelberg, 1953), 85.

[66] Both subgroups are *deverbal*, whereas only the second possesses an adjectival form.

T4:	V	ot	N_g	$\rightarrow N_{sb}$	V^{n1}
1.	otstuplenie	ot	principov	$\not\rightarrow$ *principy	otstupajut
	'a retreat	from	principles'	'principles	retreat'
2.	jarost'	ot	bessmyslic	$\rightarrow$ bessmys-licy	jarjajut
	'fury	becau-se of	absurdities'	'absurdities	infuriate [X]'
3.	svet	ot	fonarja	$\rightarrow$ fonar'	svetit
	'light	from	the lantern'	'the lantern	shines'

In the causal (2) and the source (3) examples the dependent noun can play the actor role as the subject of the verb. In the ablative example (1), however, the role of N^2 is restricted to that of an object of the verb. This situation is unique for the *Ablative group*. For the deverbal subgroup of the ablative category, T4 is the sole transformational characterization. This subgroup is illustrated by examples 1–19 in Table 2.

The possibility of T3 (N^1 *ot* $N^2 \rightarrow A^{n1}$ *ot* N^2; *očiščenie ot skverny* 'a cleansing of vileness' → *čistyj ot skverny* 'free from vileness') characterizes the *adjectival subgroup* represented by examples from 20 through 39. The head words of this subgroup have the same list of root morphemes as the *Ablative group* occurring in connection with A *ot* N constructions (pp. 98—100). In general, it would appear that the *adjectival subgroup* is characterized by a somewhat closer derivational kinship to nominal constructs than are the members of the *deverbal subgroup*. The fact that the *ot* accompanies the root in all of its transforms (*svobodnyj ot* 'free from', *svoboda ot* 'freedom from', *osvoboždat' ot* 'to free from') demonstrates that the tie between the lexeme and the preposition is extremely close. This feature seems to be typical for those cases characterized by the phenomenon called *strong government* in traditional Russian grammar. Indeed, the characteristic feature of all examples belonging to *Ablative semantic groups* of the structural types, V, N, or A + *ot* + N seems to be that of strong government.[67]

The last four examples of the adjectival subdivision (33 through 36) form a subgroup that, while showing the same transform features as examples 20 through 32, are somewhat different semantically. The head nouns *zaščita* 'defense', *pomošč'* 'assistance', *bezopasnost'* 'security', and *lekarstvo* 'medicine' all share the use of *ot* in the sense of 'against'. These examples are of particular interest in that they can be viewed as presenting a semantic parallel to the *Countermeasure group (sredstvo ot kašlja* 'remedy against coughing', *zontik ot*

[67] The concept of strong government and of different degrees of government is discussed in the chapter on verbal constructions. In particular, see pages 114 and 136—137.

solnca 'umbrella against sun'), which also uses *ot* in the meaning of 'against', but has head nouns that are not related to verbs.[68]

The *Ablative verbal subgroup* is sharply defined from the transformational point of view. No exceptions were observed to its transform pattern. The *adjectival subgroup* also displays a high degree of uniformity in its transformational responses. Some deviation is displayed in the atypical pluses for T1 and T2 in examples 30, 31, and 32. Both *zavisimost'* 'independence' and *otličie* 'difference' occupy somewhat special places in this group. In most of their occurrences they are bound not only with *ot* but also with a preceding preposition *v* 'in'. They are both complex prepositions rather than preposition *v* plus noun and preposition *ot* plus noun. It is of interest that, although the constituent structure of these units is quite different from that of *svobodnyj ot gneta* 'liberation from oppression', they retain the same transformational characteristics as the free combinations of N^1 *ot* N^2 of the *Ablative group*.

The deverbal derivation of the head nouns of the ablative category is clearly reflected in their suffix patterns. Of the twenty-three head nouns, eleven display the verbal noun suffix *-enie*; five have the *-ost'* suffix used to form abstract nouns from participles and adjectives; and four are verbal nouns having a zero suffix. The head nouns of the *deverbal* and *adjectival subgroups* show no significant differences in regard to their suffix patterns.

The two subgroups do display different patterns in regard to prefixation. In the deverbal subgroup, we have: *ot-* nine times; *iz-* twice; and once each for *s-*, *u-*, *vy-;* and, somewhat anomalously, *pere-*.[69] With the exception of the latter, these prefixes display a general ablative meaning. In contrast, the head nouns of the adjectival subgroup show the following prefixes: *o-* three times, *za-* and *ot* twice each, and one zero suffix. In the latter group, the meaning of ablation tends to be expressed by the root of the head noun rather than by an ablative prefix plus root as in the deverbal examples.

The prefix pattern of the deverbal subgroup also contrasts sharply with that of the deverbal head nouns of the *Causal group (e.g., vostorg ot uspexov* 'delight because of successes'), which displays a similar suffix pattern but where prefixes of the general ablative meaning are rare.[70]

The transformational discrimination of the two subgroups of the ablative category appears to coincide with the semantic differences that are intuitively felt to exist between them. The deverbal head nouns of the first subgroup

[68] See pages 74–75 below for a discussion of the *Countermeasure group*.

[69] The occurrence of *pere-dyška* 'respite' in this list of prefixes, which otherwise signal 'motion away from', may be explained by the fact that the root lexeme *-dyx* occurs with *ot* in all of its forms. Thus the root neutralizes the prefix.

[70] The prefix *u-* occurs five times in head words of the *Causal group*, but never in the ablative meaning: *ustalost'* 'tiredness', *udovol'stvie* 'satisfaction', *utomlennost'* 'weariness', *ulybka* 'smile', and *ubytok* 'loss'. The prefix *ot-* occurs once *(otčajanie* 'despair').

refer to an action in process. Compare this with the class meaning of head nouns of the *Causal group* where N^1 typically refers to an emotional state. The adjective-related second subgroup contains, for the most part, examples expressing the idea of elimination or opposition. The deviation of *zavisimost'* 'dependence' from this pattern may be connected with the fact that it is a phraseological calque from French.[71]

The semantic peculiarities of the group *zaščita* 'defense', *pomošč'* 'assistance', *bezopasnost'* 'security', and *lekarstvo* 'medicine' have already been noted. Of these, *pomošč'* is of particular interest in that it is one of the few head nouns that is inherently ambiguous in its combination with *ot: pomošč' ot ljudej* may have either the meaning of 'help against people' or of 'help provided by people'. In the latter sense it undergoes the set of transforms typical for the *Communication group* (V). To illustrate:

	Ablative Meaning 'opposition'	Communication Meaning 'assistance'
T1: →	—	*pomošč' ljudej* 'the assistance of people'
T2: →	—	*ljudskaja pomošč'* 'human assistance'
T3: →	*pomoščnyj ot ljudej* 'auxiliary against people'	—
T4: →	*pomogat' ot ljudej* 'to assist against people'	—
T5: →	—	*ljudi pomogajut* 'people assist'
T6: →	—	*pomošč' ot ljudej (k nam)* 'assistance from people (to us)'

2.3.1.3. *Phenomenon-Source Group*

Examples of this group have a relational meaning similar to examples of the *Communication-Originator group* (*pis'mo ot brata* 'letter from brother') but are distinguished from the latter by the fact that members of the *Communication-Originator group* have animate dependent nouns and hence

[71] The writer is indebted to Gerta H. Worth for this observation. It should be further noted that *zavisimost'* occurs only rarely as an independent item in the N^1 *ot* N^2 formula. In the great majority of cases it is found as a part of the complex preposition *v zavisimosti ot, cf., dans la dépendence de*. See pages 62–63 for a discussion of complex prepositional structures of the type *v* N *ot*.

TABLE 3

Transform Features of 'N¹ ot N²' Units of the Phenomenon-Source Group

	N^1	*ot*	N^2	T1: $\rightarrow N^1 N^2_g$	T2 $\rightarrow A^{n2} N^1$	T3: $\rightarrow A^{n1}$ *ot* N^2	T4: $\rightarrow V^{n1}$ *ot* N^2	T5: $\rightarrow N^2_{sb} V^{n1}$	T6: $\rightarrow N^1$ *ot* N^2 *do* N^3
1.	svet 'light	ot from	fonarja the lantern'	+	+	+	+	+	−
2.	svet 'light	ot from	spički the match'	+	+	+	+	+	−
3.	blesk 'brilliance	ot from	volokon the filaments'	+	−	+	+	+	−
4.	otblesk 'reflection	ot from	morja the sea'	+	+	+	+	+	−
5.	otblesk 'reflection	ot from	stekla the glass'	+	−	+	+	+	−
6.	luči 'rays	ot from	stekla the glass'	+	+	+	+	+	−
7.	iskry 'sparks	ot from	stekla the glass'	−	−	+	+	+	−
8.	zajčiki 'reflections of a ray	ot from	solnca the sun'	−	+	−	−	−	−
9.	ten' 'shadow	ot from	parka the park'	+	+	+	+	+	−
10.	ten' 'shadow	ot from	zontika the umbrella'	+	+	+	+	+	−
11.	ten' 'shadow	ot from	derev'ev the trees'	+	+	+	+	+	−
12.	ten' 'shadow	ot from	list'ev the leaves'	+	−	+	−	+	−
13.	temnota 'darkness	ot from	sten the walls'	+	+	+	+	+	−
14.	t'ma 'darkness	ot from	tuč the clouds'	+	+	+	+	+	−
15.	mrak 'darkness	ot from	zatmenija the eclipse'	+	−	+	+	+	−
16.	moroz 'frost	ot from	l'da the ice'	+	+	+	+	+	−
17.	xolodok 'chill	ot from	kusta the bush'	+	+	+	−	+	−
18.	teplo 'warmth	ot from	pečki the stove'	+	+	+	+	+	−
19.	žar 'heat	ot from	solnca the sun'	+	+	+	+	+	−

TABLE 3 (*cont.*)

	N^1	*ot*	N^2	T1: → $N^1 N^2_g$	T2: → $A^{n2} N^1$	T3: → A^{n1} *ot* N^2	T4: → V^{n1} *ot* N^2	T5: → $N^2_{sb} V^{n1}$	T6: → N^1 *ot* N^2 *do* N^3
20.	svežest'	ot	vetra	+	+	+	+	+	–
	'freshness	from	the wind'						
21.	suxost'	ot	pustyni	+	+	+	+	+	–
	'dryness	from	the desert'						
22.	syrost'	ot	zemli	+	+	+	+	+	–
	'damp	from	the earth'						
23.	par	ot	galušek	+	+	+	+	+	–
	'steam	from	the dumplings'						
24.	par	ot	parovoza	+	+	+	+	+	–
	'steam	from	the locomotive'						
25.	pena	ot	valov	+	–	+	+	+	–
	'foam	from	the billows'						
26.	zapax	ot	pišči	+	+	+	+	+	–
	'smell	from	the food'						
27.	veter	ot	zemli	+	+	+	+	–	–
	'wind	from	the land'						

head nouns that have co-occurrence privileges with animate nouns.[72] The dependent nouns as well as the head nouns of the *Phenomenon-Source group* are inanimate. In general five of the six transformations utilized in the study of homomorphic N^1 *ot* N^2 constructions are possible for examples of this type.

Source:	N^1 *ot* N^2	*svet ot fonarja* 'light from the lantern'
T1:	→ $N^1 N^2_g$	*svet fonarja* 'lantern's light'
T2:	→ $A^{n2} N^1$	*fonarnyj svet* 'lantern light'
T3:	→ A^{n1} *ot* N^2	*svetlyj ot fonarja* 'alight from the lantern'
T4:	→ V^{n1} *ot* N^2	*svetit ot fonarja* '[it] shines from the lantern'
T5:	→ $N^2_{sb} V^{n1}$	*fonar' svetit* 'the lantern shines'

Transformation 1 (T: → $N^1 N^2_g$) converts the phrase into a subjective genitive construction (*otblesk ot morja* 'reflection from the sea' → *otblesk morja* 'sea's

[72] More precisely, words of the *Communication-Originator group* have head nouns that transform into verbs requiring animate nouns as subjects. The latter role is filled by N^2: *e.g.*, *podarok ot sultana* 'a present from the sultan' → *sultan podarit* 'the sultan presents'.

reflection'). This description finds its formal demonstration in T5, which restates the dependent noun as the subject of a verb derived from the head noun *(otblesk ot morja* 'reflection from the sea' → *more otbleskivaet* 'the sea reflects'). The second transformation (T: → $A^{n2} N^1$) indicates the attributive nature of the relationship between N^1 and N^2 *(veter ot zemli* 'wind from the land' → *zemnoj veter* 'land wind'). T3 indicates that the head noun may also be restated as a qualitative adjective whose primary function is the description of a condition or state *(pena ot valov* 'foam from the billows' → *penistyj ot valov* 'foamy from the billows'). In transformation 4 the head noun is rewritten as a verb with the rest of the construction remaining constant *(par ot galušek* 'steam from the dumplings' → *parit ot galušek* '[it] steams from the dumplings').

There are a number of exceptions to the transformational pattern. The failure of *zajčiki ot solnca* 'reflections of a ray from the sun' (8) to undergo transformations 1 and 3–5 is because *zajčiki* is here used in its secondary and metaphorical meaning, whereas in all of the requisite derived forms only the primary meaning 'hare' obtains. Example 7, *iskry ot stekla* 'sparks from the glass' → *iskry stekla* 'the glass' sparks', was rejected by the informant on semantic grounds, although *luči stekla* 'the glass' rays' from *luči ot stekla* 'rays from the glass' was accepted. Several examples fail to undergo T2 (T: → $A^{n2}N^1$) due to the absence of appropriate adjective forms derivable from N^2, *e.g.*, *mrak ot zatmenija* 'darkness from the eclipse' where *zatmenie* does not possess an adjectival form. Transform 5 has one exception: *veter ot zemli* 'wind from the land' (27) cannot become *zemlja veet* 'the land blows'.

With few exceptions, the head words of this group are simple non-derived nouns. Only one example of the group has a prefix — *otblesk* 'reflection', although the non-prefixed form *blesk* 'brilliance' also occurs. Only five of the twenty-one head words have suffixes: *xolodok* 'chill', *syrost'* 'damp', *svežest'* 'freshness', *suxost'* 'dryness', and *zajčik* 'reflection of a sunray'. None of these suffixes appear to be significantly related to the meaning or classification of the *Phenomenon-Source group* as are the *-enie* and *-ost'* suffixes in the *Causal group*, for example *(cf.* pp. 63–64). All of the examples, except *zajčiki ot solnca* 'reflections of a ray from the sun', have N^1's that are etymologically related to verbs (T4 and T5). It is of interest, however, that the type of derivational relation between N^1 and the corresponding verb is very different from that in examples of the *Ablative group* in which the line of derivation is direct — *otklonenie* 'deviation' → *otklonjat'* 'to deviate'. In the *Source group* the derivational tie, while still evident, is less immediate. Derivationally, the head nouns of the *Phenomenon-Source group* fall between those of the *Ablative* and *Causal groups*, on the one hand, and on the other, those of the *Component-Aggregate group (ključ ot biblioteki* 'key to the library') where the derivational connection between N^1 and a cognate verb is remote, if present at all.

TABLE 4

Transform Features of 'N¹ *ot* N²' *Units of the Trace-Origin Group*

	N^1	*ot*	N^2	T1: → $N^1 N^2_g$	T2: → $A^{n2} N^1$	T3: → A^{n1} *ot* N^2	T4: → V^{n1} *ot* N^2	T5: → $N^2_{sb} V^{n1}$	T6: → N^1 *ot* N^2 *do* N^3
1.	sledy	ot	seti	−	+	−	−	+	−
	'marks	from	the net'						
2.	sledy	ot	kolenej	−	+	−	−	+	−
	'marks	from	the knees'						
3.	sledy	ot	pal'cev	+	+	−	−	+	−
	'marks	from	the fingers'						
4.	poteki	ot	slez	−	+	−	−	+	−
	'streaks	from	tears'						
5.	poteki	ot	kapl'	+	−	−	−	+	−
	'streaks	from	drops'						
6.	pjatno	ot	puli	−	+	+	+	+	−
	'a spot	from	the bullet'						
7.	pjatno	ot	likera	−	+	+	+	+	−
	'a spot	from	the liquor'						
8.	pjatno	ot	želtka	−	+	+	−	+	−
	'a spot	from	the yolk'						
9.	pjatno	ot	kraski	−	−	+	−	+	−
	'a spot	from	the paint'						
10.	polosy	ot	knuta	−	+	+	−	+	−
	'stripes	from	the whip'						
11.	dyry	ot	pul'	−	+	+	−	+	−
	'holes	from	the bullets'						
12.	dyry	ot	pogon	−	+	+	−	+	−
	'holes	from	the stripes'						
13.	srezy	ot	lopaty	−	+	−	−	+	−
	'slices	from	the spade'						
14.	breš'	ot	vystrela	−	−	−	−	−	−
	'a breach	from	the shot'						
15.	vyboina	ot	puli	−	+	−	−	+	−
	'a dent	from	the bullet'						
16.	voronki	ot	bomb	−	+	+	−	−	−
	'craters	from	the bombs'						
17.	šramy	ot	oskolkov	−	+	−	−	−	−
	'scars	from	the fragments'						
18.	šramy	ot	udara	−	+	−	−	−	−
	'scars	from	the blow'						

Semantically, the head words of the *Phenomenon-Source group* display a strikingly close unity. Of the twenty-one head words, six (*svet* 'light', *[ot]blesk* 'brilliance, reflection', *luči* 'rays', *zajčiki* 'reflections of sunbeams', and *iskry* 'sparks') refer to light. These are semantically counterbalanced by *ten'* 'shadow', *mrak* 'gloom', *t'ma* and *temnota* 'darkness'. *Xolodok* 'chill', *moroz* 'frost', and *teplo* 'warmth', *žar* 'heat' represent another such pairing. The concept dampness figures in three examples — *syrost'* 'damp', *par* 'steam', and *pena* 'foam' and is opposed to *suxost'* 'dryness'. Finally, the noun *zapax* 'odor', *svežest'* 'freshness', and *veter* 'wind' fill out this list of terms referring to natural phenomena. A final point which serves to buttress the establishment of such a group on transformational grounds is that many of the verbs cognate to N^1 in the group are marked by the syntactic feature of 'impersonality', *e.g.*, *svetaet* '[it] is getting light', *stemneet* '[it] is getting dark', *morozit* '[it] is freezing'. This property is characteristic of verbs dealing with phenomena of nature.

2.3.1.4. *Trace-Origin Group*

The transformational characterization of the *Trace-Origin group* is less sharply defined than that for the other semantic categories. The two transforms that most consistently apply to examples of this group are T2 and T5. These are illustrated in the following:

N^1 ot N^2	→	T2: → A^{n2} N^1
srezy ot lopaty		*lopatnye srezy*
'slices from the spade'		'spade slices'
		T5: → N^2_{sb} V^{n1}
		lopata srežet
		'the spade slices'

The remaining transforms are generally negatively characterized, although four of the ten heads also admit T3: *pjatnistyj ot pul'* 'spotted from the bullets' ← *pjatna ot pul'* 'spots from the bullets' and *dyra* 'hole', *voronka* 'crater', and *polosa* 'stripe' with the adjectival transforms *dyrjavyj* 'full of holes', *voronkovyj* 'cratered', and *polosatyj* 'striped'.

Both of the possible transformations show a number of exceptions. Example 5, *poteki ot kapl'* 'streaks from the drops', fails to conform to the pattern because the adjectival form of *kaplja* has the transferred meaning of 'very small' rather than the etymological meaning of the noun root of a 'drop of liquid'. Example 14 is negative in that *vystrel* 'shot' lacks an adjectival form as does *kraska* 'paint'.

Derivationally the list of head words presents a mixed picture, although they are predominantly of nominal origin. *Breš'* (French *brèche)* and *šram*

TABLE 5

Transform Features of 'N^1 ot N^2' Units of the Communication-Originator Group

	N^1	*ot*	N^2	T1: → $N^1 N^2_g$	T2: → $A^{n2} N^1$	T3: → A^{n1} *ot* N^2	T4: → V^{n1} *ot* N^2	T5: → $N^2_{sb} V^{n1}$	T6: → N^1 *ot* N^2 *do/k* N^3
1.	podarok 'present	ot from	sultana the sultan'	+	+	−	−	+	+
2.	zapiska 'note	ot from	mamy mamma'	+	+	−	−	+	+
3.	zapiska 'note	ot from	Ivanova Ivanov'	+	−	−	−	+	+
4.	pis'mo 'letter	ot from	sestry [one's] sister'	+	+	−	−	+	+
5.	pis'mo 'letter	ot from	Ljuby Ljuba'	+	+	−	−	+	+
6.	otkrytka 'post card	ot from	Kuz'mina Kuz'min'	+	−	−	−	−	+
7.	konvert 'envelope	ot from	Anny Anna'	+	+	−	−	−	+
8.	poklony 'greetings	ot from	znakomyx acquaintances'	+	−	−	−	+	+
9.	sovety 'advice	ot from	druzej friends'	+	−	−	−	+	+
10.	sovety 'advice	ot from	rodni kin'	+	−	−	−	+	+
11.	razgovor 'conversation	ot from	obščestva the society'	+	+	−	−	+	+
12.	pomošč' 'aid	ot from	ljudej people'	+	+	−	−	+	+
13.	deputaty 'deputies	ot from	rabočix the workers'	+	+	−	−	−	+
14.	ob''javlenie 'declaration	ot from	komendanta the commandant'	+	+	−	−	+	+
15.	naznačenie 'appointment	ot from	ministra the minister'	+	+	−	−	+	+
16.	počtenie 'respect	ot from	detej children'	+	−	−	−	+	+
17.	napadenie 'attack	ot from	kirgizov the Kirghiz'	+	+	−	−	+	+

(German *Schramme)* can be excluded from consideration on the grounds that they have not been sufficiently assimilated into the Russian derivational system to develop related adjectival or verbal forms. *Sled* 'mark', *pjatno* 'spot', *dyra* 'hole', *polosa* 'stripe', and *voronka* 'crater' are of nominal origin, whereas the three prefixed forms *poteki* 'streaks', *vyboina* 'dent', and *srezy* 'slice' are of verbal origin.[73]

On the whole, this group is weakly defined in terms of formal criteria and relies heavily on meaning. On the other hand, its examples do not undergo any of the combinations of transformation that would mark them as belonging to one of the other formally defined groups. Consequently, from the formal point of view, they must be viewed as a negatively defined residue category.

2.3.1.5. *Communication-Originator Group*

The *Academy Grammar* lists a semantic category with the label 'origin'.[74] The examples include both of the following types of phrases: *poklony ot otca* 'greetings from father' and *svet ot fonarja* 'light from the lantern'. The reaction of these two types of examples under transformation shows that they are very different in their inner syntactic structure.[75]

T1: $\rightarrow N^1 N^2_g$	*poklony otca* 'father's greetings'	*svet fonarja* 'lantern's light'
T2: $\rightarrow A^{n2} N^1$	*otcovskie poklony* 'paternal greetings'	*fonarnyj svet* 'lantern light'
T3: $\rightarrow A^{n1}$ *ot* N^2	—	*svetlyj ot fonarja* 'alight from the lantern'
T4: $\rightarrow V^{n1}$ *ot* N^2	—	*svetit ot fonarja* '[it] shines from the lantern'
T5: $\rightarrow N^2_{sb} V^{n1}$	*otec klanjaetsja* 'father greets'	*fonar' svetit* 'the lantern shines'
T6: $\rightarrow + k N^3$	*poklony ot otca k detjam* 'greetings from father to children'	—

The most obvious difference between these two types is that examples of the first type have animate nouns as the object of the preposition. A less obvious

[73] *Sled* stems from CS **slědъ* (Vasmer, *II*, 658); *pjatno* < CS **pęt'no* (Vasmer, *II*, 478); *voronka* and *dyra* are also non-derived nouns in their present meaning (Vasmer, *I*, 229 and 386). *Potek, srez,* and *vyboina* are marked as being derived from verbs by virtue of their prefixes *po-*, *s-*, and *vy- (poteč', srezat', vybit').*

[74] *AG, II*, 1, 250–1.

[75] The type represented by *svet ot fonarja* is treated in detail under the heading of the *Phenomenon-Source group*, pp. 50–53.

but very important consequence of this is that the type of noun that can play the role of the head word is very different in the two types of examples. The list of head words, which can appear in examples of the *poklony ot otca* 'greetings from father' type, is restricted to those referring to actions, or more accurately to the results of actions that can be performed by animate beings. The list of words that can appear as head nouns in examples of the *svet ot fonarja* 'light from the lantern' type are unmarked in this respect and it is the unmarked group that displays the fewer transformational restrictions.

Transformations 1 and 2 illustrate the possessive-attributive nature of the relationship between N^1 and N^2. These syntactic reflexes, taken together with the negative results for transforms 3 (T: $\rightarrow A^{n1}$ *ot* N^2) and 4 (T: $\rightarrow V^{n1}$ *ot* N^2), indicate that the relationship between N^1 and N^2 for the *Communication-Originator group* is that of actor and the result of his activity. This is borne out by T5, which restates the two units in the form of subject and predicate *(otec klanjaetsja* 'father greets'). Lastly, the examples of the *Communication-Originator* type are characterized by the possibility of being expanded by further prepositional complementation (T6), *e.g.*, *poklony ot otca k detjam* 'greetings from father to children'.

Transformation 1 shows no negative responses. The second transform, however, displays minuses for six of the phrases. Two of these are due to the fact that a surname is the object of the preposition. Surnames, in contrast to given names, do not form adjectives in Russian. In example ten, N^2, *znakomye* 'acquaintances', already has the form of an adjective thus precluding the possibility of contrasting the two usages. The remaining three exceptions are due to semantic shifts between nominal and adjectival forms. For example, in example sixteen, the T2 reformulation of *deti* 'children' as an adjective modifying *početenie* 'respect' is perfectly possible, but yields a phrase meaning 'childish respect' rather than the desired 'children's respect'.

Transformation 5 (T: $\rightarrow N^2_{sb} V^{n1}$, *komendant ob''javljaet* 'commandant declares' $\rightarrow$ *ob''javlenie ot komendanta* 'declaration from the commandant') has three negative responses. *Deputat* 'deputy' and *konvert* 'envelope' are both borrowings lacking verb forms in Russian. The remaining exception, *otkrytka,* is derived from the verb *otkryt'* and possesses the transferred meaning 'post card' rather than the verbal meaning 'to open'.

The primary morphological feature of this group has already been noted — the animacy of N^2. The head noun presents a much less uniform picture, although its membership also is sharply restricted, at least on the lexical level. Morphologically the head nouns split into two major groups: *podarok* 'present', *pis'mo* 'letter', *poklon* 'greeting', *sovet* 'advice', *razgovor* 'conversation', and *pomošč'* 'aid', versus *ob''javlenie* 'declaration', *naznačenie* 'appointment', *početenie* 'respect', and *napadenie* 'attack'. Both are derived from verbs, but it would appear that two different layers of derivation are involved. The first list is

TABLE 6

Transform Features of 'N¹ ot N²' Units of the State-Cause Group

	N^1	*ot*	N^2	T1: → $N^1 N^2_g$	T2: → $A^{n2} N^1$	T3: → A^{n1} *ot* N^2	T4: → V^{n1} *ot* N^2	T5: → $N^2_{sb} V^{n1}$	T6: → N^1 *ot* N^2 *do* N^2
1.	radost'	ot	vstreči	+	–	+	+	+	–
	'joy	because of	the meeting'						
2.	radost'	ot	(izbavlenija)[76]	+	–	+	+	+	–
	'joy	because of	(the salvation)'						
3.	jarost'	ot	bessmyslic	–	–	+	+	+	–
	'fury	because of	absurdities'						
4.	gordost'	ot	(fakta)	–	–	+	+	+	–
	'pride	because of	(the fact)'						
5.	gore	ot	uma	+	–	+	+	–	–
	'grief	because of	cleverness'						
6.	smuta	ot	(fakta)	–	–	+	+	+	–
	'disturbance	because of	(the fact)'						
7.	pokoj	ot	ljudej	–	–	+	+	+	–
	'peace	because of	the people'						
8.	vozbuždenie	ot	boja	–	–	+	+	+	–
	'agitation	because of	the battle'						
9.	skuka	ot	knig	–	–	+	+	+	–
	'boredom	because of	books'						
10.	naslaždenie	ot	papirosy	–	–	–	+	+	–
	'enjoyment	because of	the cigarette'						
11.	goreč'	ot	komedii	–	–	+	–	+	–
	'bitterness	because of	the comedy'						
12.	udovol'stvie	ot	soprikosnovenija	+	–	+	+	+	–
	'pleasure	because of	the touch'						
13.	udovletvorenie	ot	(slučaja)	–	–	+	+	+	–
	'satisfaction	because of	(the event)'						
14.	vostorg	ot	goroda	–	–	+	+	+	–
	'ecstasy	because of	the town'						
15.	vostorg	ot	uspexov	+	–	+	+	+	–
	'ecstasy	because of	successes'						
16.	ustalost'	ot	vnimanija	–	–	+	+	–	–
	'tiredness	because of	attention'						
17.	utomlennost'	ot	žizni	–	–	+	+	+	–
	'weariness	because of	life'						
18.	smjatenie	ot	zrelišča	–	–	+	+	+	–
	'confusion	because of	the sight'						
19.	zamešatel'stvo	ot	vstreči	–	–	–	+	+	–
	'embarrassment	because of	the meeting'						

[76] See pages 61–62 and especially footnote 77 regarding the items in parentheses.

TABLE 6 (*cont.*)

	N^1	*ot*	N^2	T1: $\rightarrow N^1 N^2_g$	T2: $\rightarrow A^{n2} N^1$	T3: $\rightarrow A^{n1}$ *ot* N^2	T4: $\rightarrow V^{n1}$ *ot* N^2	T5: $\rightarrow N^2_{sb} V^{n1}$	T6: $\rightarrow N^1$ *ot* N^2 *do* N^3
20.	zamešatel'stvo	ot	ljudej	–	–	–	+	+	–
	'embarrassment	because of	the people'						
21.	mučenie	ot	vetra	–	–	–	+	+	–
	'torment	because of	the wind'						
22.	otčajanie	ot	(položenija)	+	–	+	+	+	–
	'despair	because of	(the situation)'						
23.	legkost'	ot	nedoedanija	+	–	+	+	+	–
	'lightness	because of	starvation'						
24.	obida	ot	(zvona)	–	–	+	+	+	–
	'resentment	because of	(the ringing)'						
25.	opjanenie	ot	izbytka	–	–	+	+	+	–
	'drunkenness	because of	excess'						
26.	vpečatlenie	ot	forta	–	–	+	+	+	–
	'impression	because of	the fort'						
27.	rumjanec	ot	zloupotreblenija	–	–	+	+	+	–
	'a flush	because of	ill-usage'						
28.	paralič	ot	maljarii	–	–	+	+	+	–
	'paralysis	because of	malaria'						
29.	revmatizm	ot	sapog	–	–	+	–	–	–
	'rheumatism	because of	the boots'						
30.	izžoga	ot	bljuda	–	–	+	+	+	–
	'heartburn	because of	the dish'						
31.	žar	ot	ožoga	–	–	–	–	+	–
	'fever	because of	a burn'						
32.	smert'	ot	ženy	–	–	+	+	+	–
	'death	because of	[one's] wife'						
33.	smert'	ot	klinka	–	–	+	+	+	–
	'death	because of	a blade'						
34.	povreždenie	ot	vyrubki	–	–	+	+	+	–
	'damage	because of	the cutting down'						
35.	ulybka	ot	orfografii	–	–	–	+	+	–
	'a smile	because of	the orthography'						
36.	ubytki	ot	požara	–	–	+	+	–	–
	'losses	because of	the fire'						
37.	slezy	ot	ljubvi	+	+	–	+	+	–
	'tears	because of	love'						
38.	posledstvija	ot	dejstvija	+	–	–	+	+	–
	'consequences	because of	the action'						
39.	šum	ot	dviženija	–	–	+	+	+	–
	'noise	because of	the movement'						

probably closed except for the occasional inclusion of new words on the basis of analogy with words already included. The appearance of *otkrytka* 'post card' and *konvert* 'envelope' in the list serves as illustration of this process. The second group is still productive and could easily be expanded, *e.g.,privetstvija* 'salutations', *rekomendacija* 'recommendation', *soobščenie* 'communication', *etc.*

The semantic unity of the head nouns is apparent. With the marginal exceptions of sixteen and seventeen, all refer to some form of communication between people.

2.3.1.6. *State-Cause Group*

The set of six transforms used to isolate and characterize the various semantic groups within the N^1 *ot* N^2 construction provides a unique set of specifying features for examples of the *Causal group*. With some variation, the pattern is that transformations 3–5 are possible. To illustrate:

		T3: A^{n1} ot N^2 *jarostnyj ot bessmyslic* 'furious because of absurdities'
N^1 ot N^2 *jarost' ot bessmyslic* 'fury because of absurdities'	→	T4: V^{n1} ot N^2 *raz''jarjat'sja ot bessmyslic* 'to become furious because of absurdities'
		T5: N^2_{sb} V^{n1} *bessmyslicy raz''jarjajut* 'absurdities infuriate'

Additionally, T1, which involves deletion of the preposition, is possible for about one-quarter of the examples *(radost' ot vstreči* 'joy because of meeting' → *radost' vstreči* 'meeting's joy'). Transforms 2 (T: → A^{n2} N^1) and 6 (T: → N^1 *ot* N^2 + *do* N^3) are rarely, if ever, possible.

Apart from these transformational features, examples of this type display certain constructional peculiarities, which, if not unique to causal examples, are at least of more common occurrence in this group than in other semantic categories of the N^1 *ot* N^2 construction. In six cases the role of the dependent noun is played by one of the demonstrative pronouns instead of one specific noun. Although exact statistics were not kept, it is clear that the relative frequency of demonstrative pronouns as the object of the preposition was higher in examples of the causal category than in examples of the other groups. The pronominal elements in all six cases refer to a clause that describes the causal situation, *e.g.*, . . . *gordost' ot togo, čto obo mne poslali nastojaščuju tele-*

grammu . . . 'pride because of the fact that they had sent a real telegram about me'.[77] On the semantic level, an interesting correlate of the use of the demonstrative pronoun is that N^1 in all cases refers to an emotion *(radost'* 'joy', *obida* 'resentment', *gordost'* 'pride', *udovletvorenie* 'satisfaction', *smuta* 'confusion', *otčajanie* 'despair').

The second constructional feature that showed a higher relative frequency in the *Causal group* than elsewhere was that certain common head words *(vosxiščenie* 'delight', *vostorg* 'ecstasy', and *otčajanie* 'despair') occur in the prepositional case following the preposition *v*.[78] That this is not a wholly free syntactic combination is attested by the recent seventeen volume Academy of Sciences dictionary, which gives individual sublistings for the set expressions *byt' v vosxiščenii* 'to be in rapture' and *byt' v vostorge* 'to be in ecstasy'.[79] Both of these words are syntactically parallel to *otčajanie* 'despair' in that they occur in the expression *prixodit' v* 'to enter into a state of': (1) *vosxiščenie,* (2) *vostorg,* and (3) *otčajanie*.[80]. Additionally, these three head nouns show an obvious semantic kinship.

These factors, taken together with the fact that all three are often coupled with *ot* to indicate causality, lead to the conclusion that the examples in question do not represent $N^1 + ot + N^2$ structures, but are complex prepositions of the structural type *v* N_p *ot.* This interpretation would make them parallel to complex prepositions of the type *v zavisimosti ot* 'in dependence on', *v otličie ot* 'in contrast to', *etc.*[81] These latter examples also serve to counter

[77] Since the transforms operate only upon N^1 *ot* N^2 units, appropriate nouns were substituted for the pronouns in the examples. The substitutions were judged acceptable by the native informant. The substitutions are indicated in Table 6 by parentheses enclosing the inserted word.

[78] In addition to these three, the noun *smjatenie* 'confusion' also occurred in the form *v* N_p.

[79] *Slovar' sovremennogo russkogo literaturnogo jazyka, II,* cols. 732 and 738; *VIII,* col. 1687.

[80] The nouns *zamešatel'stvo* 'embarrassment' and *jarost'* 'fury' might marginally be added to this group since both also occur in the expression *prixodit' v* N^1_a *ot* N^2. They do not, however, occur in set expressions of the type *byt' v* N_p nor do they exhibit the syntactic peculiarities of *vosxiščenie, vostorg,* or *otčajanie,* which are discussed in the following paragraph.

[81] V. S. Bondarenko, *Predlogi v sovremennom russkom jazyke* (Moscow, 1961), 63. Bondarenko, who also is the author of the section on prepositions in the *Academy Grammar,* includes a large number of complex prepositions of the type *v zavisimosti ot* in the cited work, but does not extend his classification to include the word-combinations under discussion *(v vostorge ot* 'in ecstasy from'). Nor are the latter so classified in the following two major studies on secondary prepositions: A. M. Finkel', *Proizvodnye pričinnye predlogi v sovremennom russkom literaturnom jazyke* (Kharkov, 1962); E. T. Čerkasova, "K izučeniju obrazovanija russkix otymennyx predlogov", *Issledovanija po grammatike russkogo literaturnogo jazyka: sbornik statej,* eds. N. S. Pospelov and N. Ju. Švedova (Moscow, 1955), 73–139.

the possible objection that the lexical meaning of a phrase such as *v vosxiščeni ot* 'in delight from' or *v vostorge ot* 'in ecstasy from' is too concrete to become grammaticalized and function primarily as a grammatical rather than a lexical unit. Even a preposition consisting of one word may retain a high degree of lexical meaning — as, for example, the preposition *blagodarja* 'thanks to'.

Transformation 3, which converts N^1 to an adjective, is the key element in the characterization of the *Causal group*. One morphological expression of the close relationship of the causal examples to adjectival formations is the occurrence of the suffix *-ost'* in six of the head words of the causal examples as opposed to its infrequency among the head nouns of the other two semantic categories, which permit T3. The suffix *-ost'*, according to the *Academy Grammar*, is the most productive suffix in CSR used to form abstract nouns with the meaning of property, quality, and state. Its primary use is in the formation of such nouns from the stems of descriptive adjectives.[82]

Another indication of the close connection between the semantic category of causality and the presence of head words, which are derived from adjectives, is provided by the analysis of A *ot* N constructions. In this group it is shown that approximately two-thirds of all of the examples examined expressed causal relations.[83]

Six of the head nouns do not undergo the adjectivization transformation. In two of these cases the explanation lies in a shift of meaning between the nominal and the adjectival form. The usual situation in such cases is that a given noun will have a basic meaning and one or more transferred or metaphorical meanings, whereas its derived adjective refers to only the primary meaning. Take, for example, the phrase *žar ot ožoga*, which means 'a fever because of a burn'. The primary meaning *žar* is 'heat' while 'fever' is listed as a secondary meaning. The derived adjective, *žarnyj*, refers only to the primary meaning of 'heat'.

The nouns *zamešatel'stvo, naslaždenie* both lack appropriate adjectival forms. *Zamešatel'stvo* 'confusion' lacks a corresponding adjective. *Naslaždenie* 'enjoyment' is cognate with the adjective *sladkij* 'sweet' but the meanings have become widely divorced. The head nouns of the remaining two exceptions, *slezy ot ljubvi* 'tears because of love' and *ulybka ot ortografii* 'a smile because of the orthography', both have corresponding adjectives *(sleznyj* and *ulybočnyj)*, but their A^{n1} *ot* N^2 transforms were rejected as nonsensical.

Transformation 4, which restates N^1 as a verb (T: N^1 *ot* $N^2 \rightarrow V^{n1}$ *ot* N^2), is possible in all but three cases. This transformation simply recasts the N^1 *ot* N^2 *(smjatenie ot zrelišča* 'embarrassment because of the sight') in parallel verbal

[82] *AG, I*, 252. The *-ost'* suffix is also commonly used to form abstract nouns from past passive participles, *i.e.*, from the adjectival form of the verb.

[83] The transformational basis for this correlation is stated in detail in the chapter on A *ot* N constructions, pages 96–98.

form *(mjastis' ot žrelišča* 'to be embarrassed because of the sight'). The verbal transforms all have the meaning 'to be in the state or assume the state referred to by the root of the word': *vostorgat'sja ot goroda* 'to become ecstatic because of the town', *vozbuždat'sja ot boja* 'to become agitated because of the battle', *ustat' ot vnimanija* 'to tire because of attention', *mučit'sja ot vetra* 'to be tormented because of the wind', *op'janet' ot izbytka* 'to become drunk because of excess'.

Transformation 3 demonstrated the morphological relationship of the head noun to adjectives *(gordost'* 'pride' → *gordyj* 'proud'). The fourth transform shows that many of the N's are of verbal derivation. Nine of the examples considered are verbal nouns in *-enie*. The verbs from which these nouns are derived are a particular sort. For example, *op'janenie* 'drunkenness' is immediately derived from the verb *(o)p'janet'* 'to become drunk'. This verb, however, is derived from the adjectival form *p'janyj* 'drunk'. Other verbs in this list do not have such close derivational ties with adjectives, but all describe states rather than actions *(otčajat'sja* 'to despair', *umeret'* 'to die', *naslaždat'sja* 'to enjoy', *etc.)*. The three head nouns that fail to undergo the fourth transformation are *revmatizm* 'rheumatism', *žar* 'fever', and *goreč'* 'bitterness'. The first of these is a foreign borrowing with no verbal form. The second word, *žar*, is used in a transferred secondary meaning of 'fever', whereas the cognate verb, *žarit'* 'to fry, roast', does not include this particular meaning in its semantic spectrum. The final word, *goreč'*, lacks a verb with the abstract meaning 'to embitter'. The related verbs *ogorčit'* (transitive) and *gorevat'* (intransitive) mean 'to grieve'. Again, this is a problem of transferred meaning.

Transformation 5 (T: $\rightarrow N^2_{sb}\, V^{n1}$), which restates the second noun as the subject of a verb derived from N^1, reformulates the passive-like causal construction (N^1 = verbal nouns; N^2 = agent) in an active form: *naslaždenie ot papiros* 'enjoyment because of cigarettes' → *papirosa naslaždaet (ranenogo soldata)* 'the cigarette gives pleasure to (the wounded soldier)'. This transformational relationship obtains for about 90 per cent of the examples collected. It does not seem unreasonable to regard the reversible transformation N^1 *ot* $N^2 \leftrightarrow N^2_{sb}$ $V^{n1}_t\, N_{ob}$ as being parallel to the full active-passive transformation of the type $N^1_{sb}\, V_t\, N^2_{ob} \leftrightarrow N^2\, V_{pp}\, N^1_i$: *žena ub'et muža* 'the wife kills the husband' ↔ *muž ubit ženoj* 'the husband is killed by the wife'. The parallel between the verbal active-passive transformation and its nominal analogue was even closer in Old Russian where *ot* + N^3 was regularly used to indicate the agent in passive constructions, *e.g.*, . . . *a dĕmoni* PROKLINAEMI OT" *blagovĕrnyx*" MUŽ *i* OT" *vĕrnyx*" ŽEN"[84] 'but the demons are accursed by true-believing husbands and by faithful wives'.

[84] T. P. Lomtev, *Očerki po istoričeskomu sintaksisu russkogo jazyka* (Moscow, 1956), 403. It is further noted that the *ot* + N of the construction was supplanted by the use

This chain of relationships may be described as follows:

	PASSIVE		ACTIVE
Modern Russian:	$N^1\ V_{pp}\quad N^2_i$ *on vozbužden boem* 'he is agitated by the battle'		
Old Russian:	$N^1\ V_{pp}$ ot + N^2 *on vozbužden ot boja* 'he is agitated by the battle'	↔	N^2_n V N^1_a *boj vozbuždaet ego* 'the battle agitates him'
Modern Russian:	N^V ot N^2 *ego vozbuždenie ot boja* 'his agitation by [because of] the battle'		

The parallel between the Old Russian construction $N^1\ V_{pp}$ *ot* + N^2 and the modern Russian N^V *ot* + N^2 in their use of *ot* + N^2 to mark the agent role is particularly significant from the point of view of equating the *Causal group* of the N^1 *ot* N^2 constructional type with passive participial constructions. The fact that it is an adjectival form of the verb *(i.e.*, the passive participle) that occurs in the analogous verbal form of the passive-causal construction provides further support for our observation about the adjectival nature of the head nouns of the *Causal group*.

The four exceptions to T5 are: *gore* 'grief', *revmatizm* 'rheumatism', *ustalost'* 'tiredness', and *ubytok* 'loss'. The transform *um ogorčaet* 'the mind inflicts grief' was rejected by the informant. It may be that the source phrase *gore ot uma* 'grief because of intelligence', due to its use as the title of the Griboedov play, has become fixed in Russian and is restricted in its permutation possibilities. The second example, *revmatizm* 'rheumatism', is a foreign loan word, which lacks a verbal form. The final two cases *ustalost'* 'tiredness' and *ubytok* 'loss' possess only intransitive verbal forms *(ustat'* 'to tire' and *ubyt'* 'to become smaller').

The fact that eight of the head words undergo T1 (T: → $N^1\ N^2_g$) shows that for particular word-combinations possession as well as causality is construed as playing a role in the relationship of N^1 and N^2. That this is a property of only certain combinations of words and not of the constructional type as

of a noun in the instrumental case. At least one relic of the earlier stage is preserved as a fixed phrase in modern Russian: *ot ruki napisano* 'written by hand', *Slovar' russkogo jazyka,* comp. S. I. Ožegov (Moscow, 1960), 679.

a whole is shown by the pair of examples *vostorg ot uspexov* 'ecstasy because of successes' and *vostorg ot goroda* 'ecstasy because of the town'. The former permits the omission of the *ot (vostorg uspexov* 'ecstasy of successes'); whereas the latter, *vostorg ot goroda,* does not allow such a change.

Thus the three transformations (3–5), which formally isolate the *Causal group* from the other semantic groups within the N^1 *ot* N^2 construction, also provide a considerable degree of insight into the inner structure of the group. The superiority of the transform analysis to one purely in terms of morphological derivational criteria is particularly clear-cut in this group. From the point of view of morphological structure, the head nouns of the *Causal group* fall into three disparate classes. The first of these includes the deadjectivals in *-ost': radost'* 'joy', *jarost'* 'fury', *gordost'* 'pride', and also *ustalost'* 'tiredness' and *utomlennost'* 'weariness' whose origin is participial. *Rumjanec* 'blush' ← *rumjanyj* 'rosy' also is a member of the deadjectival group, as is *goreč'* 'bitterness', which may be traced back to *gor'kij* 'bitter'. Verbal nouns constitute a second derivational group: *vozbuždenie* 'agitation', *naslaždenie* 'enjoyment', *smjatenie* 'embarrassment', *mučenie* 'torment', *otčajanie* 'despair', *vpečatlenie* 'impression', *povreždenie* 'damage', *op'janenie* 'drunkenness', *udovletvorenie* 'satisfaction', and also *zamešatel'stvo* 'embarrassment', *posledstvie* 'consequence', and *udovol'stvie* 'pleasure'. The remaining morphological group consists largely of nouns that have only remote derivational ties with other parts of speech: *smuta* 'disturbance', *pokoj* 'peace', *skuka* 'boredom', *vostorg* 'ecstasy', *obida* 'resentment', *šum* 'noise', *sleza* 'tear', *ubytok* 'loss', *ulybka* 'smile', *smert'* 'death', *žar* 'fresh', *izžoga* 'heartburn', *paralič* 'paralysis', and *revmatizm* 'rheumatism'.

From the purely semantic point of view, the great majority of head nouns found in the causal category display a marked similarity in that they have a strong tendency to refer to emotional states. The largest group of exceptions is formed by words referring to illness, injury, or death: *smert'* 'death', *žar* 'fever', *izžoga* 'heartburn', *paralič* 'paralysis', *revmatizm* 'rheumatism', and *povreždenie* 'damage'; with the exception of the last, all of these belong to the third derivational group.

It is of interest that many of the head nouns possess antonyms: *radost'* 'joy' — *grustnost'* 'sadness', *legkost'* 'lightness' — *tjažest'* 'heaviness', *gordost'* 'pride' — *styd* 'shame', *skuka* 'boredom' — *živost'* 'animation', *smjatenie* 'confusion' — *spokojstvo* 'peacefulness', *etc.* This type of relationship is typical of words referring to qualities the expression of which is the primary function of adjectives.[85] This correlation brings us back again to the centrality of the adjectival derivation that underlies the *Causal group.*

[85] *AG, I,* 280. The author of the section on adjectives, N. Ju. Švedova, notes this capability of qualitative adjectives to enter into antonymic pairs as one of their typical features.

TABLE 7

Transform Features of 'N^1 ot N^2' Units of the Component-Aggregate and the Container-Designation Groups[86]

	N^1	*ot*	N^2	T1: $\to N^1 N^2_g$	T2: $\to A^{n2} N^1$	T3: $\to A^{n1}$ *ot* N^2	T4: $\to V^{n1}$ *ot* N^2	T5: $\to N^2_{sb} V^{n1}$	T6: $\to N^1$ *ot* N^2 *do/k* N^3
1.	ključ	ot	goroda	+	+	−	−	−	−
	'key	to	the town'						
2.	ključ	ot	kaliti	+	+	−	−	−	−
	'key	to	the gate'						
3.	ključ	ot	senej	+	+	−	−	−	−
	'key	to	the hallway'						
4.	ključ	ot	biblioteki	+	+	−	−	−	−
	'key	to	the library'						
5.	ključ	ot	škafa	+	+	−	−	−	−
	'key	to	the cupboard'						
6.	gil'zi	ot	mauzerov	+	+	−	−	−	−
	'cartridge cases	to	Mausers'						
7.	gil'zi	ot	vintovok	+	+	−	−	−	−
	'cartridge cases	to	rifles'						
8.	p'edestal	ot	pamjatnika	+	+	−	−	−	−
	'pedestal	to	a monument'						
9.	cepočka	ot	časov	+	+	−	−	−	−
	'a chain	to	a watch'						
10.	cep'	ot	lampadki	+	+	−	−	−	−
	'a chain	to	an icon lamp'						
11.	šeluxa	ot	podsolnuxov	+	+	−	−	−	−
	'husks	to	sunflower seeds'						
12.	šeluxa	ot	semeček	+	+	−	−	−	−
	'husks	to	[sunflower] seeds'						
13.	obertki	ot	paketov	+	+	−	−	−	−
	'wrappings	to	packages'						
14.	poplavki	ot	setej	+	+	−	−	−	−
	'floats	to	nets'						
15.	probka	ot	šampanskogo	+	−	−	−	−	−
	'cork	to	a champagne bottle'						
16.	ščepa	ot	kresta	+	+	−	−	−	−
	'chip	to	the cross'						

[86] The Table contains the examples for two similar but distinct semantic groups represented by numbers 1–39 and 40–49 respectively. The two groups are discussed in sections VII and VIII.

TABLE 7 (*cont.*)

	N^1	*ot*	N^2	T1: $\rightarrow N^1 N^2_g$	T2: $\rightarrow A^{n2} N^1$	T3: $\rightarrow A^{n1}$ *ot* N^2	T4: $\rightarrow V^{n1}$ *ot* N^2	T5: $\rightarrow N^2_{sb} V^{n1}$	T6: $\rightarrow N^1$ *ot* N^2 *do/k* N^3
17.	oglobljа 'shaft	ot to	tačanki a cart'	+	+	–	–	–	–
18.	dyrka 'hole	ot to	bublika a bagel'	+	+	–	–	–	–
19.	dyra 'hole	ot to	štanov the pants'	+	+	–	–	–	–
20.	sidenija 'seats	ot to	stul'ev the chairs'	+	–	–	–	–	–
21.	nosik 'spout	ot to	čajnika the teapot'	+	+	–	–	–	–
22.	rukojatka 'handle	ot to	šila the awl'	+	+	–	–	–	–
23.	lezvie 'blade	ot to	britvy the razor'	+	+	–	–	–	–
24.	peryško 'feather	ot to	veera the fan'	+	+	–	–	–	–
25.	vorotničok 'collar	ot to	bluzki the blouse'	+	+	–	–	–	–
26.	krjuk 'hook	ot to	lampy the lamp'	+	+	–	–	–	–
27.	rukojatka 'handle	ot to	zvonka the bell'	+	+	–	–	–	–
28.	rukava 'sleeves	ot to	žiletki the waistcoat'	+	+	–	–	–	–
29.	poloski 'stripes	ot to	perednika the apron'	+	–	–	–	–	–
30.	prjažka 'buckle	ot to	pojasa the belt'	+	+	–	–	–	–
31.	doski 'boards	ot to	zabora the fence'	+	+	–	–	–	–
32.	pni 'stumps	ot to	osokorej the poplars'	+	+	–	–	–	–
33.	general 'general	ot of	armii the army'	+	+	–	–	–	–
34.	činovnik 'official	ot of	pravitel'stva the government'	+	+	–	–	–	–
35.	podkovki 'heels	ot to	sapog the boots'	+	+	–	–	–	–

TABLE 7 (*cont.*)

	N^1	*ot*	N^2	T1: → $N^1 N^2_g$	T2: → $A^{n2} N^1$	T3: → A^{n1} *ot* N^2	T4: → V^{n1} *ot* N^2	T5: → $N^2_{sb} V^{n1}$	T6: → N^1 *ot* N^2 *do/k* N^3
36.	busy 'beads	ot to	monista the necklace'	+	+	–	–	–	–
37.	steklo 'glass	ot to	lampoček the lamps'	+	+	–	–	–	–
38.	stearin 'stearin	ot from	sveči the candle'	+	+	+	–	–	–
39.	skobka 'bracket	ot to	zvonka the bell'	+	+	–	–	–	–
40.	butylka 'bottle	ot for	vina wine'	(+)	+	–	–	–	–
41.	banočka 'can	ot for	mazi salve'	(+)	–	–	–	–	–
42.	banka 'can	ot for	monpans'e lozenges'	(+)	–	–	–	–	–
43.	banka 'can	ot for	konservov preserved food'	(+)	+	–	–	–	–
44.	žestjanka 'tin box	ot for	konservov canned goods'	(+)	+	–	–	–	–
45.	korobka 'box	ot for	gil'z cartridges'	(+)	+	–	–	–	–
46.	korobka 'box	ot for	papiros cigarettes'	(+)	+	–	–	–	–
47.	korobka 'box	ot for	botinok boots'	(+)	+	–	–	–	–
48.	kartonka 'carton	ot for	torta a cake'	(+)	+	–	–	–	–
49.	futljar 'case	ot for	violončeli a cello'	(+)	+	–	–	–	–

2.3.1.7. *Component-Aggregate Group*

This is one of the most frequently occurring types of the N *ot* N construction and is perhaps the most sharply defined from all points of view — the transformational, the morphological, and the semantic.

The first of the two transformations that define examples of this group is T1 (T: → $N^1 N^2_g$); *ključ ot biblioteki* 'key to the library' → *ključ biblioteki* 'library's key' or *general ot armii* 'general of the army' → *general armii* 'army's general'. In examples of this group, the preposition *ot* may be deleted with full retention of grammaticalness. Furthermore, the prepositionless transform differs in meaning from its source phrase only to a small extent. Compare the following pairs: *p'edestal ot pamjatnika* 'pedestal to the monument' — *p'edestal pamjatnika* 'the monument's pedestal'; *lezvie ot britvy* 'blade to the razor' — *lezvie britvy* 'razor's blade'; *činovnik ot pravitel'stva* 'official of the government' — *činovnik pravitel'stva* 'government's official'. The *Academy Grammar* notes the similarity of such pairs and remarks that they are opposed in that in the prepositional construction the dependent noun is represented as being separated from the object named by the head noun.[87] It would appear, however, that this opposition is more a function of context than of the inherent meaning of the word-combination. For example, in the sentence *Oni vzjali činovnika ot pravitel'stva i poslali ego za granicu* 'They took the official from the government and sent him abroad', the idea of separation is clearly expressed and the deletion of *ot* substantially alters the meaning of the phrase. On the other hand, in the sentence *Činovnik ot pravitel'stva ležal na divane i kuril* 'An official of the government lay on the divan and smoked', the meaning is basically the same with or without *ot*. Thus, taken in isolation, the semantic difference between *p'edestal ot pamjatnika* 'pedestal to the monument' and *p'edestal pamjatnika* 'monument's pedestal' is quite small. The *Academy Grammar* asserts that the use of prepositions between two nouns, a phenomenon which has developed with particular vigor in the nineteenth- and twentieth-centuries, arises by analogy with semantically similar verbal constructions.[88] V. V. Vinogradov makes the following observation on this line of development: "Prepositional-nominal constructions, originally connected with verbs and having depended on them, with the development and (increasing) complexity of the grammatical structure of the language, began to unite themselves directly to nouns, for example: *mandariny* ['tangerines'], *dostavlennye* ['shipped'] or *privezennye iz Gruzii* ['brought in from Georgia'] — *mandariny iz Gruzii* ['tangerines from Georgia'] *(cf.* also: *mandariny Gruzii* . . . . ['Georgia's tangerines']"[89]

Although such a line of evolution has undoubtedly occurred in connection with nouns derivationally related to verbs *(izbavljat' ot vraga* 'to save from the enemy' → *izbavlenie ot vraga* 'salvation from the enemy'), a more economical explanation for the rise of N^1 *ot* N^2 constructions (where N^1 is not derivationally related to a verb) is that they are an analytic expansion of non-prepositional $N^1\ N^2_g$ constructions. Synchronically and transformationally, this is clearly the case. The use of the preposition may be viewed here simply as an analytic device to reduce the multiple ambiguity of the semantically overloaded $N^1\ N^2_g$ construction. The enormous semantic range expressed by the genitive in Russian is reflected in Roman O. Jakobson's definition of it as

[87] *AG, II*, 1, 250.
[88] *AG, II*, 1, 51.
[89] *AG, II*, 1, 51–2.

the case which " . . . focuses upon the extent to which the entity takes part in the message".[90] The insertion of the *ot* between certain types of nouns occurring in the N^1 N^2_g construction more sharply delineates one of the segments of this very broad spectrum.

The second transformation restates the N^1 *ot* N^2 construction as A^{n2} N^1: *ključ ot škafa* 'key to the cupboard' → *škafnyj ključ* 'cupboard key'; *rukojatka ot šila* 'handle to the awl' → *šil'naja rukojatka* 'awl handle'. This adjectivization transformation affords a formal basis for the characterization of the relationship between N^1 and N^2 as attributive in that adjectives constitute the morphological nucleus for the syntactic relationship of attribution.

No exceptions to T1 were noted. The two exceptions to T2, *sidenija ot stul'ev* 'seats to the chairs' and *poloski ot perednika* 'stripes to the apron', fail to undergo the adjectivization transformation because neither *stul* nor *perednik* have adjectival forms. It is to be noted that the head nouns of the *Component-Aggregate group* display a marked semantic homogeneity. In most cases they specify concrete objects that are closely connected with or attached to the equally concrete referents of the dependent nouns. All of the examples share the common notion of physical contiguity.

2.3.1.8. *Container-Designation Group*

The last ten examples (40–49) in Table 7 represent a small but distinct class wherein the head nouns indicate a container and the dependent nouns — that which it was designed to hold.

This group is very similar to the *Component-Aggregate group* just discussed. Transformationally, the *Container-Designation group* is opposed to the former group only by T1, which is marked in Table 7 by a parenthesized plus, *e.g.*, (+). The reason for this is that from the purely formal, grammatical point of view, examples of the *Container group* admit the deletion of *ot*. It is only from the point of view of our second criterion that the two groups are opposed. The second criterion specifies that a uniform type of semantic relationship must exist between any member of a given set of source phrases and the corresponding member of the transformed set. If this systematic correlation does not obtain for an example, it is not a member of that class.[91] If we compare the semantic relationship between N^1 and N^2 under T1 for several examples from the *Container-Designation* and the *Component-Aggregate groups*, significant differences in the syntactic structures of the source phrases become apparent. To illustrate: *butylka ot vina* refers to a bottle made for the purpose of holding wine, but not being so used. The product of T1, *butylka vina*, on the other hand, indicates that the bottle contains wine. The same semantic distinction holds

[90] Roman O. Jakobson, "The Relationship between the Genitive and the Plural", *Scando-Slavica*, III (1957), 181.

[91] See page 39 above for a fuller statement of this requirement.

for the other members of the *Container-Designation group*. In contrast, *ključ ot biblioteki*, an example of the *Component-Aggregate group*, refers to a key belonging to the library, although possibly detached from it at the moment.

Thus the nature of the relationship between the two nouns in each of the two groups is quite different, although it is only under transformation that the difference is clearly defined.[92] If we transform a number of examples of the majority *Component-Aggregate group*, each of the resulting transforms will have the same relationship to its source phrase as indicated in the example *ključ ot biblioteki* 'key to the library'. When, however, we encounter an example of the morphologically identical and semantically similar *Container-Designation* type, we find the same correlation does not hold. Such a shift signals the presence of a different syntactic and semantic type. This is confirmed by the fact that the new type of semantic correlation between N^1 and N^2 is consistent for all members of the newly postulated group. This last is shown in the following series of oppositions:

EMPTY CONTAINERS:
banočka ot mazi, žestjanka ot konservov, futljar ot violončeli
'can for salve' 'tin box for canned goods' 'case for a cello'
FULL CONTAINERS:
banočka mazi, žestjanka konservov, futljar violončeli
'can of salve' 'tin box of canned goods' 'case of cello'

The second transform (T: → $A^{n_2} N^1$; *papirosnaja korobka* 'cigarette box' → *korobka ot papiros* 'box for cigarettes') illustrates that in this group as in the closely akin *Component-Aggregate group* the relationship of N^2 to N^1 is attributive and may be expressed in an adjectival form.

There are no exceptions to T1. Two of the examples, however, fail to undergo the adjectival transform, T2. The first of these, *banočka ot mazi* 'can for salve', fails because the adjectives derived from *maz'* 'salve' refer to the ideas of 'smear' or 'grease' and the second, *banka ot monpans'e* 'can for lozenges', a French loan word, has no adjective form in Russian.

Morphologically, the head words of the *Container-Designation group* are all derived from nominal roots. It is of interest that most of the head words as well as many of the dependent ones are foreign borrowings.[93]

[92] A second non-transformational demonstration of the uniqueness of the *Container-Designation group* is that its and only its examples may substitute *iz-pod* for the preposition *ot*, *e.g.*, *butylka ot vina* ↔ *butylka iz-pod vina*, but not **ključ iz-pod biblioteki*.

[93] According to Vasmer, *butylka* 'bottle' is borrowed from the French *bouteille* (*I*, 155); *karton(ka)* 'carton' is either from the German *Karton* or directly from the French *carton* (*I*, 536); *futljar* 'case' is from the German *Futteral* (*III*, 222). *Žestjanka* 'tin box' → *žest'*, which is a borrowing from Turkotataric or Mongolian (*I*, 422). *Korobka* 'box' and *banka* 'can' are both native Slavic noun forms, although the former may be related to Latin *corbis* (*I*, 629 and I, 51).

TABLE 8

Transform Features of 'N¹ *ot* N²' *Units of the Countermeasure Group*[94]

	N¹	*ot*	N²	T1: → $N^1 N^2_g$	T2: → $A^{n2} N^1$	T3: → A^{n1} *ot* N^2	T4: → V^{n1} *ot* N^2	T5: → $N^2_{sb} V^{n1}$	T6: → N^1 *ot* N^2 *do/k* N^3
1.	sredstvo	ot	kašlja	–	+	–	–	–	–
	'remedy	against	coughing'						
2.	poroški	ot	nervov	–	+	–	–	–	–
	'powders	against	nerves'						
3.	maz'	ot	vesnušek	–	+	–	–	–	–
	'salve	against	freckles'						
4.	židkost'	ot	klopov	–	+	–	–	–	–
	'liquid	against	bedbugs'						
5.	setka	ot	komarov	–	+	–	–	–	–
	'net	against	mosquitoes'						
6.	zontik	ot	solnca	–	+	–	–	–	–
	'umbrella	against	the sun'						
7.	parasolik	ot	solnca	–	+	–	–	–	–
	'parasol	against	the sun'						
8.	tenty	ot	solnca	–	+	–	–	–	–
	'tents	against	the sun'						
9.	naves	ot	doždej	–	+	–	–	–	–
	'awning	against	the rains'						
10.	tabletka	ot	boli	–	–	–	–	–	–
	'tablet	against	pain'						
11.	sredstvo	ot	bessonicy	–	–	–	–	–	–
	'remedy	against	insomnia'						
12.	panaceja	ot	bed	–	–	–	–	–	–
	'panacea	against	misfortunes'						
13.	krem	ot	zagara	–	–	–	–	–	–
	'cream	against	sunburn'						
14.	palka	ot	sobak	–	–	–	–	–	–
	'stick	against	dogs'						
15.	butylka	ot	vina	(+)	+	–	–	–	–
	'bottle	for	wine'						
16.	banka	ot	konservov	(+)	+	–	–	–	–
	'can	for	preserved food'						
17.	žestjanka	ot	konservov	(+)	+	–	–	–	–
	'tin box	for	preserved food'						

[94] Table 8 also contains six examples of the *Container-Designation group* (15–20) for purposes of comparison.

TABLE 8 (*cont.*)

	N^1	*ot*	N^2	T1: $\to N^1 N^2_g$	T2: $\to A^{n2} N^1$	T3: $\to A^{n1}$ *ot* N^2	T4: $\to V^{n1}$ *ot* N^2	T5: $\to N^2_{sb} V^{n1}$	T6: $\to N^1$ *ot* N^2 *do/k* N^3
18.	korobka 'box	ot for	botinok boots'	(+)	+	–	–	–	–
19.	kartonka 'carton	ot for	torta a cake'	(+)	+	–	–	–	–
20.	futjar 'case	ot for	violončeli a cello'	(+)	+	–	–	–	–

2.3.1.9. *Countermeasure Group*

Examples of this group (*e.g.*, *poroški ot nervov* 'powders against nerves') constitute a small but strongly marked semantic class. From the point of view of meaning, they are similar to the *Ablative group* (*osvoboždenie ot gneta* 'liberation from oppression') and particularly to the small subset of the group containing the head words *zaščita* 'defense', *bezopasnost'* 'security', *pomošč'* 'aid', and *lekarstvo* 'medication'. Notwithstanding the semantic similarity of the head words of the two groups, they are strongly opposed in their derivational composition and their transformational reflexes. The head words of the *Ablative group* are derivationally related to verbs (*zaščiščat'* 'to defend', *obezopasit'* 'to secure', *pomogat'* 'to aid', and *lečit'* 'to treat') and also to adjectives (*zaščitnyj* 'defensive', *bezopasnyj* 'secure', *pomoščnjy* 'auxiliary', and *lečebnyj* 'medicinal') and, more importantly, can be transformed into parallel constructions using these forms, *e.g.*, *zaščita ot opasnosti* 'defense against danger' → *zaščiščat' ot opasnosti* 'to defend against danger' or → *zaščitnyj ot opasnosti* 'defensible against danger'. Neither of these transformations are possible for members of the *Countermeasure group*. Transformationally the examples of this latter group are most similar to the *Component-Aggregate group* (*p'edestal ot pamjatnika* 'pedestal to a monument') and the *Container-Designation group* (*butylka ot vina* 'bottle for wine').[95] All three of these are united to each other and are opposed to the *Ablative group* in that they admit T2, which restates N^2 as an adjective modifying N^1. Compare *klopinaja židkost'* 'bedbug liquid' ← *židkost' ot klopov* 'liquid against bedbugs' with the impossibility of this transformation

[95] The unity of these groups may also be shown non-transformationally by the fact that they and only they permit the replacement of *ot* by *dlja*. *Cf. butylka ot vina* ↔ *butylka dlja vina; poroški ot želudka* ↔ *poroški dlja želudka* and *p'edestal ot pamjatnika* ↔ *p'edestal dlja pamjatnika*.

for *žaščita ot opasnosti* 'defense against danger'. In the first case, the dependent noun may function as an adjectival attribute of N^1, whereas in the second N^2 is restricted to an object role.

The members of the *Countermeasure group* are characterized by only one transformation, *i.e.*, T2, which rewrites N^2 as an adjective modifying N^1 *(komarinaja setka* 'mosquito net' → *setka ot komarov* 'net against mosquitoes'). T1, which is possible for the *Component-Aggregate (ključ biblioteki* 'library's key') and marginally so for the *Container-Designation group* [(+)] *(butylka vina* 'bottle of wine'), is impossible for the examples of the *Countermeasure group*. It yields transformed phrases that are, in most cases, nonsensical *(sredstvo kašlja* 'remedy of coughing', *poroški nervov* 'powders of nerves', *naves doždej* 'awning of the rains', *tenty solnca* 'tents of the sun') or that, in a few cases *(židkost' klopov* 'liquid of bedbugs' or *setka komarov* 'net of mosquitoes'), present total inversions of the meaning of the source phrase.[96]

Six of the examples of the *Countermeasure group* fail to undergo T2. *Palka ot sobak* 'stick against dogs' cannot be so transformed because the only derived attributive form is a possessive adjective that would yield the nonsensical phrase *sobač'ja palka* 'a doggish stick'. *Panaceja ot bed* 'panacea against misfortunes' fails to undergo transformation because the resulting phrase *(bedstvennaja panaceja)* means 'unfortunate panacea'. *Bessonica* of *sredstvo ot bessonicy* 'remedy against insomnia' is probably a calque *(cf.* French *insomnie)*. *Krem ot zagara* 'cream against sunburn' and *maz' ot vesnušek* 'salve against freckles' do not admit the adjectival transformation since the derived adjectives *(zagorelyj* 'sunburned' and *vesnuščatyj* 'freckled') yield semantic absurdities when used as direct attributes of *krem* and *maz'*.

Derivationally, the head words of this group (with the exception of the deadjectival *židkost'* 'liquid') are characterized by the possession of nominal roots. Like the list of the head nouns of the *Container-Designation group*, a relatively large number of them *(panaceja* 'panacea', *zontik* 'umbrella', *parasolik* 'parasol', *tent* 'tent', *krem* 'cream') are of non-Russian origin.

2.3.1.10. *Temporal Group*

The *Academy Grammar*, together with many other Russian grammars, contains a classificational category with the label *temporal* as one of the semantic subgroups of the N^1 *ot* N^2 constructional type. The following list contains some typical examples:

1. *razvitie ot kolybeli* 'development from the cradle'
2. *mečty ot junyx let* 'dreams from [one's] young years'

[96] This last feature again unites this class with the *Ablative group*. Compare, for example, *palka ot sobak* 'stick against dogs' → *palka sobak* 'stick of the dogs' with *otklonenie ot zakona* 'deviation from the law' → *otklonenie zakona* 'deviation of the law'.

3. *vremja ot vremeni* 'from time to time'
4. *čas ot času* 'from hour to hour'
5. *pis'mo ot pjatogo sentjabrja* 'letter of the fifth of September'
6. *postanovlenie ot vtorogo marta* 'resolution of the second of March'
7. *otnošenie ot desjatogo ijunja* 'memorandum of the tenth of June'
8. *gazeta ot prošloj nedeli* 'paper of last week'

Such lists also usually contain examples of the type N^1 *ot* N^2 *do* N^3 *(e.g., vremja ot polnoči do rassveta* 'time from midnight to dawn'). In the present work these are treated elsewhere under the heading of unanalyzable N^1 *ot* N^2 *do* N^3 constructions of the range type.[97]

The examples listed above fall into three groups: 1–2, 3–4, and 5–8. It should be noted that an adjective or numeral modifying N^2 is a frequent feature in the first group (1–2) and an obligatory one in the third type (5–8). The first two groups are archaisms in Modern Russian.[98] Examples 1–2 may be formally separated from the remaining cases by an expansion transformation (T: $\rightarrow N^1$ *ot* N^2 *do* N^3; *mečty ot [junyx] let do starosti* 'dreams from (one's) [young] years to old age'). This transform, in effect, modernizes the construction and permits its reassignment to the N^1 *ot* N^2 *do* N^3 *Range group*. The use of *ot* to express temporal meaning in N^1 *ot* N^2 phrases in Modern Russian has been supplanted by the preposition *s*: *mečty s junyx let* 'dreams since [one's] young years' or *s detstva* 'since childhood' versus the older *ot detstva* 'from childhood'.

Examples 3–4 represent a small set including (besides 3 and 4) *god ot godu* 'from year to year' and *den' oto dnja* 'from day to day'. In addition to their distinctive lexical nature these may be isolated by the use of an adverbialization transform: T: N^1 *ot* $N^2 \rightarrow Q^n$ *(vremja ot vremeni* 'from time to time' $\rightarrow$ *vremenami* 'from time to time'). The remaining examples, while formally admitting adverbialization transformations, have somewhat different meanings in their adverbial forms *(časami* 'for hours', *godami* 'for years', *dnjami* 'for days'). This transform formally demonstrates that these examples are not nominal constructions at all, but simply compound temporal adverbs.

The final group, examples 5–8, is the only living type of temporal N^1 *ot* N^2 construction. This usage, a highly restricted one, is found almost exclusively in official correspondence and documents.[99] Transformationally, examples of

[97] See pages 43–44.

[98] T. P. Lomtev, *Očerki po istoričeskomu sintaksisu russkogo jazyka* (Moscow, 1956), 355–6. Lomtev further notes that in Old Russian the combination *ot* N could be used in a temporal sense either independently (. . . *i v''staet' ot'' nošči*, ... 'and he gets up after the night') or in conjunction with *do* N *(ot'' utra do poludnja* 'from morning to noon'). In later Russian the independent use of *ot* N died out and in the nineteenth- and twentieth-centuries only *ot* N *do* N is used in a temporal sense. Exceptions to this are archaisms such as 1–4 above.

[99] *Sovremennyj russkij jazyk, II,* "Sintaksis", ed. E. M. Galkina-Fedoruk (Moscow, 1958), 70.

this group are uniquely characterized by the preposition deletion transform T1: N^1 *ot* (A) $N^2 \rightarrow N^1$ (A) N^2 *(pis'mo ot pjatogo sentjabra* 'letter of the fifth of September' → *pis'mo pjatogo sentjabrja* 'letter of the fifth of September'). Examples of this type also partially undergo the transform T2: N^1 *ot* $N^2 \rightarrow$ A^{n2} N^1 *(otnošenie ot [desjatogo] ijunja* 'memorandum of [the tenth] of June' → *ijun'skoe otnošenie* 'June memorandum'). The failure of the whole of the source phrase to undergo the adjectivization transformation is not due to any peculiarity of temporal constructions, but to a general restriction on modifiers of dependent nouns in transformations of this structural type, *i.e.*, N^1 *ot* A N^2. *Cf. rukojatka ot zvonka* 'handle to the bell' → *zvonkovaja rukojatka* 'bell handle', but *rukojatka ot dvernogo zvonka* 'handle to the door bell' ↛ **dvernaja zvonkovaja rukojatka* 'door bell handle'.[100]

These two transformational possibilities, which are also characteristic of the *Component-Aggregate* semantic type *(ključ ot škafa* 'key to the cupboard'), provide a formal basis for the attributive description assigned to both of these groups by the *Academy Grammar*.[101]

The most noteworthy fact about the examples of the *Temporal group* is the extremely high degree of lexical restriction upon both N^1 and N^2. This holds true for both the surviving archaic forms (1–4) and the living but stylistically restricted date examples (5–8). These observations lead to the conclusion that a temporal subdivision of the N^1 *ot* N^2 construction is at best an extremely marginal phenomenon in Modern Russian and perhaps even non-existent from the strictly grammatical point of view. Its only distinctive features are lexical ones.

2.4. CONCLUDING REMARKS

In the preceding sections it has been shown that the N^1 *ot* N^2 construction subsumes some ten different semantic groups.[102] Nine of these (all but the *Temporal group)* may be isolated and characterized by their differing transform potentials. These nine groups, together with their transform characteristics, are summarized in table 9.

[100] One exception to this was noted: *ob''javlenie ot pervogo maja* 'declaration of the first of May' → *pervomajskoe ob''javlenie* 'May Day declaration'. There are also marginal cases of the type: *pis'mo ot prošlogo goda* 'letter of last year' → *prošlo-godnoe pis'mo* 'last year's letter'. For a discussion of the transform features of modifiers of dependent genitive substantives, see Dean S. Worth, "Transformation Criteria for the Classification of Predicative Genitive Constructions in Russian", *1961 International Conference on Machine Translation of Languages and Applied Language Analysis, II* (London, 1961), 725–35.

[101] *AG, II*, 1, 251.

[102] This figure does not include the *Range group*, which occurs only in the N^1 *ot* N^2 *do* N^3 format. The *Spatial group*, which occurs predominantly in the double preposition construction, is, however, included since it, unlike members of the *Range group*, does transform into an N^1 *ot* N^2 structure.

TABLE 9

Transform Features of 'N^1 ot N^2' Units: Summary

	N^1	*ot*	N^2	T1: $\to N\,N^2_g$	T2: $\to A^{n2}\,N^1$	T3: $\to A^{n1}$ *ot* N^2	T4: $\to V^{n1}$ *ot* N^2	T5: $\to N^2_{sb}\,V^{n1}$	T6: $\to N^1$ *ot* N^2 *do/k* N^3
I.	*Spatial:*								
	uxod	ot	doma	−	−	−	+	−	+
	'departure	from	the house'						
II.	*Ablative:*								
	otklonenie	ot	zakona	−	−	(+)	+	−	−
	'deviation	from	the law'						
III.	*Phenomenon-Source:*								
	svet	ot	fonarja	+	+	+	+	+	−
	'light	from	the lantern'						
IV.	*Trace-Origin:*								
	srez	ot	lopaty	−	+	−	−	+	−
	'slice	from	the spade'						
V.	*Communication-Originator:*								
	pis'mo	ot	brata	+	+	−	−	+	+
	'letter	from	[one's] brother'						
VI.	*State-Cause:*								
	jarost'	ot	bessmyslicy	−	−	+	+	+	−
	'rage	because of	an absurdity'						
VII.	*Component-Aggregate:*								
	ključ	ot	biblioteki	+	+	−	−	−	−
	'key	to	the library'						
VIII.	*Container-Designation:*								
	butylka	ot	vina	(+)	+	−	−	−	−
	'bottle	for	wine'						
IX.	*Countermeasure:*								
	setka	ot	komarov	−	+	−	−	−	−
	'net	against	mosquitoes'						

The transformationally defined semantic groups shown in Table 9 may wno be compared with the semantic groups listed by the *Academy Grammar*.[103] The latter lists seven intuitively based semantic groups. The foregoing analysis yields ten semantic groups and thus is somewhat more precise. Its real superiority, however, lies in its formal basis. Nine of the ten semantic groups have sets of transformationally defined features that characterize them. Also of great importance is the fact that, in addition to yielding a formal taxonomy

[103] The full list may be found on page 25.

of the homomorphic groups within the N^1 *ot* N^2 structure, the system affords a degree of insight into the *sub-surface* syntactic structure of the different types of source phrases. Thus we can now say that in groups VII–IX the relationship between N^2 and N^1 is attributive *because* they can be transformed into the structure A^{n2} N or that the relationship between N^1 and N^2 in groups I and II is objective *because* they can be restated as V^{n1} *ot* N.

The head nouns in the examples of Table 9 form the following list: 1) *uxod* 'departure', 2) *otklonenie* 'deviation', 3) *svet* 'light', 4) *srez* 'slice', 5) *pis'mo* 'letter', 6) *'jarost'* 'rage', 7) *ključ* 'key', 8) *butylka* 'bottle', and 9) *setka* 'net'. This sequence of nouns may be described as representing a spectrum in terms of the degree of verbality of the nouns. The minimum or zero degree of verbality is found at the higher end *(setka* 'net') and the maximum degree at the lower end *(uxod* 'departure'). Inspection of Table 9 shows that the transformational correlate of the higher degrees of verbality is the admissibility of T4 and for the lower degrees — T2.

Another type of correlation may also be noted in this list. Although no formal proof can be marshalled for the assertion, it seems likely that ties of what is traditionally called *strong government* prevail at the maximum verbality end of the scale and that these ties become progressively weaker as one nears the zero verbality end of the scale. *Setka ot komarov* 'net against mosquitoes' is a clear-cut example of *weak government,* whereas *uxod ot doma* 'departure from the house' is an equally sharply defined example of *strong government.*[104] Lastly, the transform analysis provides a clear-cut answer to the question of which word determines the semantic classification of a given example. The authors of the *Academy Grammar* as well as a great many other Russian grammarians hold that it is the dependent noun that determines the relational meaning of an example.[105] Our analysis, with its demonstration of the high degree of uniformity in both transformational characterization and morphological derivation of the head nouns *within* each group (and of the con-

[104] For an attempt to provide a formal definition of these two vague syntactic relationships for $V(P)N_{dp}$, see Ju. D. Apresjan, "O sil'nom i slabom upravlenii (opyt količestvennogo analiza)", *Voprosy jazykoznanija*, 3 (1964), 32–49; L. N. Iordanskaja, *Dva operatora dlja obrabotki slovosočetanij s "sil''nym upravleniem"* (Moscow, 1961). Also, see pages 114 and 136–137 for a more detailed discussion of strong and weak government.

[105] *AG, II*, 1, 52. V. V. Vinogradov states that in certain types of NPN constructions the diversity of relational meanings is due to "... the explanatory functions expressed by the dependent nouns ...." L. N. Popova in her investigation of causal relations (see page 26 footnote 14 above) notes that "Many investigators consider the chief factor which conditions the meaning of weakly governed prepositions ... [to be] the lexical meaning of the dependent noun". (p. 191.) That this view of the primacy of the dependent noun is not restricted to grammarians of the traditional school is shown by V. P. Manolova's comment on the problem as quoted on pages 32 – 33 above.

sequent differences *between* the head words of each group), shows that it is the head noun that normally determines the semantic classification of an example. In many, if not most, cases it is sufficient to know the head word in order to assign an example to the correct category. For example, given the word *glupost'* 'stupidity' as N^1 of N^1 *ot* N^2, it is reasonably certain that by virtue of its derivational history (deadjectival) and its consequent transform potential that the example will fall into the *State-Cause group* (VI).

In some cases, such as *pis'mo ot brata* 'letter from [one's] brother' it appears that the key factor in making a classification is that N^2 is animate. This is only indirectly the case. It can be argued equally well that the animacy of N^2 is a function of N^1. In other words, only N^2's in the grammatical class of animate beings have co-occurrence privileges with nouns belonging to deverbal nouns of the class of *pis'mo* 'letter', *i.e.*, *brat pišet* 'the brother writes'. Thus in almost all cases it can be shown that N^1 is the controlling factor in the classification of N^1 *ot* N^2 units.

3

TRANSFORM ANALYSIS OF A *ot* N CONSTRUCTIONS

3.1. INTRODUCTION

Russian adjectival constructions with dependent *ot* phrases are much less numerous than their verbal and nominal counterparts. Adjectives serve as the grammatical head of *ot* constructions in about 8 per cent of the *ot* usages encountered in our sample text as opposed to approximately 16 per cent for nouns and 68 per cent for verbs.[1] The frequency with which adjectives serve as the head of *ot* N is somewhat surprising when it is considered that adjectives are non-nuclear syntactic units and in comparison with verbs and nouns they serve as construction heads only marginally.

Like its nominal counterpart, the N^1, A *ot* N^2 construction subsumes a number of different semantic groups. This is illustrated by the following four examples: *lico, mokroe ot slez* 'a face wet from tears'; *starik, čistyj ot grexa* 'an old man pure of sin'; *derevo, blizkoe ot doma* 'a tree close to the house'; *syn, slepoj ot roždenija* 'a son blind from birth'. This chapter treats the problem of formally isolating and characterizing the different semantic groups contained within the single morphological framework N^1, A *ot* N^2 by means of analytic transformations.

The initial part of the chapter examines several earlier treatments of the problem by Russian specialists on syntax. First, A. M. Peškovskij's views on the classification of A(P)N units are discussed. This is followed by an examination of the analysis of the N^1, A *ot* N^2 construction made by N. N. Prokopovič in the *Academy Grammar*.[2] Following this, two studies discussing the expression

[1] K. Paustovskij, *Povest' o žizni*, 2 vols. (Moscow, 1962). The figures above are based on a count of some 1,100 examples of *ot* constructions from the text of this book. The overall distribution of nouns, verbs, and adjectives in CSR is 40.7%, 21.0%, and 12.5% respectively. È. A. Štejnfel'dt, *Častotnyj slovar' sovremennogo russkogo literaturnogo jazyka* (Tallin, 1963), 37.

[2] Akademija Nauk SSSR, Institut jazykoznanija, *Grammatika russkogo jazyka* (Moscow, 1954; 2nd ed. 1960), *II*, 1, 301–2 and 307–9.

of causal relations by means of the N^1, A *ot* N^2 construction are analyzed. Finally, a transformational treatment of adjectival constructions is examined in detail.

The second part of the chapter consists of an original transformational analysis of the N^1, A *ot* N^2 construction and a discussion comparing the results of the analysis to that of the foregoing works. The chapter ends with a brief overview of the results of our analysis of adjectival constructions.

3.2. SURVEY OF LITERATURE

Traditional treatments of APN constructions generally offer a dual approach to their description – grammatical and notional. The problem of syntactic homonymy is usually treated only implicitly within the context of the second of these approaches.

A. M. Peškovskij emphasizes the grammatical approach to the description of A(P)N units, although his treatment is so brief as to be more a set of suggestions for the analysis of the constructional type rather than a classificatory system in itself.[3] Initially it is pointed out that adjectives, in and of themselves, generally are not capable of government except in so far as they are related to a verb. The only noted exceptions to this are the instrumental of limitation *(slabyj duxom* 'weak in spirit'), which occurs primarily with predicate adjectives, and the quantitative genitive of the superlative construction *(mudrejšaja iz žen* 'the wisest of wives'). All other cases of government by adjectives involve some type of relationship to a verb. These fall into two groups: 1) those where the adjective construction is identical with a parallel verbal construction *(ustalyj ot čego-to* 'tired because of something' = *ustat' ot čego-to* 'to tire because of something') and 2) those cases where the adjectival construction does not fully parallel the verbal construction *(sveduščij v čem* 'knowledgeable about something' – *vedat' čto* 'to know something'). The latter type subsumes a variety of subtypes, each reflecting different types of relationships between the adjectival and the verbal construction. In sum, Peškovskij's treatment of constructions headed by an adjective (A[P]N) comes down to the following: adjectives do not serve as construction heads unless they are in some way related to verbs; if they are related to verbal constructions, they are to be analyzed in terms of their verbal equivalents.[4] The problem of the multiple ambiguity of individual APN constructions is not touched upon.

[3] A. M. Peškovskij, *Russkij sintaksis v naučnom osveščenii,* 7th ed. (Moscow, 1956), 326–7.

[4] See pages 106–108 below for a survey of Peškovskij's treatment of verbal constructions.

N. N. Prokopovič utilizes both the grammatical and the notional approaches discussed above.[5] Unfortunately no attempt is made to integrate the two views. It is noted that the circle of adjectival constructions of the type APN has considerably expanded in CSR, especially since the middle of the nineteenth-century, and that the A *ot* N type is of particular frequency. This expansion assertedly has taken place under the influence of verbal constructions of the type V(P)N. This is attested by the large number of A(P)N constructions that parallel the verbal constructions in structure and meaning. The interrelations between the two constructional types are given in the following schematization:[6]

I. A(P)N parallel to V(P)N in structure and meaning
- A. A(P)N fully duplicates V(P)N
  1. *krasnyj ot smuščenija — krasnet' ot smuščenija*
     'red because of embarrassment' — 'to redden because of embarrassment'
  2. *otličnyj ot drugix — otličat'sja ot drugix*
     'different from others' — 'to differ from others'
  3. *svobodnyj ot raboty — osvobodit'sja ot raboty*
     'free from work' — 'to free one's self from work'
- B. A(P)N partially duplicating V(P)N in structure and meaning typical for V *ot* N
  1. *poslušnyj zovu — poslušat' zov*
     'obedient to the call' — 'to obey the call'
  2. *polnyj sena — napolnjat' senoj*
     'full of hay' — 'to fill with hay'

II. A(P)N not parallel to V(P)N in structure
- A. A(P)N semantically similar to V(P)N
  1. *koričnevyj ot zagara*
     'brown because of suntan'
  2. *udobnyj dlja sidenija*
     'convenient for sitting'
- B. A(P)N not semantically similar to V(P)N
  1. *žalkij svoeju slabost'ju*
     'pitiable in his own weakness'
  2. *dobryj po nature*
     'good by nature'

[5] *AG, II*, 1, 301–2 and 308–9.
[6] *AG, II*, 1, 302.

III. A(P)N parallel or not parallel to V(P)N but expressing relations not possible for latter

1. *zagorelyj do krasnoty*
   'sunburned to redness'
2. *sladkij do pritornosti*
   'sweet to cloyingness'

The *Academy Grammar*'s treatment of the interrelations of adjectival and verbal prepositional constructions is quite similar to that of Peškovskij's, although it makes much heavier use of semantic criteria, particularly in regard to II and III. Having made this survey of derivational relationships of A(P)N constructions as a whole, Prokopovič turns to a purely notional semantic description of individual constructions, *e.g.*, A *ot* N. No attempt is made to determine whether the derivational patterns examined in the earlier section have any bearing upon the problem of isolating and classifying the different semantic groups subsumed within the A *ot* N framework. According to Prokopovič, all A *ot* N units are united by the fact that the A is supplemented by a limitational meaning expressed by PN. Within the framework of this general semantic categorization, the *Academy Grammar* presents the following semantic groupings:[7]

I. Causal Relations: *seryj ot pyli* 'gray because of dust'
   A = feature *(priznak)*
   N = cause of A

II. Spatial Relations: *blizkij ot goroda* 'close to town'
   A = spatial feature
   N = concrete meaning

III. Temporal Relations: *gluxonemoj ot roždenija* 'deaf-mute from birth'
   A = constant feature
   N = event, phenomenon from the time of which A appears

IV. Ablative Relations: *svobodnyj ot predrassudkov* 'free from prejudices'
   A = feature of being freed, distinguished, excluded from
   N = object from which someone is freed, distinguished, *etc.*

Of the above, the *Causal group* is by far the most common and is highly productive. The *Spatial* and *Temporal groups* are each restricted to a handful of lexical items, although the primary restriction in the *Spatial group* falls on A and in the *Temporal group* on N. The great majority of the temporal examples

[7] *AG, II*, 1, 308–9. The observation that the addition of the PN to A somehow "limits" the meaning of the adjective is of a very little interest, since the addition of any dependent linguistic unit will limit the meaning of the constructional head, *i.e.*, modification = limitation.

involve the PN, *ot roždenija* 'since birth'. The *Ablative group* is composed of a small group of adjectives with the meaning of 'deprivation' or 'ablation'. Thus the sole criteria used in the isolation and characterization of the different semantic subgroups is meaning. It will subsequently be shown that the formal derivational data illustrated in the foregoing description of A(P)N units in relation to corresponding V(P)N units can be used to differentiate among the semantic groups of the former. For example, the causal unit *seryj ot pyli* 'gray because of dust' can be transformed to *seret' ot pyli* 'to become gray because of dust', whereas this is not possible for the spatial example *blizkij ot goroda* 'close to town', *i.e.*, **priblizit'sja ot goroda* 'to approach from town'.

Considerable information about the *Causal group* of A *ot* N constructions is provided by the studies of L. N. Popova and L. N. Zasorina.[8] Popova examines the expression of causal meaning on two levels — the semantic and the syntactic. The semantic structure of A and N is subjected to detailed scrutiny since "In the case of the adjective . . . , the chief factor conditioning the meaning of the preposition is the concrete correlation of the meanings of the head and the dependent words in a given word-combination".[9] The head adjectives and the dependent nouns are each found to fall into a number of semantic groups. These semantic groups in their relative frequency of occurrence are as follows: Adjectives — 1) color *(krasnyj* 'red'); 2) physical feature *(mokryj* 'wet'); 3) psychological quality *(serdityj* 'angry'); 4) characterizing feature *(smešnoj* 'funny'); and 5) bodily feature *(slepoj* 'blind'); Dependent nouns — a) feelings *(zlost'* 'malice'); b) physical state *(natuga* 'strain'); c) quality *(zastenčivost'* 'shyness'); d) action *(beg* 'running'); e) phenomenon of nature *(solnce* 'sun'); f) object-substance *(krov'* 'blood'); and g) animate object *(ranenyj* 'wounded man'). These groupings of different types of adjectives and nouns cannot be interchanged at random. Certain groups of A occur either not at all or only rarely with some groups of N and quite commonly with others. In other words, each group of A has a certain characteristic set of co-occurrence privileges in terms of groups of N. Popova's findings on this count are illustrated in the following table in which the letters refer to the semantic groups of N listed above. Marginal A–N combinations are indicated in parentheses.

[8] L. N. Popova, "O značenii predloga v sovremennom russkom jazyke (Predlog ot + roditel'nyj padež v značenii pričiny)", *Učenye zapiski Leningradskogo gosudarstvennogo universiteta*, 235 *(= Serija filologičeskix nauk)*, vyp. 38 (1958), 190–208; L. N. Zasorina, "Opyt sistemnogo analiza predlogov sovremennogo russkogo jazyka (Predlogi so značeniem pričiny)", *Učenye zapiski Leningradskogo gosudarstvennogo universiteta*, 301 (1961) *(= Serija filologičeskix nauk)*, vyp. 60, 64–81.

[9] Popova, 202.

		zlosti	*natugi*	*zastenčivosti*	*bega*	*solnca*	*krovi*	*ranenyj*
Color	*(krasnyj)*:	a	b	c	d	e	f	(g)
Physical feature	*(mokryj)*:	—	b	—	d	e	f	—
Psychological quality	*(serdityj)*:	a	—	—	—	—	—	—
Characterizing feature	*(smešnoj)*:	(a)	(b)	—	—	—	—	—
Bodily feature	*(slepoj)*:	—	—	—	—	(e)	(f)	—

Thus, according to Popova, adjectives with the meaning of external features (*i.e.*, the color and physical feature groups) have by far the greatest range of co-occurrence privileges in the construction A *ot* N. The nouns fall into two general classes: abstract — indicating feelings, states, qualities and actions, and concrete — indicating objects, substances, phenomena of nature, and occasionally animate beings. In concluding her survey of the semantic characteristics of A *ot* N, Popova notes that the pattern of semantic interrelationships of A and N is similar to that found for causal verbal constructions of the type V *ot* N.[10]

Popova finds that the head adjectives of the A *ot* N causal construction display certain semantic peculiarities that are a function of their syntactic role in the sentence.[11] It is asserted that adjectives used in causal constructions act in a predicative or semi-predicative function and predicativeness is a requisite condition for the expression of causal meaning.[12] Failing this, the word-combination assumes a supplementary objective nuance. Compare, for example, the following examples:

1. *Guby — to li ot černiki, to l' ot xoloda černy.*
   'The lips [were] black either from the bilberry or from the cold'.
2. *Sljunul na grud' černye ot krovi zuby.*
   'He slobbered out on his chest the black from blood teeth'.

In 1, where the subject and APN are separated by a predication, the latter functions as an independent member of the sentence (or in other cases as an isolated clause). Semantically, "... the preposition indicates the cause of a quality or property that remains itself independently of the cause that has evoked it."[13] In 2, where APN is not separated from the noun it modifies by

[10] *Loc. cit.*

[11] Popova's findings on the syntactic function and the related semantic shift are almost exactly paralleled by the observations of L. N. Zasorina in her 1961 study cited on page 85, footnote 8. The same corpus was used for both studies. See page 119.

[12] Popova, 201.

[13] *Loc. cit.*

a predication, it is not an independent member of the sentence, but acts as a complex attribute of the modified noun. In this type of sentence, the *ot* is supposed to introduce a supplementary meaning into the name of the quality itself, *i.e.*, it gives a causal-limitational meaning to the APN.

According to Popova, only certain semantic groups of descriptive adjectives can freely fulfill predicative or semi-predicative functions, because the predicate usage entails a shift of their meanings. According to Vinogradov the usual non-predicative use of adjectives is "The expression of a permanent feature which is thought of as being outside of temporal limitations . . ."[14] In contrast to this, in all of the examples of causal *ot* constructions examined by Popova, the head adjective " . . . did not designate constant invariant qualities, but properties whose appearance is limited in time, properties appearing only at the moment of the presence of that object, substance, *etc.* which is expressed by the dependent noun in the genitive case."[15]

The only transformational study of the Russian A(P)N construction that has thus far been published is that of T. M. Nikolaeva.[16] The study covers all Russian constructions in which an adjective is the head word, *i.e.*, AN, AV, QA, and APN. The latter structural type, as the most diversified, receives the greatest amount of attention. The APN units are broken down first by preposition and then by the case of N. Once the lowest morphological level is reached (in our case A *ot* N), analytic transformations are used to isolate the different semantic groups within the A *ot* N framework. According to Nikolaeva, "TA consists of the transformation of constructions having one and the same morphological structure (and the same formula in terms of word classes) into other constructions identical to the transformed in meaning."[17]

Unlike Papp or Manolova, whose work was discussed in the preceding chapter, Nikolaeva explicitly notes the problem raised by the semantic invariancy requirement and also specifically states what operations are and are not admissible in the transformational process. According to Nikolaeva, the condition calling for the semantic identity of the source phrase and its transform refers to the extralinguistic situation.[18] The problem of disagreement among inform-

[14] V. V. Vinogradov, *Russkij jazyk: grammatičeskoe učenie o slove* (Moscow–Leningrad, 1947), 270.

[15] Popova, 200.

[16] T. M. Nikolaeva, "Transformacionnyj analiz sočetanij s prilagatel'nym—upravljajuščim slovom", *Transformacionnyj metod v strukturnoj lingvistike*, ed. S. K. Šaumjan (Moscow, 1964), 142–68. There is also a transformational study of Russian adjectives by A. V. Isačenko that, unfortunately, does not touch upon the APN type of construction. A. V. Isačenko, "Transformacionnyj analiz kratkix i polnyx prilagatel'nyx", *Issledovanija po strukturnoj tipologii*, ed. T. N. Mološnaja (Moscow, 1963), 61–93.

[17] Nikolaeva, 142.

[18] *Loc. cit.* It should be noted that this is not the formulation of the semantic invariancy requirement utilized in the present study. See page 39.

ants and the relativity of judgments about *grammaticalness* is also touched upon. The primary grammatical requirement imposed upon the transformations is that the source phrase and its transform have the same lexical roots. Within this morphological context, the following operations are admissible:[19]

1. change of the preposition:
   skol'zkij ot rosy → skol'zkij posle rosy
   'slippery from the dew' → 'slippery after the dew'
2. change of the flexion of N in accord with 1:
   blizkij ot nee → blizkij k nej
   'near from her' → 'near to her'
3. addition and deletion of P:
   neobxodimyj dlja ženščiny → neobxodimyj ženščine
   'indispensible for a woman' → 'indispensible to a woman'
4. change of one part of speech into another:
   on trudno rešaetsja → ego trudno rešit'
   'he decides with difficulty' → 'it is difficult to decide it'
5. insertion of conjunctions:
   dovol'no prijatnyj → dovol'nyj i prijatnyj
   'rather pleasant' → 'content and pleasant'

The above outlined conditions require some comment. The first matter is that of the semantic invariance condition. Nikolaeva notes the theoretical weakness of this requirement and observes that on the practical level one can speak about the sameness of meaning "... only with a high degree of approximation."[20] The hazards of determining 'sameness' versus 'non-sameness' are inadvertently illustrated by the examples of the sort: *dalekij ot meločej* 'far from trifles' and *dalekij dlja meločej* 'far for trifles' or *dovol'no prijatnyj* 'rather pleasant' and *dovol'nyj i prijatnyj* 'content and pleasant'. The asserted semantic 'sameness' of these phrases and their transforms is somewhat obscure. Such examples are frequent.

The second matter of interest is that concerning the preservation of root morphemes in the transforms. This requirement, apparently adopted from Zellig Harris' definition of the transformational process,[21] seems to be violated by operations 1 and 5. These call for the insertion of new lexical units — prepositions and conjunctions. It is true that these are function words, but they nonetheless have a considerable degree of lexical meaning. This is particularly

[19] *Ibid.*, 145. The examples are supplied by the present writer from various parts of Nikolaeva's article.

[20] *Ibid.*, 142.

[21] See page 16 for a discussion of Harris' views.

true of the complex prepositions, such as *po otnošeniju k* 'in relation to' or *nesmotrja na* 'in spite of', which possess explicit and stable lexical meanings. Nikolaeva's admission of the substitution of prepositions in the face of the requirement that there be full retention of roots implies that she regards prepositions, simple and complex, as purely formal grammatical units. If this is in fact the case, it should be so stated.[22]

The transformations proposed for the analysis of the A *ot* N unit are all of the preposition substitution type, *e.g.*, can A P^1 N be rewritten as A P^2 N with full retention of meaning? Nikolaeva presents the following as the results of her analysis of the A *ot* N construction:[23]

	A	ot	N	*k* 'to'	*s* 'with'	*posle* 'after'	*iz-za* 'on account of'	*dlja* 'for'
1.	*mokryj*	*ot*	*slez*	—	—	—	—	—
	'wet	because of	tears'					
2.	*skol'zkij*	*ot*	*rosy*	—	—	+	—	—
	'slippery	because of	the dew'					
3.	*ustalyj*	*ot*	*znoja*	—	—	—	+	—
	'tired	because of	the heat'					
4.	*ustalyj*	*ot*	*xod'by*	—	—	+	+	—
	'tired	because of	the walk'					
5.	*blednyj*	*ot*	*straxa*	—	+	—	+	—
	'pale	because of	terror'					
6.	*čistyj*	*ot*	*zavisti*	—	—	—	—	—
	'free	of	envy'					
7.	*slepoj*	*ot*	*roždenija*	—	+	—	—	—
	'blind	since	birth'					
8.	*blizkij*	*ot*	*nee*	+	—	—	—	+
	'near	to	her'					
9.	*dalekij*	*ot*	*meločej*	—	—	—	—	+
	'far	from	trifles'					

[22] Other arguments against the acceptance of preposition substitution as a type of analytic transformation are given in connection with the critique made of V. P. Manolova's *Transformation of Russian Syntagms of the Type* $S + S$, $S + P$, $V + S$, $V + P + S$ (Moscow, 1962). See pages 33—34.

[23] Nikolaeva, 156. The order of examples has been altered to facilitate discussion of the results. The original order of the items is 1, 6, 2, 3, 8, 7, 4, 5, and 9. In addition to being subjected to the listed transformations in the form of isolated word-combina-

The above description of the transform features of the nine examples raises a number of questions. In terms of the semantic classificatory scheme of the *Academy Grammar*, examples 1–5 express causal relations, examples 6 and 7 express ablative and temporal relations respectively, and the remaining two examples (8 and 9) — spatial relations. Unfortunately, the above-listed transformational specifications show no systematic relationship to the semantic groups. For example, none of the five causal examples share the same set of transform features nor do the two spatial examples. On the other hand, the causal example *mokryj ot slez* 'wet because of tears' and the ablative example *čistyj ot zavisti* 'free of envy' both share the same transformational specifications. The author summarizes the shortcomings of her analysis as follows: "The most serious apprehensions in the use of the described method are aroused not by the fact that combinations which are clearly close in meaning are fragmented into still smaller groups, but by the fact that the unity of combinations with the same type of admissible transformations is doubtful in many cases."[24] This observation is well documented by the material on A *ot* N. In the final analysis, Nikolaeva's results for the A *ot* N construction show only that in selected examples certain other prepositions can be substituted for *ot* with greater or lesser retention of the original meaning of the *ot* phrase.

Nikolaeva's study of adjectival constructions and Manolova's transform analysis of nominal and verbal constructions both rely very heavily on transformations involving the substitution of prepositions. Taken together, they serve to demonstrate that, even aside from the theoretical problems raised by preposition substitution, the method is not particularly effective in isolating the different semantic groups contained within a single constructional type.

The preposition substitutions work on a semi-lexical level. Transformations that operate on the grammatical level offer a much better hope for the resolution of multiply ambiguous homomorphic constructions. The use of such transformations is illustrated in the following original transform analysis of A *ot* N units.

tions, these examples were also subjected by Nikolaeva to the same transformations after being set in the context of a predication, *e.g.*, *on — mokr ot slez* 'it is wet because of tears', *on — čistyj ot zavisti* 'he is free of envy'. This was done in order to determine what effect, if any, their syntactic role might have on their transform potential. For the *ot* units, the only difference in the behavior of the adjectival examples in the predicative context is that *on — ustal iz-za xod'by* 'he is tired on account of the walk' is not possible, whereas the isolated word-combination *ustal ot xod'by* 'tired because of the walk' is.

[24] Nikolaeva, 151.

3.3. ANALYSIS OF N^1, A *ot* N^2 UNITS[25]

The general outline of the transform analysis of the adjectival construction is similar to that of the N *ot* N units, although less complex. As in the case of the nouns, the transforms are subject to the dual criteria of semantic invariance and grammaticalness.[26]

All of the examples of the structural type N^1, A *ot* N^2 are subjected to a set of six transformations. The units are then classified and described in terms of their responses to the transformations. The transformations that are used in the analysis of the N^1, A *ot* N^2 units are as follows:

T1:	N^1, A ot N^2	→	$N^1 - A^{n2}$
	lico, černoe ot pota		*lico — potnoe*
	'a face black because of sweat'	→	'the face [is] sweaty'
T2:	N^1, A ot N^2	→	N^1 V^a ot N^2
	glaza, mokrye ot slez		*glaza moknut ot slez*
	'eyes wet because of tears'	→	'eyes become wet because of tears'
T3:	N^1, A ot N^2	→	N^1, V_{ppp} N^2_i
	glaza, belye ot nenavisti		*glaza, vybelennye nenavist'ju*
	'eyes white because of hate'	→	'eyes whitened with hatred'
T4:	N^1, A ot N^2	→	N^2 V N^1
	voda, mutnaja ot doždja		*dožd' mutit vodu*
	'water muddy because of rain'	→	'rain muddies the water'
T5:	N^1, A ot N^2	→	X V N^1 ot N^2
	čelovek, otličnyj ot drugix		*X otličaet čeloveka ot drugix*
	'a man different from the others'	→	'X distinguishes [this] man from the others'
T6:	N^1, A ot N^2	→	N^1 Q^a ot N^2
	dom, dalekij ot goroda		*dom daleko ot goroda*
	'a house far from town'	→	'a house away from town'

Examples of the structural type N^1, A *ot* N^2 fall into four groups on the basis of their response to the above-listed transformations.[27]

[25] The unit under examination is A *ot* N; since the adjective is usually dependent upon a noun, the entire construction (N^1, A *ot* N^2) is taken as the string being subjected to transformation.

[26] A full statement of these criteria and the procedural details of the analysis will be found on pages 38—39.

[27] The transformations that are possible for a given example are indicated by a plus mark. Examples of the written-out transforms of the source phrase are given above in the illustration of the transformations.

GROUP:					T1	T2	T3	T4	T5	T6
Causal:	*lico'*	*černoe*	*ot*	*pota*	+	+	+	+	−	−
	'a face,	black	because of	sweat'						
Ablative:	*čelovek,*	*otličnyj*	*ot*	*drugix*	−	−	−	−	+	−
	'a man	different	from	the others'						
Spatial:	*dom,*	*dalekij*	*ot*	*goroda*	−	−	−	−	−	+
	'a house,	far	from	town'						
Temporal:	*mužik,*	*gluxonemoj*	*ot*	*roždenija*	−	−	−	−	−	−
	'a peasant	deaf-mute	since	birth'						

Having briefly illustrated the transformations used in the analysis of the N^1, A *ot* N^2 units and the transform features of each of the semantic subgroups subsumed within the N^1, A *ot* N^2 constructions, we now turn to a more detailed examination of each group.

TABLE 10

Transform Features of 'N^1, A *ot* N^2' *Units of the Causal Group*

	N^1	, A	*ot*	N^2	T1: → N^1—A^{n_2}	T2: → N^1 V^a *ot* N^2	T3: → N^1 V_{ppp} N^2_i	T4: → N^2 V N^1	T5: → X V^a N^1 *ot* N^2	T6: → Q *ot* N^2 *do* N^1
1.	guby	, černye	ot	xoloda	+	+	+	+	−	−
	'lips	, black	because of	cold'						
2.	guby	, černye	ot	černiki	−	+	+	+	−	−
	'lips	, black	because of	the bilberries'						
3.	lico	, černoe	ot	zagara	+	+	+	+	−	−
	'face	, black	because of	sunburn'						
4.	stol	, černyj	ot	kraski	+	+	+	+	−	−
	'table	, black	because of	paint'						
5.	kryši	, černye	ot	ljudej	+	+	+	+	−	−
	'roofs	, black	because of	people'						
6.	glaza	, krasnye	ot	vodki	−	+	+	+	−	−
	'eyes	, red	because of	vodka'						
7.	glaza	, krasnye	ot	znoja	+	+	+	+	−	−
	eyes	, red	because of	heat'						

TABLE 10 (*cont.*)

	N^1	, A	*ot*	N^2	T1: $\rightarrow N^1 — A^{n2}$	T2: $\rightarrow N^1\ V^a\ ot\ N^2$	T3: $\rightarrow N^1\ V_{ppp}\ N^2_i$	T4: $\rightarrow N^2\ V\ N^1$	T5: $\rightarrow X\ V^a\ N^1\ ot\ N^2$	T6: $\rightarrow Q\ ot\ N^2\ do\ N^1$
8.	čelovek	, krasnyj	ot	volnenija	+	+	+	+	–	–
	'a man	, red	because of	excitement'						
9.	starik	, krasnyj	ot	negodovanija	+	+	+	+	–	–
	'an old man	, red	because of	indignation'						
10.	kotly	, krasnye	ot	ržavčiny	+	+	+	+	–	–
	'kettles	, red	because of	rust'						
11.	Ivanov	, belyj	ot	gneva	+	+	+	+	–	–
	'Ivanov	, white	because of	anger'						
12.	pekar'	, belyj	ot	muki	+	+	+	+	–	–
	'a baker	, white	because of	flour'						
13.	glaza	, belesye	ot	nenavisti	+	+	+	+	–	–
	'eyes	, whitish	because of	hate'						
14.	lica	, zelenye	ot	užasa	+	+	+	+	–	–
	'faces	, green	because of	terror'						
15.	barži	, zelenye	ot	soldat	+	+	+	+	–	–
	'barges	, green	because of	soldiers'						
16.	nebo	, bagrovoe	ot	zari	+	+	+	+	–	–
	'sky	, purple	because of	the dawn'						
17.	starik	, bagrovyj	ot	duxoty	+	+	+	+	–	–
	'an old man	, purple	because of	stuffiness'						
18.	Ivanov	, blednyj	ot	gneva	+	+	+	+	–	–
	'Ivanov	, pale	because of	anger'						
19.	vse	, blednye	ot	ustalosti	+	+	+	+	–	–
	'all	, pale	because of	tiredness'						
20.	ženščina	, ryžaja	ot	vesnušek	+	+	–	–	–	–
	'a woman	, reddish	because of	freckles'						
21.	doroga	, ryžaja	ot	navoza	+	+	–	–	–	–
	'road	, reddish	because of	dung'						
22.	mal'čiki	, serye	ot	goloda	+	+	–	–	–	–
	'boys	, grey	because of	hunger'						
23.	šineli	, serye	ot	izvestki	+	+	–	–	–	–
	'overcoats	, grey	because of	lime'						
24.	noč'	, sedaja	ot	dyma	+	+	–	–	–	–
	'night	, grey	because of	smoke'						
25.	oblomki	, sedye	ot	soli	+	+	–	–	–	–
	'debris	, grey	because of	salt'						
26.	on	, sinij	ot	medikamentov	–	+	+	+	–	–
	'he	, blue	because of	drugs'						

TABLE 10 (*cont.*)

	N^1	, A	*ot*	N^2	T1: $\rightarrow N^1 — A^{n_2}$	T2: $\rightarrow N^1 V^a$ *ot* N^2	T3: $\rightarrow N^1 V_{ppp} N^2_i$	T4: $\rightarrow N^2 V N^1$	T5: $\rightarrow X V^a N^1$ *ot* N^2	T6: $\rightarrow Q$ *ot* N^2 *do* N^1
27.	negocianty	, sizye	ot	brit'ja	+	+	−	−	−	−
	'merchants	, bluish	because of	shaving'						
28.	veršiny	, rozovye	ot	lučej	+	+	−	−	−	−
	'heights	, rosy	because of	the [sun's] rays'						
29.	ona	, golubovata	ot	blednosti	+	+	−	−	−	−
	'she	, bluish	because of	[her] paleness'						
30.	lico	, pestroe	ot	mazkov	+	+	+	+	−	−
	'face	, motley	because of	daubs'						
31.	lica	, temnye	ot	bessonicy	+	+	+	+	−	−
	'faces	, dark	because of	insomnia'						
32.	mešoček	, temnyj	ot	pota	+	+	+	+	−	−
	'a small bag	, dark	because of	sweat'						
33.	oblački	, jarkie	ot	solnca	+	+	−	−	−	−
	'clouds	, bright	because of	the sun'						
34.	skamejka	, teplaja	ot	solnca	+	+	+	+	−	−
	'a bench	, warm	because of	the sun'						
35.	golyš	, gorjačij	ot	znoja	+	+	+	+	−	−
	'pebble	, hot	because of	the heat'						
36.	pal'cy	, xolodnye	ot	volnenija	+	+	+	+	−	−
	'fingers	, cold	because of	excitement'						
37.	plečo	, xolodnovatoe	ot	kupanija	+	+	+	+	−	−
	'shoulder	, cool	because of	bathing'						
38.	glaza	, mokrye	ot	slez	+	+	+	+	−	−
	'eyes	, wet	because of	tears'						
39.	mesjac	, mokryj	ot	doždja	−	+	+	+	−	−
	'month	, wet	because of	rain'						
40.	t'ma	, vlažnaja	ot	blizosti (reki)	+	+	+	+	−	−
	'darkness	, damp	because of	the nearness (of the river)'						
41.	listy	, syrye	ot	kraski	+	+	−	−	−	−
	'pages	, damp	because of	paint'						
42.	pole	, krovavoe	ot	sveta	+	+	+	+	−	−
	'field	, bloody	because of	the light'						
43.	starik	, potnyj	ot	duxoty	−	+	−	−	−	−
	'an old man	, sweaty	because of	the stuffiness'						
44.	povod'ja	, skol'zkie	ot	rosy	+	+	−	−	−	−
	'reins	, slippery	because of	the dew'						

TABLE 10 (*cont.*)

	N^1	, A	*ot*	N^2	T1: → N^1—A^{n2}	T2: → N^1 V^a *ot* N^2	T3: → N^1 V_{ppp} N^2_i	T4: → N^2 V N^1	T5: → X V^a N^1 *ot* N^2	T6: → Q *ot* N^2 *do* N^1
45.	stol	, lipkij	ot	kraski	+	+	−	−	−	−
	'table	, sticky	because of	paint'						
46.	jabloni	, tjaželye	ot	plodov	+	+	+	+	−	−
	'apple trees,	heavy	because of	the fruits'						
47.	voda	, mutnaja	ot	doždja	+	+	+	+	−	−
	'water	, muddy	because of	rain'						
48.	ulica	, zvonkaja	ot	vorob'ev	−	+	−	−	−	−
	'street	, aring	because of	sparrows'						
49.	derev'ja	, ustalye	ot	znoja	+	+	−	−	−	−
	'trees	, tired	because of	the heat'						
50.	starik	, ustalyj	ot	zabot	+	+	−	−	−	−
	'an old man,	tired	because of	worries'						
51.	duša	, ustalaja	ot	žizni	+	+	−	−	−	−
	'soul	, tired	because of	life'						
52.	Antoščenko,	zaskoruzlyj	ot	krovi	+	+	−	−	−	−
	'Antoščenko,	hardened	because of	blood'						
53.	mal'čik	, odurelyj	ot	žira	+	+	+	+	−	−
	'boy	, crazy	because of	the grease'						
54.	kapitalisty	, poluumnye	ot	straxa	+	+	−	−	−	−
	'capitalists	, half-crazy	because of	terror'						
55.	lico	, glupovatoe	ot	ulybki	+	+	−	−	−	−
	'a face	, dullish	because of	a smile'						
56.	kulačka	, zlaja	ot	soznanija	+	+	+	+	−	−
	'kulak [f.]	, evil	because of	consciousness'						
57.	ruka	, smešna	ot	popytok	−	+	−	−	−	−
	'a hand	, ludicrous	because of	attempts'						
58.	on	, polubol'noj	ot	vozbuždenija	+	+	−	−	−	−
	'he —	, half-sick	because of	excitement'						
59.	ljudi	, poročnye	ot	skuki	+	+	+	+	−	−
	'people	, vicious	because of	boredom'						
60.	ja	, p'jan	ot	xod'by	+	+	+	+	−	−
	'I —	, drunk	because of	the walk'						
61.	ja	, p'jan	ot	radosti	+	+	+	+	−	−
	'I	, drunk	because of	joy'						
62.	ja	, xmelen	ot	razgovorov	+	+	+	+	−	−
	'I	, drunk	because of	the conversations'						
63.	kusok	, nozdrevatyj	ot	starosti	+	+	+	+	−	−
	'a piece	, holey	because of	age'						

3.3.0.1. *Causal Group*

Examples expressing causal meaning account for the great majority of N^1, A *ot* N^2 units both in absolute numbers and in terms of the number and variety of roots that are used. The causal units are formally characterized by the admissibility of transformations 1–4.

T1 recasts the N^1, A *ot* N^2 unit into the form N^1—A^{n2} *(lico, černoe ot pota* 'face black because of sweat' → *lico — potnoe* 'face [is] sweaty'). This transformation reflects the fact that N^2 can function as an attribute of N^1 just as the A does. As a matter of conjecture, it may be that in some cases there is a transformational relationship between dual adjective attributive constructions of the type AAN *(potnoe, černoe lico* 'sweaty black face') and N^1, A *ot* N^2 causal units *(lico, černoe ot pota* 'face black because of sweat').

T2 converts the N^1, A *ot* N^2 units into a parallel verbal construction of the form N^1 V^a *ot* N^2: *nebo, bagrovoe ot zari* 'sky purple because of the dawn' → *nebo bagroveet ot zari* 'sky becomes purple because of the dawn'. This transformation is the most effective of the four in isolating the causal examples from the other semantic groups and is also prerequisite to the remaining two transformations that characterize the causal units. If T2 is not possible, then T3 and T4 are automatically excluded.[28] The second transformation relies on the fact that many descriptive adjectives in Russian have derived verbal forms with the meaning 'to assume the quality specified by the root'. Of the forty-one different adjective roots represented in the causal examples, thirty-four possess such parallel verb forms and, consequently, undergo T2.

The third and fourth transformations rest in turn upon the fact that many of the derived intransitive 'becoming' verbs have secondary derived factitive forms, *e.g.*, *glupyj* 'stupid' → *glupet'* 'to become stupid' → *oglupit'* 'to make stupid'. The existence of such derivational chains makes possible transformational series of the type *mužik, xmel'noj ot vodki* 'peasant drunk because of vodka' → *mužik xmeleet ot vodki* 'a peasant becomes drunk because of vodka' → *vodka xmelit mužika* 'vodka intoxicates the peasant'. The derived factitive forms are less productive than the deadjectival 'becoming' verbs and occur for only twenty-one of the forty-one verbs represented in the causal examples.[29] The reason why some *-et'* verbs have corresponding factitive forms while

[28] Two exceptions to this were noted. The adjective *smešnoj* 'laughable' lacks a form **smešnet'* meaning 'to become laughable', but has a factitive form *smešit'* meaning 'to make someone laugh'. The deverbal adjective *gorjačij* 'hot' also lacks a 'becoming' verbal form, but has a transitive equivalent *gorjačit'* 'to make hot', *i.e.*, 'to excite'.

[29] See page 147 for a discussion of the process from the point of view of verbal constructions. It is of interest that the proportion of derived factitive verbs to 'becoming' verbs is approximately the same for the examples of the intransitive verbal construktions as for the adjective examples examined here.

others do not is not altogether clear, but it would appear that in general the more frequent verbs are much more likely to have the factitive form than less frequent verbs *(i.e., černet'/černit'* 'to become black/to blacken' and *zelenet'/zelenit'* 'to become green/to make green' versus *ryžet'* 'to become ruddy' or *sizet'* 'to become dove-colored'). In some cases T3 is impossible because the *-it'* form of the root has a different meaning. For example, *golubit'* does not mean 'to make blue' but 'to caress' *(cf. golubčik* 'my dear fellow'); *serit'* does not mean 'to make grey', but 'to cover with sulphur'.

T3 (T: $\rightarrow$ N^1 V_{ppp} N_i^2) is a passive transformation of T4, *e.g.*, (T3) *mužik, oxmelennyj vodkoj* 'a peasant made drunk by vodka' $\rightarrow$ (T4) *vodka xmelit mužika* 'vodka makes drunk the peasant'. This transformation is of particular interest in that it demonstrates (at least for a part of the examples) the formal relationship of verbal passive constructions to adjectival constructions of the type under discussion, *i.e., mužik, xmel'noj ot vodki* 'a peasant drunk because of vodka' and *mužik oxmelennyj vodkoj* 'a peasant made drunk by vodka'.[30] The relationship in OR was even more striking in that the agent of the action expressed by passive participles could be indicated by *ot* + N.[31] Thus, from both the synchronic transformational and the diachronic points of view, there is a close connection between causal adjectival *ot* constructions and passive verbal constructions.[32]

The derivational basis of the causal examples has already been touched upon in the description of the transformations. With a handful of exceptions, the adjectives form their derived 'becoming' verbs by means of the formant *-e-*.[33] There are three cases in which the line of derivation goes in the opposite direction, *i.e.*, from V to A: *ustalyj* 'tired' $\leftarrow$ *ustat'* 'to tire', *zaskoruzlyj* 'hardened' $\leftarrow$ *zaskoruznut'* 'to become hardened' and *odurelyj* 'crazed' $\leftarrow$ *oduret'* 'to become stupid'. Such cases, however, are the exception rather than the rule for the causal construction type.

Examination of the material illustrated by the above transformation raises an important point about the direction of derivation on the syntactic as opposed to the morphological level. In morphological derivational series of the type *černyj* $\rightarrow$ *černet'* $\rightarrow$ *černit'* 'black' $\rightarrow$ 'to become black' $\rightarrow$ 'to blacken', the line of derivation is clearly A $\rightarrow$ $V_{et'}$ $\rightarrow$ $V_{t'}$.[34] On the syntactic level, however, the line of derivation among the constructions is:

[30] The suffixal *-n-* in both the adjectival and the participial forms constitutes another formal marker of this relationship on the historical plane.

[31] See pages 64–65 for an illustration of this.

[32] This connection also exists with regard to the N *ot* N units. See pages 64–65.

[33] See pages 148–149 for a detailed discussion of the derivational characteristics of deadjectival verbs.

[34] See page 147 for supporting evidence.

guby černejut ot xoloda	→	*guby, černye ot xoloda*
N^1 V_{et} ot N^2		N^1, A ot N^2
'lips become black because of the cold'	→	'lips black because of the cold'
	↘	*xolod černit guby*
		N^2 V N^1
		'cold blackens the lips'

In other words, at the morphological level, the adjective form is basic; whereas on the syntactic level, the construction headed by the derived verb serves as the derivational model for a parallel adjectival construction. This line of development finds support in two facts. First, as was noted by Peškovskij, adjectives do not normally serve as construction heads except in so far as they are related to a verb. Secondly, it was observed by both Popova and Zasorina that the expression of causal meaning in A *ot* N units was heavily dependent on the presence of a (semi-) predication. The proposed line of constructional derivation N^1 V *ot* $N^2 \rightarrow N^1$, A *ot* N^2 is in accord with these observations. Thus, the causal examples of the N^1, A *ot* N^2 illustrate that the direction of derivation on the syntactic constructional level can in some cases run counter to that of the morphological or word level.

3.3.0.2. *Ablative Group*

The *Ablative group* is comprised of a small number of adjectives that undergo only one of the listed transformations: T5: → X V^a N^1 *ot* N^2, *pole, svobodnoe ot neprijatelja* 'field free from the enemy' → *X osvoboždaet pole ot neprijatelja* 'X frees the field of the enemy'. This transformation isolates the following list of examples from their homomorphic counterparts expressing other semantic relations.

1. *rabočij,*	*svobodnyj*	*ot*	*gneta*
'a worker,	free	from	oppression'
2. *odežda,*	*čistaja*	*ot*	*snega*
'clothes,	free	of	snow'
3. *ugol,*	*bezopasnyj*	*ot*	*napadenija*
'a corner,	secure	from	attack'
4. *delo,*	*tajnoe*	*ot*	*postoronnix*
'a matter,	secret	from	outsiders'
5. *žizn',*	*osobennaja*	*ot*	*vsex*
'a life,	apart	from	all [others]'
6. *student,*	*otličnyj*	*ot*	*drugix*
'a student,	different	from	others'
7. *veroispovedanie,*	*otdel'noe*	*ot*	*pročix*
'a denomination,	separate	from	others'

The *Academy Grammar* gives the following tautological semantic definition of this group: " . . . the feature expressed by the adjective is complemented by an indication of the object . . . from which someone is freed, distinguished or isolated . . . ."[35] In contrast, T5 uniquely isolates this group in a completely formal manner.

T5 demonstrates that N^1 can function as the object of a verb derived from A: *starik, čistyj ot grexa* 'an old man pure from sin' → *X očiščaet starika ot grexa* 'X purifies the old man of sin'. This would seem, in part, to suggest a similarity of the ablative examples to those causal units that permit N^1 to be restated as the object of V^a, *e.g.*, *lico, zelenoe ot užasa* 'a face green because of horror' → *užas zelenit lico* 'horror turns the face green'. This overlooks the difference in the role of *ot* + N in the two types, however. In the ablative examples, a *de novo* subject must be introduced and *ot* + N be retained as a complement of the verb. It can never be restated as the subject of the verb. Thus, in the causal type, the *ot* + N can function as the actor, whereas in the ablative type the prepositional unit can only play the role of an object.

A second transformation, not listed in Table 10, that further opposes the ablative examples to the causal is the reflexive transformation of the type N^1, V *ot* N^2 → N^1 V_{sja} *ot* N^2: *student, otličnyj ot drugix* 'a student different from others' → *student otličaetsja ot drugix* 'a student distinguishes himself from others'.[36] This provides a convenient intermediate stage between the source phrase and T5 *(X otličaet studenta ot drugix* 'X distinguishes the student from others').

The adjectives of the *Ablative group* are of a different lexical layer from those of the *Causal group*. This difference is reflected in their typical derivational and transformational pattern *teplyj* 'warm' → *teplet'* 'to become warm' → *oteplit'* 'to make warm, to winterize'. The ablative adjectives also are members of derivational series, but of a very different sort, *e.g.*, *otdel'nyj* 'separate' and *otdelit'* 'to separate', *otdelit'sja* 'to get separated'. In this group the derivational relationship between A and V is not so clear-cut as it is for the causal series. In particular, the ablative adjectives do not form intransitives in *-et'* with stadial meanings. Furthermore, their intransitive forms in *-sja* are derived directly from the transitive verb forms and have passive meanings. This is shown by the *-sja* transform: *žizn', osobennaja ot vsex* 'a life apart from all [others]' → *žizn' obosobljaetsja ot vsex* 'a life stands apart from all [others]' → *X obosobljaet žizn' ot vsex* 'X isolates a life from all [others]'.

One final point of opposition between these adjectives and those of the *Causal group* is that the ablative adjectives are characterized by the syntactic

[35] *AG*, *II*, 1, 329.

[36] This transformation restates the *Ablative group* in the form in which they occur in the N^1 V_{sja} *ot* N^2 construction. See pages 169–172 for the analysis of the verbal units.

property of strong government.[37] This is reflected transformationally by the fact that the *ot* N is retained under transformation for the ablative units *(gorod, bezopasnyj ot napadenija* 'a town secure from attack' → *obezopasit' gorod ot napadenija* 'to secure a town from attack'), whereas it disappears in transitive verb transformations of the causal units *(voda, mutnaja ot doždja* 'water muddy because of rain' → *dožd' mutit vodu* 'rain muddies the water').

3.3.0.3. *Spatial and Temporal Groups*

The spatial and temporal examples constitute small marginal groups whose identifying characteristics are more lexical than grammatical. The examples of the two groups are opposed to their causal and ablative homomorphs chiefly by the fact that the transformations that characterize those groups are not admissible for spatial and causal examples.

In all of the examples collected only three different adjective roots were found with spatial meaning in the constructional format N^1, A *ot* N^2. These are represented in the three following examples:

1. *dom, blizkij ot lesa*
   'a house close to the forest'
2. *gorod, dalekij ot Moskvy*
   'a town far from Moscow'
3. *soldaty, krajnie ot (levogo) kryla*
   'the soldiers extreme from the (left) flank'

Native speakers of Russian judge these phrases to be only semigrammatical. The more usual form of such spatial examples involves a predication between the head noun and the adjective phrase, *e.g.*, *Kiti posmotrela na ego lico, kotoroe bylo na takom blizkom ot nee rasstojanii* . . . . 'Kitty looked at his face which was at such close distance from her . . . .' Cases like those indicated by examples 1–3, where there is no explicit predication, are usually expressed adverbially, that is, the fully grammatical form of such phrases is *dom blizko ot lesa* 'house close to the forest', *gorod daleko ot Moskvy* 'a town far from Moscow'. This adverbial form can be used as the specifying transform for the spatial examples, *i.e.*, T6: N^1, A *ot* $N^2 \rightarrow N^1\ Q^a$ *ot* N^2; *dom, blizkij ot lesa* → *dom blizko ot lesa*. This transformation will not work, however, for *krajnij* 'extreme' since its adverbial form means 'extreme(ly)' in a non-spatial transferred sense only.

The only examples of N^1, A *ot* N^2 units with a temporal meaning were:

1. *mužik, gluxonemoj ot roždenija*
   'a peasant, deaf-mute since birth'

[37] See pages 171–172 for a discussion of strong government in connection with de-adjectival ablative examples of the type $N^1\ V_{sja}$ *ot* N^2.

2. *syn, slepoj ot mladyx nogtej*
   'a son, blind since childhood'
3. *starik, slepoj ot kolybeli*
   'an old man, blind since the cradle'
4. *devuška, bol'naja ot detstva*
   'a girl, sick since childhood'

All of these are fixed phraseological units in which the N component cannot be altered. The use of *ot* in this sense has been supplanted in CSR by the preposition *s* 'since' in all cases except the first. These examples are formally isolated from those of the other semantic groups of the structural type by the fact that they do not undergo transformation.

In sum, it must be concluded that no spatial or temporal categories exist for N^1, A *ot* N^2 units in the sense that *Causal* and *Ablative groups* do. There are only a small number of individual phraseological units with spatial or temporal meaning.

3.4. CONCLUDING REMARKS

The foregoing analysis has been directed toward the resolution of the syntactic ambiguity inherent in the construction N^1, A *ot* N^2. More specifically, it has tried by means of analytic transformations to isolate and characterize the different semantic types ascribed to the construction by traditional grammars.

The transformations formally specify two groups — the *Causal*, which accounts for the great majority of N^1, A *ot* N^2 units, and the much smaller, but strongly marked, *Ablative group*. The remaining two semantic groups, *Spatial* and *Temporal*, traditionally assigned to the construction are primarily phraseological units and do not stand on the same level as the preceding two groups.

Two other points of general interest were brought to light in the analysis. It was noted by Popova and Zasorina that the causal adjectival units were characterized by the presence of a predication between the adjective and the head noun. The transformations corroborate this assertion in that in each of them the adjective is restated either as a verb, a predicate adjective, or in one case as an adverb. This predicativeness is not, however, restricted to causal examples, but applies to all A *ot* N units.

The second point is that concerning the opposing directions of the derivational process on the morphological and the syntactic levels. This phenomenon may be illustrated in the following manner:

Morphological derivation: *krasnyj* → *krasnet'*
Syntactic derivation: *krasnyj* + *ot* ← *krasnet'* + *ot*

The above outlined process has very important consequences for APN constructions and clarifies an otherwise anomalous situation. Derivationally, adjectives are much more closely related to nouns than to verbs, but constructions in which adjectives function as grammatical heads are modeled not on nominal but on verbal constructions. This rather paradoxical situation can be explained, at least in part, in terms of a feedback process operating between the two linguistic levels of syntax and morphology.

4

TRANSFORM ANALYSIS OF N^1 V *ot* N^2 CONSTRUCTIONS[1]

4.1. INTRODUCTION

Russian verbal prepositional constructions, like their nominal counterparts, display a high degree of syntactic homomorphy. Consider, for example, the following word-combinations: *uxodit' ot raboty* 'to leave work', *oberegat' ot raboty* 'to protect from work', and *zabolet' ot raboty* 'to fall ill because of work'. From the formal (grammatical) point of view, at least on the surface level, the three phrases are identical in that they each consist of a verb, the preposition *ot*, and the dependent noun *rabota*. On a deeper level, however, it is self-evident that the type of syntactic relationship between the verbs and the nouns is quite different. This underlying structural difference is wholly apart from the lexical meaning of the individual words involved. It is this underlying structural difference unaccompanied by any differences in the surface grammar that constitutes this particular type of syntactic homonymy.

Traditional treatments of Russian grammar try to resolve this sort of homonymy by means of a notional taxonomy describing the different semantic-relational groups within the N^1 V *ot* N^2 structure. Since it is not possible to elaborate formal procedures for assigning examples to them, the taxonomies offered by these grammars are both vague and, not infrequently, contradictory. Perhaps the most striking feature uniting these descriptions is their failure to make any statement of the criteria that the authors have used in making up their classificational systems.

The initial part of this chapter will examine some of the classificational systems developed for N^1 V *ot* N^2 units and will devote particular attention to the types of criteria used by the authors in their systems. First we will

[1] N^1 V *ot* N^2 will be used as a cover symbol subsuming three types of verbs: 1) unmarked intransitive verbs *(černet'* 'to become black'), 2) marked intransitive verbs *(kolebat'sja* 'to vacillate'), and 3) transitive verbs *(uvesti* 'to lead off'). When it is necessary to discriminate among these types, the following symbols will be used: 1) Vø; 2) Vsja; and 3) Vt.

examine and compare three general treatments of the problem by A. A. Šaxmatov, A. M. Peškovskij, and the writers of the recent *Academy Grammar*. Following this, three recent and more specialized studies, all dealing primarily with the expression of causal relations by N^1 V *ot* N^2 units, will be examined. One transformationally oriented study is also briefly touched upon.

The second part of the chapter presents an original transform analysis of the N^1 V *ot* N^2 construction. Following an introductory statement, the analysis is presented in three sections: 1) N^1 $V_{\emptyset}$ *ot* N^2, 2) N^1 V_{sja} *ot* N^2, and 3) N^1 V_t N^2 *ot* N^3.

4.2. SURVEY OF LITERATURE

Traditional treatments of syntactic homonymy in verbal prepositional constructions fall into two groups that differ more in emphasis than in substance. The first and less sophisticated approach focuses on the particular meaning thought to be displayed by P in a given VPN construction. After the preposition is assigned the proper interpretation, examples are grouped on the basis of a supposed communality of meaning of the preposition. This is the approach adopted by A. A. Šaxmatov in his *Sintaksis*.[2] The following meanings for *ot* in V *ot* N constructions are listed.[3]

I. With verbs of movement, *[ot]* designates the starting point of the movement.
   1. *Sofija ot sebja vyxodit.*
      'Sofija goes out of her room.'
   2. *Ot vsex storon narod tolpilsja.*
      'The people crowded together from all sides.'

II. *[Ot]* designates the place from which one or another action starts to be revealed.
   1. *Sami istoriki Napoleona rasskazyvajut, čto ešče ot Smolenska on xotel ostanovit'sja.*
      'The historians of Napoleon themselves recount that already from Smolensk he wanted to stop.'

III. *[Ot]* designates the beginning, the original cause of a corresponding action.
   1. *Nečego [ee] doprašivat'. Ot menja vse. Moj grex, moe i delo.*
      'There is nothing to ask [her]. It is all because of me. My sin and my doing.'

[2] A. A. Šaxmatov, *Sintaksis russkogo jazyka*, 2nd ed. (Leningrad, 1941). Photomechanic reprint (The Hague, 1963).

[3] Šaxmatov, 378–9. Only representative examples are given.

2. *Meždu tem imperator, ustavši ot tščetnogo ožidanija ....*
   'Meanwhile the emperor having tired of unavailing waiting ....'
3. *Ja uznal i poljubil ego po slučaju bolez'ni mladšego brata moego, ešče mladenca, kotoryj ot ospy neskol'ko dnej ne mog raskryvat' glaz.*
   'I got to know and love him on the occasion of the illness of my younger brother, still an infant, who, for several days, was not able to open his eyes because of smallpox.'
4. *Stepan Stepanovič byl v mundire, i ot mundira li, ili ot drugix pričin P'er uvidal pered soboj sovsem drugogo čeloveka.*
   'Stepan Stepanovič was in uniform and whether it was because of the uniform or because of other reasons, Pierre saw before him a completely different person.'

IV. *[Ot]* designates the performer of an action expressed by the passive voice.[4]
1. *Dušen'ka uže ostavlena ot vsex.*
   'Dušen'ka [was] already forsaken by everyone.'
2. *I ot poslednej — ot tebja ja budu zabyt ....*
   'And by the latter — [and] by you I shall be forgotten ....'

V. *[Ot]* designates an object or phenomenon which the subject escapes, leaves (behind), or avoids.
1. *On ot vsego žalsja i xoronilsja.*
   'He shrank from and hid himself from everything.'
2. *Ot nee čuždalsja.*
   '[He] shunned her.'
3. *Menja oberegali ot truda.*
   '[They] guarded me from labor.'

VI. *[Ot]* designates a person on whose behalf an action proceeds, [a person] who is its source or performer.
1. *Pošlite; tol'ko, požalujsta, ne ot menja, — otvečala Nasten'ka.*
   'Send [it], only, please, not on my behalf — Nasten'ka answered.'
2. *Ja ne znala, čto vy tože ot žil'cov živete.*
   'I did not know that you also live from the lodgers.'

VII. *[Ot]* designates a person or object left without attention, neglected, forgotten.
1. *Ot živogo muža vspomjanula pokojnika.*
   '[She] recalled [her] deceased [husband] rather than [her] live husband.'

[4] This group, although not so indicated, is archaic in CSR.

VIII. *[Ot]* designates a moment of time from which an action is revealed.
1. *Ja ot rodu ruž'ja v ruki ne bral.*
'I from birth have not taken a gun into my hands.'
2. *I s tex por, kak priedet iz seminarii, vse raz ot razu xuže da xuže.*
'And since then, when [he] comes from the seminary, every time it is worse and worse.'

An examination of Šaxmatov's category headings shows that what is referred to as the meaning of *ot* is, in fact, the ontological meaning of the dependent noun. In other words, it is tacitly assumed that the generic meaning of the dependent noun determines the meaning of *ot* in each group. In sum, Šaxmatov's system amounts to a semantic interpretation of each example grouping them, and using a somewhat generalized paraphrase of the meaning of N^2 as a class label. The purely ad hoc nature of this procedure is especially evident in groups II and VII, the class labels of which are so narrow that they could apply to little beyond the particular examples given.

Šaxmatov realized that such an approach inevitably must be restricted to a very low level of generality. In a note to the discussion of prepositional constructions, he observes that it would have been better to treat them in terms of a priori categories (spatial, causal, *etc.)* within the morphological framework imposed by the construction head.[5]

It is this latter course that has been adopted by many of Šaxmatov's successors — including Peškovskij, Vinogradov, and the other authors of the *Academy Grammar*. This second approach, instead of focusing on the different meanings of a given preposition, takes a more abstract view of the problem of homonymy within the V *ot* N structure. This system entails the adoption of a number of a priori logical categories, with examples classified by being assigned to the appropriate category.

Šaxmatov treated prepositional constructions in the portion of his work dealing with isolated word-combinations. A. M. Peškovskij examines them under the general heading of the secondary members of the sentence.[6] The material on word-combinations with verb heads is broken down into two major sections. First, those constructions consisting of verb plus dependent noun are presented. The latter are arranged by case and then largely on the basis of semantic criteria, *e.g.*, verbs expressing removal *(izbegat'* 'to avoid', *etc.)*, verbs expressing goal *(dostigat'* 'to attain', *etc.)*. The second major section treats

[5] Šaxmatov, 552.

[6] A. M. Peškovskij, *Russkij sintaksis v naučnom osveščenii*, 7th ed. (Moscow, 1956), 283–340. Most subsequent Russian works on syntax have combined the organizational approaches of Šaxmatov and Peškovskij and present the material on prepositional constructions twice, once under word-combinations and once under the secondary members of the sentence.

verbal prepositional constructions. Unlike the foregoing section the subdivision is not by case but by preposition since Peškovskij considers the prepositions and not the case endings of the noun as the basic expression of the relationship between the object and the action.[7] Each preposition is then described in terms of a priori semantic categories. The following analysis of the V *ot* N construction is given.[8]

I. Spatial — also termed separative *(otdelitel'nyj)* or removal *(udalitel'nyj)*

A. Verbs of movement: N = starting point

a. *udaljat'sja ot berega*
'to move away from the shore'

b. *idti ot stolba*
'to walk from the pillar'

B. Verbs not connected with the idea of movement

1. Indicate removal without departure

a. *otkazat'sja ot čego*
'to decline something'

b. *uderživat'sja ot čego*
'to refrain from something'

c. *storonit'sja ot čego*
'to step aside from something'

2. Indicate a starting point without subsequent removal

a. *skažite emu ot menja*
'tell him from me'

b. *otličat'sja ot čego*
'to distinguish one's self from'

c. *v ètoj kartine est' nečto ot primitivov*
'in this picture there is something of the primitives'

II. Temporal — completely analogous to the spatial meaning. The *ot* indicates that the time named by the noun is the initial moment of the action. In modern Russian, the temporal use of *ot* is found only in a few semi-adverbial phrases:

a. *ot rodu ne igral*
'[he] had not played from birth,' *i.e.*, 'never played'
ot mladyx nogtej privyk
'accustomed from early childhood'

[7] Peškovskij, 304.
[8] Peškovskij, 315–6.

b. *ot rodu*
'from birth'
god ot godu
'with each passing year'
den' oto dnja
'with each passing day'
ot veka
'from time immemorial'

III. Causal

a. *pogibnut' ot požara*
'to perish because of the fire'
b. *stradat' ot grubosti nravov*
'to suffer from coarseness of temperaments'

IV. Modal *(sposob)* — only in semi-adverbial expressions
a. *skazat' ot duši*
'to say from the soul'
b. *skazat' ot čistogo serdca*
'to say from a pure heart'

V. With the verbs *lečitsja* 'to undergo a cure' and *vyzdorovet'* 'to recover' *(ot čaxotki* 'from tuberculosis'*)*

Peškovskij's classification of the different semantic groups subsumed within the N^1 V *ot* N^2 construction graphically illustrates the inadequacies of non-formal classificational schemes. Three of the five categories are at best marginal phenomena each consisting of a handful of fixed *ot* N phrases. From the point of view of their grammatical characterization, two of the three, temporal and modal, are identically described as semi-adverbial. The two major categories, causal and spatial, lack any grammatical characterization. The *Spatial group* presents a rather curious spectacle in that only the first of its semantic subdivisions has anything to do with the idea of space, whereas the remaining (non-spatial) spatial examples are classified according to whether or not they indicate 'removal' or 'moving off from' *(udalenie)*. It is difficult to see any connection between the idea of removal and the examples of either of the subgroups. Further, the asserted semantic unity of the 'non-removed' subgroup is particularly obscure.

Peškovskij's analysis of N^1 V *ot* N^2 units is much inferior to that proposed for the nominal units (N^1 *ot* N^2). These were (in part) formally categorized in terms of their derivational kinship to the verbal constructions now under examination. In the verbal constructions, however, no such use of formal criteria is made.[9]

[9] See pages 24–25 for a discussion of Peškovskij's analysis of the N^1 *ot* N^2 constructions.

The *Academy Grammar* gives a much more detailed description of V *ot* N constructions than either of the preceding works.[10] If Šaxmatov focuses on the different meanings of *ot* (actually the meaning of the dependent noun) and Peškovskij on the assignment of examples to 'given' logical categories, the *Academy Grammar* classifies examples of the N^1 V *ot* N^2 construction in terms of the semantic relationship between the head verb and the dependent noun. These relations are, as with Peškovskij, labeled in terms of large a priori logico-semantic categories *(i.e.*, spatial, causal, *etc.)*.

It is noted that VPN_g constructions generally express attributive circumstantial relations (action and place, time, manner, cause, goal of completion), but can also express objective relations.[11] The *Academy Grammar*'s classification of N *ot* V constructions is presented below in schematized form.[12]

I. Objective Relations:
   A. Physical removal: *ot''exat' ot goroda* 'to depart from town'
   B. Abstract removal: *osvobodit'sja ot truda* 'to relieve [one's self] of labor'
      1. In A and B: V = activity
         N = person or object from which subject of V is removed or freed
   C. Source: *uznat' ot sekretarja* 'to find out from the secretary'
      1. V = *ždat'* 'to wait', *želat'* 'to wish', *polučit'* 'to receive', *uslyšat'* 'to hear' *etc.* (usually transitive)
         N = source of expectation, obtaining, perception

II. Causal Relations: *rastopit'sja ot znoju* 'to melt because of the heat'
      1. V = activity
         N = object, phenomenon, state calling forth the activity

III. Spatial and Temporal Relations (always with *do* 'to' + N):
   A. Spatial: *exat' ot lesa do reki* 'to go from the forest to the river'
      1. V = activity
         N = segment of space encompassed by the activity
   B. Temporal: *rabotat' ot sredy do pjatnicy* 'to work from Wednesday to Friday'
      1. V = activity
         N = segment of time encompassed by the activity

[10] Akademija Nauk SSSR, Institut jazykoznanija, *Grammatika russkogo jazyka, II*, 1 (Moscow, 1954; 2nd ed. 1960). The section on verbal word-combinations is credited to V. M. Filippova, 3.

[11] *AG, II*, 1, 138.

[12] *AG, II*, 1, 144–5.

IV. Archaic Temporal Relations (without *do* + N): *bolet' ot kolybeli* 'to be ill from the cradle'
Now mostly in fixed phrases *(pomnit' ot molodyx nogtej* 'to remember from early childhood')

V. Attributive-Circumstantial Relations: *skazat' ot (vsej) duši* 'to say from [one's] entire soul'
1. V = denoting activity plus the fixed phrases *ot čistogo serdca* 'from a pure heart', *ot vsego serdca* 'from a whole heart'
N = manner of completion of activity

The *Academy Grammar* does not state what criteria have been used in its classification of VPN constructions. However, the comparatively large number of examples and the rather detailed description of them provide enough material to permit the reader to ascertain roughly what these criteria are. Perhaps the most noteworthy single observation afforded by such an inspection is that no single type of criterion is applied with any degree of consistency.

The primary criteria utilized for isolating the different meaning groups within the V *ot* N structure are semantic. This is the approach used in the attempt to fix the unique meaning of each relational grouping by means of specifying the ontological referents of V and N in each group. For example, in the *Objective group* the V refers to an action involving removal or freeing from something while N refers to an action, person, or object. This set of specifications opposes the examples of the former group to those of the *Causal group* in which the verb refers to an action and the noun to an action, object, phenomenon, or state eliciting the action of the verb. There would appear to be a high degree of overlap in the range of these definitions. The second major area where semantic criteria are used is in the labeling of the groups. Here, however, the criteria are utilized inconsistently since groups II *(Causal)* and III A *(Spatial)* and B *(Temporal)* have semantic headings while I *(Objective)* and IV *(Attributive-Circumstantial)* have grammatical terms as labels.

From the point of view of the utilization of formal criteria, the classification scheme of the *Academy Grammar* represents an advance over the systems of both Šaxmatov and Peškovskij. The *Academy Grammar*'s system of relational classes differs substantially from that of Peškovskij's only in that it has broken down the latter's spatial category into a spatial and a large new class with the heading *Objective.* In doing this, and in other minor ways, the *Academy Grammar* has made greater use of formal criteria than has Peškovskij. In particular, the newly established *Objective group* is isolated from the *Spatial group* by restricting the latter to examples of the V *ot* N *do* N pattern.[13] The *Academy*

[13] This opposition is further supported by transformational and derivational evidence in the original analysis. See pages 133–135 below.

Grammar points out the similarity of the nonarchaic temporal examples to the spatial examples by indicating their adherence to the dual prepositional pattern. Peškovskij simply remarks that the *Temporal group* is analogous to his *Spatial group* without specifying the feature that they share. A further use of a formal feature in isolating one of the subgroups of the objective category is the specification that the verbs of the source subgroup usually have a direct object.

Although the *Academy Grammar* makes greater use of formal features than the two preceding descriptions, its failure to make full use of such criteria, even on a superficial level, is strikingly evident. For example, the statement that the verbs of the sour cegroup usually possess direct objects could easily have been bolstered by pointing out that many verbs with the general meaning 'to obtain something from some source' take their direct objects not in the accusative, but in the genitive case.[14] Similarly, the majority of verbs listed in the physical and abstract removal subgroups of the *Objective group* are characterized by the grammatical property described by Russian grammarians as strong government.[15] In other words, the *ot* N is semi-required by the head word. A closely related fact is that many of these verbs were used without *ot* but with a genitive object in earlier stages of the language. *(Cf.* Puškin's *bežal on ix besedy šumnoj* 'he fled their noisy conversation' or *ty lask moix bežiš'* 'you flee my caresses'.)[16] Lastly, the use of the ablative prefixes *ot-*, *u-*, *iz-*, *s-*, and *ob-* is strongly in evidence among examples of the *Objective group* while completely lacking in the examples of all of the other relational groups.

The similarity of the classificational schemes of Peškovskij and the *Academy Grammar* have already been noted. It may also be observed at this point that the system utilized by Šaxmatov, although based on somewhat different premises, is quite similar to the other two. If we ignore the very narrow and marginal groups II (point from which action X starts to be revealed) and VII (ignored person or object) and delete the archaic agent of a passive construction type (IV — . . . *ot tebja ja budu zabyt* . . . . ' . . . I will be forgotten by you . . . .'), we are left with a set of categories that correspond very closely to those used by Peškovskij and by the *Academy Grammar: Spatial*, *Removal*, *Source*, *Temporal*, and *Causal*. In essence, the classifications of all three of the works discussed above are based on the meaning of the dependent noun.

The drawbacks of the use of semantic criteria for the resolution of syntactic homomorphs have been demonstrated and discussed in detail in another section of the study.[17] In brief they are two: 1) there is no objective way of defin-

[14] *AG, II*, 1, 120.

[15] *Sovremennyj russkij jazyk: morfologija, sintaksis*, ed. E. M. Galkina-Fedoruk (Moscow, 1964), 271–2.

[16] Peškovskij, 296.

[17] See page 34.

ing the semantic categories themselves and 2) there is no rigorous way of assigning a given example to any particular category.

A second contrast involving the above three treatments is afforded by comparing each author's treatment of V *ot* N structures with his handling of the parallel N *ot* N and A *ot* N constructions. Šaxmatov's treatment of the three parallel constructions is completely uniform. In all three the meaning of the dependent noun is the sole criterion of classification. It has already been noted that Peškovskij's treatment of the N *ot* N and APN constructions differs from his handling of the parallel V *ot* N type. The analysis of the nominal constructions rests primarily on their degree of relatedness to parallel verbal constructions.[18] If such a relationship is found to exist, the problem of classifying the different types within the N *ot* N or A *ot* N construction is to be studied from the point of view of the nearest V *ot* N equivalent. In the latter format, however, the classification system is based almost wholly on nonformal criteria.

This same sort of discrepancy between the classificatory criteria applied to the V *ot* N construction and those used for the N *ot* N and A *ot* N constructions is to be found in the *Academy Grammar*.[19] In both of the latter cases the basis for the initial gross division of the groups is that of the derivational relation between the head word and a cognate verb.[20] For both noun and adjective heads, the first question posed in regard to gross classification is whether or not the construction duplicates a parallel verbal construction. (*Cf. spasenie ot presledovanija* 'salvation from persecution', which parallels *spasat' ot presledovanija* 'to save from persecution', as opposed to *krem ot zagara* 'cream against sunburn'; or *svobodnyj ot raboty* 'free from work', which parallels *osvobodit' ot raboty* 'to free from work', versus *koričnevyj ot zagara* 'brown because of sunburn'.) Thus the *Academy Grammar*, like Peškovskij, makes some use of derivational criteria in its classification of the nominal and adjectival structures, but falls back upon purely semantic criteria in its analysis of the verbal constructions.

Thus from the formal point of view, the analysis of V *ot* N constructions is considerably less satisfactory than that obtained for N *ot* N and A *ot* N constructions. Neither the *Academy Grammar* nor Peškovskij make any comment about this shift in criteria. The general reason, however, would appear to be as follows. The verbal constructions are viewed as basic. In a sample of some

[18] See pages 24 and 82 for a discussion of this procedure.

[19] See pages 25–26 and 83–85 above for a discussion of the classificational criteria for the N *ot* N and A *ot* N constructions respectively.

[20] This is somewhat oversimplified since the relationship between the head noun and its 'prototype' verb can be semantic as well as morphological. Thus *doroga ot pristani* 'road from the dock' is considered by the *AG* to be modeled on a verbal prototype since *doroga* names a spatial concept (*AG*, *II*, 1, 252). Consequently it is considered to be of the same status as *otxod* in *otxod ot pristani* 'departure from the dock' where the head noun is actually derived from a verb.

1,100 examples of *ot* constructions taken from running text, verbs occur as the heads of *ot* constructions in 65 to 70 per cent of all cases.[21] In view of the predominance of the verbal constructions, it is natural to view the less frequent nominal and adjectival constructions in terms of their semantic, syntactic, and derivational relationship to verbal constructions. It is apparently assumed that the line of derivation at the constructional level is unidirectional (V *ot* N → N *ot* N or A *ot* N).[22] Hence, N *ot* N and A *ot* N constructions can be analyzed in terms of verbal constructions, but not vice-versa. This view is not without morphological foundation. The morphological make-up of Russian nouns and adjectives is much closer to the surface than is that of verbs. This is reflected by the fact that nearly 40 per cent of the *Academy Grammar*'s description of noun morphology is devoted to derivation. The comparable figure for adjectives is about 46 per cent. In contrast, the two hundred page discussion of verb morphology includes about twenty-five pages of derivational material — almost exclusively on the meaning of various prefixes. Thus, in some measure, the shift from the limited use of morphological derivational criteria, for nominal and adjectival constructions, to purely semantic ones, for verbal constructions, reflects a very real difference in the derivational make-up of the different types of heads involved.[23]

Despite the problems outlined above, there is a considerable quantity of formal evidence of both a derivational and a syntactic nature that was not touched upon in the foregoing works. None of the sources examined utilized any of the syntactic properties that characterize verbs as possible accessories for the distinctive classification of constructional homomorphs. In all three classificational schemes, transitive, intransitive, and reflexive verbs[24] are mixed indiscriminately and the possibility that their differing syntactic properties might have some bearing on the meaning of a dependent *ot* N phrase is not considered. Presumably such a distinction was considered unnecessary since it can easily be demonstrated that the same type of semantic relations can be expressed by all three types. Consider, for example, the following two sets of three examples each: 1a) *ujti ot doma* 'to depart from home', b) *vesti detej ot doma* 'to lead the children from the house', c) *toropit'sja ot doma* 'to hurry

[21] The count was made of K. Paustovskij's two volume biography *Povest' o žizni* (Moscow, 1962).

[22] At the word level this is not necessarily the case. Consider, for example, the following: at the word derivational level, clearly *krasnyj* 'red' → *krasnet'* 'to become red', but at the constructional level *krasnet' ot čego-to* 'to redden because of something' → *krasnyj ot čego-to* 'red because of something'. See pages 97–98 for a discussion of this matter.

[23] Or perhaps more accurately, it reflects a very real difference in the state of our knowledge about the derivational make-up of verbals versus nominals.

[24] Henceforth, the expression 'reflexive verb' will be replaced by the term *-sja* verb or Vsja. Reflexiveness is only one of several meanings of the *-sja* suffix.

from the house'; and 2a) *zabolet' ot tifa* 'to fall ill because of typhus', b) *terpet' strax ot ugrozy* 'to suffer terror because of a threat', c) *rastopit'sja ot znoja* 'to melt because of heat'. The examples of the first set all express a spatial relationship and those of the second — a causal relationship, although each set utilizes all three types of verbs. This does not, however, show that there is no correlation between the degree of transitivity[25] and semantic categories. A more detailed investigation will show that the relative distribution of various semantic categories varies quite sharply with the degree of transitivity of the verb. Although adequate statistical data are lacking, examination of our data indicates that causal examples are relatively infrequent with transitive verbs, whereas they constitute the majority type with non-*sja* intransitive verbs.

A second syntactic feature of verbs that was not utilized involves the strong-weak government opposition. Roughly speaking, strong government can be described as the property of certain stems to predict the grammatical form of a dependent word. Although the concept itself and particularly the question of degrees of government has not yet received an adequate formal foundation, it is clear that it plays an important role in isolating the various semantic groups within syntactic homomorphs. Compare, for example, *otkazat'sja ot česti* 'to decline the honor' with *rastopit'sja ot znoja* 'to melt from heat'. The first is listed by the *Academy Grammar* as an example of the *Objective group*, whereas the second is a member of the *Causal group*. The former example is a case of strong government, the latter — of weak government. This correlation is not an isolated case. An examination of the examples given by the *Academy Grammar* under the heading of *Objective Relations* shows that most, if not all, possess the syntactic property of strong government. Conversely, the verbs of the examples expressing causal relations lack this property. The effective use of relative 'strength of government' as an analytic tool hinges upon the development of formal procedures to measure degrees of government.[26]

There are also morphological criteria that can be used for the analysis of homomorphic verbal constructions, although, as we noted above, the deriva-

[25] The term *degree of transitivity* is used here to refer to the spectrum of relationships encompassed in the traditional transitive-intransitive opposition.

[26] Two recent studies have been directed toward this end. Ju. D. Apresjan, "O sil'nom i slabom upravlenii (opyt količestvennogo analiza)", *Voprosy jazykoznanija*, 3 (1964), 32–49; L. N. Iordanskaja, *Dva operatora dlja obrabotki slovosočetanij s "sil'nym upravleniem"* (Moscow, 1961).

Unfortunately, neither of these investigations provides results on a sufficiently wide scale to be of use for the purpose at hand. Consequently we will fall back on the following criterion. A V + *ot* combination is considered to express strong government if, under that verb's listing in the 17 volume *Slovar' sovremennogo russkogo literaturnogo jazyka*, Akademij Nauk SSSR, Institut russkogo jazyka (Moscow–Leningrad, 1950/65), a separate sublisting is made for that verb plus *ot*, *i.e.*, if the combination is considered as a semi-fixed phrase. Also see pages 136–137 below for a discussion of some transformational and morphological correlates of strong government.

tional material is not so rich as it was for the nominal constructions. The nouns displayed a hierarchy in terms of their derivational degree of verbality that coincided with their semantic groupings within the structure N^1 *ot* N^2. One aspect of this relationship was reflected in the suffixation pattern. Nouns with maximum degree of verbality frequently had the suffix *-enie*, those with a lower degree often had *-ka* or zero suffixes.[27] The verbs, although not presenting a multi-tiered derivational hierarchy, do fall into certain derivational groupings — some of which have semantic correlations. The very productive deadjectival class of 'becoming' verbs ending in *-et'* *(krasnet'* 'to become red') serves as one illustration of such a derivational-semantic correlation. It might also be noted that this morphological class is negatively marked for the syntactic property of transitivity discussed above.

Finally, the studies discussed above omit any discussion of the possible significance of prefixation patterns. The presence of the ablative prefixes in the verbs of the *Academy Grammar*'s *Objective group* versus their absence in the other groupings has already been remarked upon. The use of these prefixes proves to be closely connected with the expression of various relational categories.

Some of the morphological and syntactic evidence that was neglected in the above-discussed general surveys of V *ot* N constructions has been utilized to varying degrees in more specialized studies. One of the most interesting of these is a monograph on syntactic synonymy by V. P. Suxotin.[28] The spatial usages of V *ot* N are subdivided on the basis of the presence or absence of *ot-* as the verb prefix.[29] The examples are as follows:[30]

A. Verbs with prefix *ot-*

1. *. . . ja . . . , ot''exav ot cerkvi, zasnul . . . .*
   '. . . I . . . , having left the church, fell asleep . . . .'

[27] For an interesting discussion of the degrees of derivational relationships between verbal constructions and parallel nominal constructions, see N. N. Prokopovič, "K voprosu o roli slovoobrazovatel'nyx svjazej častej reči v postroenii slovosočetanij", *Issledovanija po grammatike russkogo literaturnogo jazyka: sbornik statej*, eds. N. S. Pospelov and N. Ju. Švedova (Moscow, 1955), 140–58.

[28] V. P. Suxotin, *Sintaksičeskaja sinonimika v sovremennom russkom literaturnom jazyke* (Moscow, 1960), 14. The term *syntactic synonymy* has been used in a variety of meanings by different writers. In Suxotin's usage it refers to pairs of word-combinations that involve the same words and identical or very similar meanings, but that differ in their grammatical structure. Note that this definition excludes the possibility of having different prepositions in a pair of syntactic homonyms. It is also of interest that most of the constructional pairs that qualify as *syntactic synonyms* under Suxotin's definition also qualify as transforms of each other according to Zellig Harris' definition of the term *transformation*. See page 16.

[29] Suxotin, 17.

[30] *Loc. cit.*

2. . . . *damy otošli ot kolodca.*
   '. . . the ladies left the well.'
3. . . . *ešče odin žuk otvalilsja ot tancevavšego v vozduxe roja.*
   '. . . yet one beetle fell away from the swarm which had been dancing in the air.'
4. . . . *letčikam udalos' ottjanut' ix ot aerodroma . . . .*
   '. . . the fliers succeeded in drawing them away from the airfield . . . .'

B. Verbs without the prefix *ot-*
1. *Ja vernulsja i pošel ot nego proč'.*
   'I returned and went away from it.'
2. . . . *veter dul ot berega.*
   '. . . the wind blew from the shore.'
3. *Ot krasnyx vorot neslas' pesnja . . . .*
   'The song carried from the red gates . . . .'

Both A and B, according to Suxotin, express spatial meaning. In A, however, the meaning of separation or removal is supported by the prefix *ot-*. In the examples of group B, the direction of the motion is stressed. Suxotin further notes that the dual prepositional constructions wherein V *ot* N is supplemented by the prepositions *do* or *k* plus N^3 express the meaning of "fullness of action, movement, or feature", *e.g.*, *Glaza . . . begali ot pistoleta k rokovomu tuzu . . . .* '[His] eyes . . . ran from the pistol to the fatal ace . . . .'

Suxotin's interpretation of spatial V *ot* N constructions differs markedly from that of the *Academy Grammar*. Methodologically, his principal contribution is that of recognizing the *ot-* as the formal indicator of a basic semantic distinction within V *ot* N constructions.

A much more detailed examination is made of V *ot* N constructions expressing causal relations. The discussion of these constructions is prefaced by a brief survey of the expression of causal relations by different grammatical constructions in Russian.[31] Suxotin notes that the synthetic expression of causality by constructions such as V N_i (. . . *nevesta umerla čaxotkoju* . . . . '. . . the bride died of consumption . . . .') and V_{sja} N_i (. . . *ona načala tomit'sja žaždoj* . . . . '. . . she began to be parched by thirst . . . .') are becoming ever rarer and occur only in isolated examples in his corpus. The tendency to replace these synthetic types by analytic prepositional constructions such as *po pričine* 'for the reason', *vsledstvie* 'in consequence of', *etc.*, was noted by A. A. Potebnja nearly one hundred years ago.[32] Suxotin reports that *ot* N is the most common of these analytic causal constructions.

[31] Suxotin, 109–11.

[32] A. A. Potebnja, *Iz zapisok po russkoj grammatike* (Moscow, 1958), 468. Cited in Suxotin, 110.

The criteria of Suxotin's investigation of causal V *ot* N constructions are wholly semantic and subjective. No explanation is offered of how the causal examples were isolated from those of the other semantic groups. On the semantic level, however, a variety of rather subtle definitions of the different types of verbs and of dependent nouns occurring in causal constructions is tendered. The verbs as a whole indicate either internal states or their external manifestations and their changes.[33] The various meanings of the dependent noun include:[34] 1) the rare cases where N designates a concrete object (*. . .golova načnala idti krugom ot bumažnyx radug* . . . . '. . . [his] head started to spin because of the paper rainbows . . . .'); 2) cases where N represents not an object but its manifestation: sound, smell, taste, *etc.* (*. . . vzdragivaja ot zvuka upavšej šiški* . . . . '. . . flinching because of the sound of the pine cone which had fallen . . . .'); 3) the most frequent type in which an abstract N designates the inner state of a person, his sensations (physical and mental), his mood or feelings (*. . . poblednel ot zlosti* . . . . '. . . blanched because of malice . . . .'); and, lastly, 4) a diverse group of nouns that indicate a) various actions (*Aleksej . . . ispytyval blaženstvo ot ledenjaščego prikosnovenija* . . . . 'Aleksej . . . experienced bliss because of [her] freezing touch . . . .'), b) natural phenomenon (*ot napora vody dno reki izmenjaetsja* 'the bottom of the river changes because of the pressure of the water'), and c) various circumstantial modifiers (*. . . ona . . . rasterjalas' ot roskoši* . . . . '. . . she . . . lost [her] head because of the luxury . . . .'). Examples of subgroup a) share the characteristic that the dependent noun refers back to the subject of the verb, whereas in subgroups b) and c) the noun refers to something external to the verb subject.

This *internal/external* opposition has been partially formalized by T. P. Lomtev in his utilization of the distinction as the basis of his subclassification of causal *ot* constructions.[35] According to Lomtev, internal cause is indicated when the subject of the verb is also the bearer of the state designated by N^2, *e.g.*, *čelovek ustal ot xod'by* 'the man became tired because of walking'. External cause is indicated when the subject of the verb and the bearer of the state designated by N^2 are not the same, *e.g.*, *čelovek prosnulsja ot zvonka* 'the man woke up because of the bell'. This opposition may be schematized and transformationally demonstrated as follows: internal cause — N^1 V^1 *ot* $N^2 \rightarrow N^1$ V^{n2} *i* (N^1) V^1 (*čelovek ustal ot xod'by* 'the man became tired because of walking' $\rightarrow$ *čelovek xodil i [čelovek] ustal* 'the man was walking and [the man] became tired'); external cause — N^1 V^1 *ot* $N^2 \rightarrow$ X V^{n2} *i* $N^1 \cdot V^1$ (*čelovek prosnulsja ot zvonka* 'the man woke up because of the bell' $\rightarrow$ *X zvonil i čelovek prosnulsja* 'X rang and the man woke up').

[33] Suxotin, 111.
[34] *Ibid.*, 111–3.
[35] T. P. Lomtev, *Očerki po istoričeskomu sintaksisu russkogo jazyka* (Moscow, 1956), 383–5.

The Soviet scholar L. N. Zasorina has also made an attempt to describe causal prepositional constructions in terms of a semantic analysis of the verb and the dependent noun.[36] This investigation differs from any of the foregoing in that the semantic analysis is carried out within the framework of an explicitly stated set of assumptions and procedures. The author's aim is to determine precisely what semantic features oppose *ot, s, iz, iz-za,* and *po* to each other in their general causal meanings.[37] The method of this contrastive study consists of a series of binary semantic comparisons of synonymic prepositional constructions. Each of the five prepositions is compared with each of the remaining four in similar constructional environments. This synonymy of environment is specified as follows: the head verb is classified according to whether it indicates 1) an action, 2) a state, 3) a quality, or 4) a process of change; the dependent noun — according to whether its pecifies 1) phenomenon of nature, 2) the physical condition of a person, 3) an emotion, and so on. If two prepositions are to be compared, they must occur in environments that have head verbs of the same semantic class and dependent nouns also of a single class. Thus, "... *liš' teper' ponjala, kak* ZAKOČENELA S USTALOSTI .... '... only now did she understand how numb she had become from tiredness ....'" can be compared to "... *zakryl glaza,* — VSE TELO ZAGUDELO OT USTALOSTI .... '... he closed [his] eyes — [his] whole body ached because of tiredness ....'." since both have verbs referring to states and nouns to the physical state of a person, but not to "*Lico u Beridze* POKRASNELO S MOROZA .... 'Beridze's face became red from the frost ....'" since the dependent noun refers to a phenomenon of nature. The semantic type of head word, *i.e.*, action, state, *etc.*, is regarded as the primary classificatory feature and examples of the two prepositions being compared are grouped under each semantic verb type and only then in terms of the meaning categories of the dependent noun that are indicated above.

For the present purposes, the most important aspects of Zasorina's study are not those concerned with discriminating among the causal meanings of the various prepositions, but of certain of her procedural assumptions and descriptive statements. In particular Zasorina's indication of the primacy (albeit semantic) of the head and not the dependent noun stands in sharp contrast to the analyses previously discussed. Other less central points of interest include the author's statistics on the relative frequency of *ot* versus the remaining four prepositions with 'pure' causal meaning. An examination of all of

[36] L. N. Zasorina, "Opyt sistemnogo analiza predlogov sovremennogo russkogo jazyka (Predlogi so značeniem pričiny)", *Učenye zapiski Leningradskogo gosudarstvennogo universiteta,* 301 (1961) (= *Serija filologičeskix nauk,* vyp. 60), 64–81.

[37] The present study is, of course, concerned with the problem of formally segmenting the entire semantic spectrum of *ot* constructions. Consequently, the purely contrastive aspects of her study are only of marginal interest.

the causal usages of the five prepositions in A. Tolstoj's trilogy *Xoždenie po mukam* and L. Leonov's *Russkij les* shows the following distribution: *ot* — 72.0%, *iz-za* — 9.8%, *iz* — 8.4%, *po* — 5.8%, and *s* — 5.1%.[38]

Zasorina's analysis also reveals that, for the corpus in question, verbs of state plus *ot* N are utilized almost exclusively for the expression of causal meaning and that such constructions constitute 74 per cent of all uses of the preposition.[39] It is further noted that the use of verbs referring to actions is not conducive to the expression of causal meaning. In such an environment *ot* often assumes an ablative meaning: *e.g.*, " . . . *ot xoloda ona (Ljubka) spala v life i čulkax* . . . . ' . . . [as protection] against the cold she (Ljubka) slept in a bodice and stockings . . . .'"[40] In those contexts where *ot* does retain a causal meaning even though dependent upon action verbs, Zasorina notes that the latter usually denote involuntary action *(vzdrognut'* 'to start, to wince', *vstrepenut'sja* 'to start, to wince', *spotknut'sja* 'to stumble', *zarydat'* 'to start, to sob', *krjaknut'* 'to groan', *sopet'* 'to wheeze', *revet'* 'to roar').[41]

Zasorina's study, in spite of her attention to theoretical and procedural problems, does not touch upon one very basic point. What kind of criteria were used in determining which of the examples of *ot* (or any of the other prepositions) were causal as opposed to any of its other possible meanings? These methodological problems are brought to the fore in another article by the same author in which she explicitly notes the inadequacies of semantic analysis of isomorphic word-combinations.[42] In this article a careful examination of the criteria and procedures of transformational substitution is made. It is concluded that the evaluation of the limits of the acceptability of a substitution, *i.e.*, the limits of what constitutes the semantic invariant, is ultimately a function of the native speaker's intuition. The criterion of semantic equivalence does not lend itself to rigorous formalization, in the view of the author.[43]

The best of the traditional studies dealing with the causal meaning of *ot* is that of L. N. Popova.[44] Popova's study is unique in that she utilizes not only

[38] Zasorina, 84.

[39] *Ibid.*, 71.

[40] *Ibid.*, 68.

[41] *Ibid.*, 72.

[42] L. N. Zasorina, "Transformacija kak metod lingvističeskogo èksperimenta v sintaksise", *Transformacionnyj metod v strukturnoj lingvistike,* ed. S. K. Šaumjan (Moscow, 1964), 100–1.

[43] *Ibid.*, 106.

[44] L. N. Popova, "O značenii predloga v sovremennom russkom jazyke (Predlog ot + roditel'nyj padež v značenii pričiny)", *Učenye zapiski Leningradskogo gosudarstvennogo universiteta,* 235 (= *Serija filologičeskix nauk,* vyp. 38) (1958), 190–208. The corpus from which the author's examples are drawn is the same as that used by L. N. Zasorina.

lexical but also morphological and syntactic criteria. Noting that many investigators consider that the lexical meaning of the dependent noun is the chief factor in determining the meaning of weakly governed prepositions, Popova gives the following set of counter-examples:[45]

1. *A vot kogda u nee glaza* ot ljubvi *namoknut, kogda poduška po nočam ne budet prosyxat' ot slez, — togda ona stanovitsja nastojaščej devkoj.* (Causal relations)
   'And when her eyes fill with tears *because of love,* when the pillow will not dry out for nights on end because of the tears, — then she will become a real girl.'
2. *Ja ljublju, — vot èto istinno, — podumal on, kak by ja ni postupal, esli èto* ot ljubvi, *— èto xorošo.* (Genetic relations)
   'I love, — that's the real truth, — he thought, however I act, if it is *out of love,* — it's good.'
3. *. . . ni ženit'sja, ni vljubit'sja on ne možet, netu prav, ni uexat' za granicu* ot ljubvi, *kak byvšij graf.* (Objective relations)
   '. . . he can neither marry, nor fall in love nor does [he have] the right to go abroad *[away] from love,* like a former Graf.'

These examples, which share a single dependent noun but which all clearly express different types of semantic relationships, convincingly illustrate that the dependent noun, in and of itself, does not necessarily determine the meaning of the word-combinations. Popova asserts that there is no semantic group that does not appear in the role of the dependent noun of the causal V *ot* N constructions, although some semantic types of nouns are much less common than others in the N^2 role. Examples in which N^2 is represented by a noun referring to an object or thing *(vsja scena začernela ot kurtok, bekeš, šinelej, zazveneli, stalkivajas' štyki* 'the whole scene became black because of the jackets, bekeses, [and] overcoats, the bayonets, clashing, started to ring out') or by a noun referring to an animate being *(Ozera bukval'no vskipali ot vzletavšix utok* 'The lakes literally boiled because of the ducks which were taking off') are less frequent than those with more abstract nouns. The type represented by the last cited example is thought to represent a new usage in Russian.[46]

The characterization of the verb is considerably more complex.[47] Semantically the verbs that occur with *ot* N in a causal sense indicate change of state, involuntary action, and lastly, action. The majority of these verbs belong to one of two derivational classes. The first includes those verbs with the infinitive

[45] *Ibid.*, 192.
[46] *Ibid.*, 193.
[47] *Ibid.*, 195–6. All of the subsequently reported data on the morphological structure of the head verb are from these pages of Popova's article.

in *-et'* *(goret'* 'to burn', *gudet'* 'to whistle, to ache', *kipet'* 'to boil') and the second — those with the infinitive in *-at'* *(drožat'* 'to tremble', *groxotat'* 'to crash', *treščat'* 'to crackle'). Both groups of verbs assertedly express the meaning of state. As given by Popova, these morphological classifications are incorrect. There is not one but two classes of verbs ending in *-et'*, both often expressing state. The examples given are all members of the class belonging to the second conjugation *(goret', gorju, gorit* 'to burn'). The other, unmentioned, class of *-et'* verbs belongs to the first conjugation *(krasnet', krasneju, krasneet* 'to redden') and, in all probability, accounts for a greater per cent of the verbs in the causal V *ot* N construction than the first. Popova's second derivational class (verbs with infinitives in *-at')* is even more misleading in that there are three verb classes with infinitives in *-at'* *(čitat', čitaju, čitaet* 'to read'; *groxotat', groxoču, groxočet* 'to crash'; and *drožat', drožu, drožit* 'to tremble').

Also widely represented are *-sja* verbs indicating a change in state in external features, or in the position of inanimate objects and of phenomena, *e.g.*, *Ot sveta sveči zolotilis' ee rassypavšiesja volosy* 'Because of the light of the candle her disheveled hair shone golden'. It is noted that causal constructions with verbs referring to the involuntary action of persons are not numerous. In this context the verbs generally have the meaning 'to produce some sort of sound' *(. . . mužčiny krjaxteli ot udovol'stvij* ' . . . the men groaned because of satisfaction . . . .') or 'to perform some kind of involuntary bodily movement' *(Kak tak? — vstrepenulsja ot neožidannosti Ivan Matveič* . . . . 'How can it be? — Ivan Matveič started because of the unexpectedness . . . .'). The *-sja* verbs occur as the head of causal *ot* constructions in the ratio of one for every two of the non-*sja* intransitive verbs discussed above. Verbs that express voluntary action and particularly motion usually express not causal but ablative relations, *e.g.*, "*Podxodil on v čem-to belom, naklonivšis' ot ognja* . . . . 'He approached in something white, having leaned away from the fire . . . .'"

Popova sums up the results of her investigation of causal V *ot* N examples as follows:

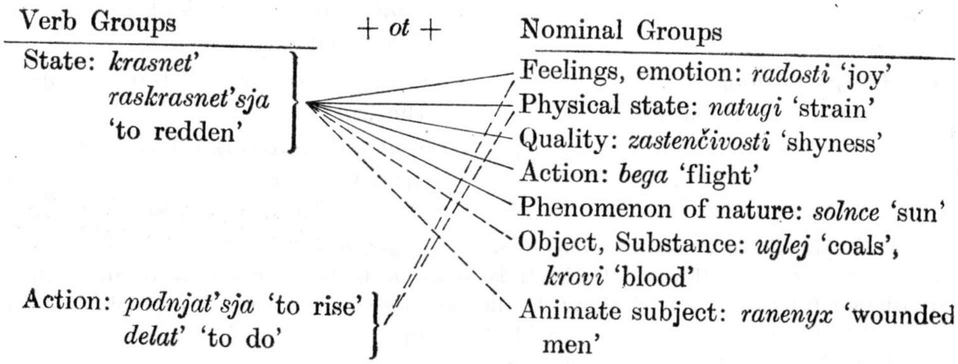

Both the noun and the verb types are in the order of the frequency of their occurrence while dotted lines indicate particularly infrequent marginal types.

Popova's study is unique in that she considers a wide range of conditioning factors. These can be summarized as follows:

A. Semantic factors:
  1. Primary importance is assigned to the lexical meanings of V and Ndp
    a. the verb typically refers to a change of state *(černet'* 'to become black') or an involuntary action *(drožat'* 'to tremble')
    b. the noun is usually abstract

B. Syntactic factors:
  1. The close interrelationship of syntactic and lexical properties is recognized
    a. verbs of the indicated semantic types are generally intransitive
    b. *ot* N in its causal meaning can directly depend only upon intransitive verbs

C. Morphological factors:
  1. The use of the *-et'* and *-at'* classes of verbs with the expression of causal meaning
  2. The use of the *-sja* morpheme as a formal marker of intransitivity

The only transformational study which treats V *ot* N constructions is that of V. P. Manolova.[48] The following analytic scheme is presented:[49]

1. *prosnut'sja ot šuma* 'to wake up because of noise' → a. *prosnut'sja iz-za šuma* 'to wake up on account of noise'
2. *smotret' ot toski* 'to look because of anguish' → a. *smotret' v toske* 'to look in anguish'
   b. *smotret' s tockoj* 'to look with anguish'
   c. *smotret' toskIivo* 'to look in an anguished way'
3. *ostat'sja ot voiny* 'to remain from the war' → a. *ostat'sja s voiny* 'to remain since the war'
   b. *ostat'sja' posle voiny* 'to remain after the war'

[48] V. P. Manolova, *Transformations of Russian Syntagms of the Types $S + S$, $S + P$, $V + S$, $V + P + S$* (Moscow, 1962). It is available to the writer only in an English translation through the U. S. Joint Publication Research Service, Washington, D. C. (= *JPRS*, 19.053) (6 May 1963), 28–71. It is apparently incomplete.

[49] *Ibid.*, 47–8. See pages 63–64 for a list of the transforms.

The methodology of Manolova's work has already been outlined and reviewed in the section on nominal constructions and will not be repeated here. The overwhelming defect of the above description is its incompleteness since only two of the traditional semantic types, causal and temporal, are illustrated. The transformations all involve the possibility of substituting various prepositions for the original *ot*. The deficiencies of this procedure have already been discussed in detail.[50]

4.3. ANALYSIS OF N^1 V *ot* N^2 UNITS

The general theoretical foundations and methodology of our analysis of the verbal units remain the same as those set forth and elaborated for the nominal constructions. The same types of transformations are used with the results subject to the twin criteria of grammaticalness and semantic invariancy.[51]

The treatment of the verbal constructions differs from that of their nominal counterparts only in one important respect. In the survey of the literature on N^1 V *ot* N^2 constructions, it was noted that none of the previous investigators discriminated between transitive and intransitive verbs or between *-sja* verbs and non *-sja* verbs within the latter category in their analyses. The present investigation makes this tripartite division the basis of its organizational format. The first section of the analysis treats N^1 V *ot* N^2 units wherein the verb is an unmarked intransitive (VØ). The second section examines those units in which the verb is a marked intransitive of the so-called "reflexive" type (Vsja). The third and final section presents an analysis of the examples containing transitive verbs (Vt).[52] Each of these three sections is prefaced by a list of the transforms used in that particular section and by examples of their operation. A brief listing of the transformationally defined semantic groups within each of the three structural types is given together with their characteristic transform features in order to help orient the reader to the following, more detailed description of each of these groups. The discussion of each of these latter groups is prefaced by a table listing the transform features of all of the examples of the group to be discussed.

Before proceeding to the analysis of the first structural type, it is necessary to stop for a moment to point out some of the problems that arise in the analysis of verbal constructions that are not present in the analysis of the

[50] See page 34.

[51] A full statement of these principles and procedures may be found on pages 38–40.

[52] The problem of verbs that are both transitive and intransitive (*e.g.*, *čitat'* 'to read' + *knigu* 'book' versus *čitat'* + #) and of marginally transitive verbs (*e.g.*, *tancevat'* 'to dance' or *vladet'* 'to possess') does not arise in our investigation. Verbs are considered transitive only if they occur in the environment V + N_{acc}.

nominal groups. The analysis of N *ot* N constructions indicated that the primary factor in determining the meaning of any given example was the degree of derivational kinship of N^1 to a cognate verb. The degree of such verbal kinship was indicated by the possibility or impossibility of various transformations. In principle this technique is equally applicable to the verbal constructions. In practice, however, this leads to the rather more difficult problem of determining and transformationally demonstrating the degree of verbality of the verb itself. For the nouns, the relative degree of verbality could be grossly estimated by examining the suffixation patterns *(e.g., -enie, -ka, -ost',* -#, *etc.)*. It is readily apparent that the nouns *osveščenie, svet,* and *svetlost'* reflect, both semantically and derivationally, differing degrees of verbality. The derivational make-up of the verbs, however, does not lie so close to the surface. From the intuitive semantic point of view, the verbs *begat'* and *dumat'* seem to differ in their degree of verbality.[53] The difference is not, however, clearly reflected in their morphological structure. This relative lack of derivational differentiation among verbs is also reflected in their transform potential which is, on the whole, less rich than was the case for the nominal constructions. Both the number and the variety of transformations that are useful in discriminating among different types of verbs are more restricted than for the nouns. Furthermore, the consistency with which a given transform is admissible (or not admissible) for the members of a particular verbal group is much more erratic than is the case with nominal constructions. In other words, there are many more seemingly unmotivated exceptions.

At first glance it would seem that the less effective performance of transform analysis in discriminating among homomorphic verbal constructions weakens our argument that the various nominal groups can be uniquely characterized by their degree of relatedness to verbs, *i.e.*, if the verbal constructions are relatively amorphous, then the derived nominal systems also will be. This is not necessarily the case. Verbal *ot* constructions account for about 70 per cent of all occurrences of the preposition, whereas nominal ones involve between 15 and 20 per cent.[54] The nominal structures are, to a much greater extent than their verbal counterparts, derived. These considerations mean that the V *ot* N constructional type, or at least some substantial part of it, forms the kernel structure(s) from which the remaining *ot* usages are derived by means of various transformations. Consequently, it is not surprising that the verbal units that comprise the core of the *ot* constructions should prove less amenable to transformation than do peripheral derived nominal or adjectival constructions.

[53] Historical evidence can be marshalled in support of this intuitive distinction. *Begat'* derives from CS **bēgēti* (Vasmer, *I*, 67–8), whereas *dumat'* is probably derived from the nominal form *duma* (Vasmer, *I*, 380).

[54] Based on an analysis of Paustovskij, *Povest' o žizni*.

4.3.1. *Dual Prepositional Constructions* N^1 V *ot* N^2 *k/do/v* N^3: *Spatial and Range Groups*

The preposition *ot* can occur in complex constructions with the prepositions *k* 'to, toward', *do* 'up to', *v* 'to', and occasionally *po* 'along'.[55] The presence of these latter prepositions and their dependents places severe restrictions upon the possible range of meaning of *ot* and of the entire N^1 V *ot* N^2 P N^3 complex that are not evident in simple N^1 V *ot* N^2 constructions.

The first transformation tests the possible deletion of the second preposition and its dependent noun. To illustrate: N^1 V *ot* N^2 *k/do/v* N^3 → N^1 V *ot* N^2 *(ljudi bežali ot klabdišča k lesu* 'the people ran from the graveyard toward the forest' → **ljudi bežali ot kladbišča* 'the people ran from the graveyard'). The response to the transform is a qualified minus (—). The informant, if pressed, will allow most of the proposed deletions, but the abbreviated form is felt to be somehow incomplete. If the speaker wishes to say that "someone walked off from the dacha" without specifying the intended destination, he would probably not say "*kto-to šel ot dači* 'someone went from the dacha'," but rather "*kto-to* U*šel ot dači* 'someone went away from the dacha'" with the prefixed form *ušel.* The non-prefixed form of the verb followed by *ot* apparently implies that the speaker has some particular destination in mind and, consequently, is usually supplemented by a prepositional clause specifying that destination.[56] The same observations apply to the verbs prefixed with *pri-*, *pro-*, *pere-*, and *pod-*. It is of particular interest that the ablative prefixes *ot-*, *u-*, *iz-*, and *s-* do not occur in the dual prepositional structures, although they are extremely common in single prepositional spatial examples.[57]

The second transformation indicates a basic divison in the dual prepositional constructions. Five of the nine *ot/do* examples permit the deletion of the verb as specified in T2: *dym stojal ot pola do potolka* 'smoke stood from the floor to the ceiling' → *dym — ot pola do potolka* 'smoke — from the floor to the ceil-

[55] The dual preposition examples are of a different structural type from the single preposition units and, consequently, are analyzed in terms of a different set of transformations. Since only two transforms are involved, they are illustrated in the discussion rather than in a prefatory section such as that given for the other structural types. The full list of examples and their transform features is given at the end of the section, in Table 11. Examples 1–18 illustrate the *Spatial group* and those from 19–24, the *Range group*.

[56] This matter of an implied destination is quite apart from the somewhat similar restrictions inherent in the determined subcategory of imperfective verbs of motion that marks the verbal action as being restricted to one destination and to one particular occasion.

There is also a small group of examples that utilizes the non-prefixed forms of *idti* without normally being accompanied by a second prepositional unit. See pages 129–132 for a description of the *Source group.*

[57] See pages 133–135 below.

TABLE 11

Transform Features of 'N^1 V *ot* N^2 *k/do/v* N^3' *Units of the Spatial and Range Groups*

N^1	V	*ot*	N^2	*k/do/v*	N^3	T1: → N^1 V *ot* N^2	T2: → N^1 — *ot* N^2 *k/do/v* N^3
1. čelovek	šel	ot	Stolypina	k	dverjam	(—)	
'the man	went	from	Stolypin	to	the doors'		
2. kto-to	šel	ot	dači	k	kalitke	(—)	—
'someone	went	from	the dacha	to	the gate'		
3. doktor	xodil	ot	nas	k	Ganne	(—)	—
'the doctor	walked	from	us	to	Hanna'		
4. ona	xodila	ot	stola	k	bufetu	(—)	—
'she	walked	from	the table	to	the buffet'		
5. ja	prišel	ot	Ficovskogo	k	sebe	(—)	—
'I	went	from	Ficovskij's				
			[place]	to	my own'		
6. imuščestvo	perešlo	ot	otca	k	synu	(—)	—
'the property	passed	from	father	to	son'		
7. ja	pereexal	ot	pana K	k	nej	(—)	—
'I	moved	from	Pan K's	to	her [place]'		
8. Sergej	pod'ezžal	ot	xutora	k	Pjatigorsku	(—)	—
'Sergey	drove up	from	the farm	to	Pjatigorsk'		
9. ljudi	bežali	ot	kladbišča	k	lesu	(—)	—
'the people	ran	from	the graveyard	to	the forest'		
10. glaza	begali	ot	pistoleta	k	tuzu	(—)	—
'[his] eyes	ran	from	the pistol	to	the ace'		
11. ljudi	perebegali	ot	dereva	k	derevu	(—)	—
'the people	ran across	from	tree	to	tree'		
12. on	skakal	ot	usad'by	k	greble	(—)	—
'he	galloped	from	the farmstead	to	the ford'		
13. on	xodil	ot	vokzala	v	akademiju	(—)	—
'he	walked	from	the station	to	the academy'		
14. ja	bežal	ot	mobilizacii	v	Odessu	(—)	—
'I	ran	from	mobilization	to	Odessa'		
15. my	projdem	ot	kraja	do	kraja	(—)	—
'we	pass	from	area	to	area'		
16. ja	prošel	ot	Alžira	do	mysa	(—)	—
'I	passed	from	Algeria	to	the cape'		
17. ono	šlo	ot	Kopani	do	Moskvy	(—)	—
'it	went	from	Kopani	to	Moscow'		

TABLE 11 (*cont.*)

	N^1	V	*ot*	N^2	*k/do/v*	N^3	T1: → N^1 V *ot* N^2	T2: → N^1—*ot* N^2*k/do/v* N^3
18.	čelovek	proxodit	ot	Moskvy	do	okrain	(−)	−
	'the man	passed	from	Moscow	to	the outskirts'		
19.	drož'	probegala	ot	zatylka	do	pjatok	(−)	+
	'the shiver	ran	from	the nape of [his] neck	to	[his] heels'		
20.	reka	zarosla	ot	berega	do	berega	(−)	+
	'the river	was overgrown	from	shore	to	shore'		
21.	vse	blistalo	ot	vorotnička	do	sapog	(−)	+
	'everything	glistened	from	[his] collar	to	[his] boots'		
22.	nivy	zašumeli	ot	okeana	do	okeana	(−)	+
	'the meadows	started to rustle	from	ocean	to	ocean'		
23.	dym	stojal	ot	pola	do	potolka	(−)	+
	'smoke	stood	from	the floor	to	the ceiling'		
24.	doroga	vela	ot	vorot	k	cerkvi	(−)	+
	'the road	led	from	the gates	to	the church'		

ing'. The opposition of the examples permitting deletion of the verb, and those examples that do not, mark sthe same division that was noted in N *ot* N constructions. The examples permitting the deletion indicate the extent or range of something *(drož' ot zatylka do pjat* 'a tremor from the nape of the neck to the heels'), whereas those not permitting the deletion specify spatial physical motion *(ona xodila ot stola k bufetu* 'she walked from the table to the buffet'). Additionally, the range function type has the characteristic that its head nouns are inanimate, whereas almost all of the noun heads for the physical motion examples are animate. The *Range group* displays a greater variety of verbs than the motion type and consists of verbs of a different semantic stratum. The physical motion group, with the exception of *skakat'* 'to gallop', has only three roots, *-id-* 'walk', *-ed-* 'ride', and *-beg-* 'run' — all verbs of motion. The verbs of the *Range group* are what might loosely be termed *stadial verbs.*[58]

[58] *Stojat'*, *zašumet'*, and marginally *blistat'* (by virtue of its alternate form *blestet')* are morphologically marked as stadial since all utilize the *-ě-* formant. *Zarasti* and *probegat'* have only a semantic claim to the classification as does *vesti* in this particular context.

Note that the verb of motion *probegat'* is, in this case, used not in its literal meaning but in the transferred sense of 'pass through' as of a shiver. In the *Range group* the dual prepositional structure appears to function as a complex predicate adjective just as was the case for the equivalent nominal construction (*e.g., partii – ot kadetov do bol'ševikov* 'the parties – from the cadets to the Bol'ševiks').

The total number of examples is too small to make a firm estimate, but it may be that there is a tendency for the *ot/k* type to be associated with the physical motion type, whereas the *ot/do* type may be found more frequently with the range function meaning.

4.3.2. *Analysis of* N^1 Vø *ot* N^2 *Units*

All of the examples of the above indicated structure are subjected to a set of four transformations and classified on the basis of their reaction. The transformations are as follows:

T1:	N^1 V ot N^2 *lodka otošla ot berega* 'the boat moved away from the shore'	→	N^1 V ot N^2 k N^3 *lodka otošla ot berega k porogam* 'the boat moved away from the shore toward the rapids'
T2:	N^1 V ot N^2 *starik poblednel ot bešenstva* 'the old man paled because of rage'	→	N^1, A ot N^2 *starik, blednyj ot bešenstva* 'the old man, pale because of rage'
T3:	N^1 V ot N^2 *veter dul ot morja* 'the wind blew from the sea'	→	N^1 ot N^2 *veter ot morja* 'the wind from the sea'
T4:	N^1 V ot N^2 *mužik op'janel ot vodki* 'the peasant got drunk because of vodka'	→	N^2 V N^1 *vodka op'janila mužika* 'vodka made the peasant drunk'

Examples of the structural type N^1 V *ot* N^2 fall into four groups in terms of their responses to the above four transformations.[59]

[59] The written-out forms of the possible permutations are given above in the illustration of the operation of the transformations.

Group:	N^1	V	ot	N^2	→	T1	T2	T3	T4
Source:	*veter*	*dul*	*ot*	*morja*		+	–	+	–
	'the wind	blew	from	the sea'					
Spatial:	*lodka*	*otošla*	*ot*	*berega*		+	–	–	–
	'the boat	moved away	from	the shore'					
Ablative:	*devuška*	*otdyxala*	*ot*	*sutoloki*		–	–	–	–
	'the girl	rested	from	the commotion'					
Causal:	*mužik*	*op'janel*	*ot*	*vodki*		–	+	–	+
	'the peasant	got drunk	because of	the vodka'					

Having briefly illustrated the transformations and the transform features of the N^1 V *ot* N^2 examples we now turn to a more detailed examination of each of the groups specified above.

4.3.2.1. *Source Group*

The first transform indicates that the examples of this group can be expanded by the addition of further prepositional complementation. Any member of the *Source group* can be set in the wider environment N^1 V *ot* N^2 *k* N^3: *zapax šel ot češui* 'the odor wafted from the scales' → *zapax šel ot češui k nosu* 'the odor wafted from the scales to the nose'. This transformation formally opposes the examples of the *Source group* to those of the *Ablative* and *Causal groups* and, on the other hand, demonstrates the similarity of the source examples to those of the *Spatial group*.[60] The examples of the *Source group* are opposed to those of the *Spatial group* by T3, which involves deletion of the verb: N^1 V *ot* N^2 → N^1 *ot* N^2, *zvon isxodil ot oružija* 'a peal issued from the weaponry' → *zvon ot oružija* 'peal from the weaponry'. This demonstrates that in the *Source group* the verb is a grammatically and semantically neutral link (and hence dispensible), whereas in the *Spatial group* the verb occupies a much more central place.

An examination of morphological evidence shows several points of difference between the derivational composition of the verbs of the *Source group* and that of the verbs of the *Spatial group*. There are numerous restrictions on the verb in the *Source group*. The first of these is lexical. In the examples collected, the number of verbs that enter into the *Source group* is very small: *idti* 'to walk', *isxodit'* 'to issue from', *letet'* 'to fly', *dut'* 'to blow', and perhaps marginally, *otlivat'* 'to pour out'. Within this small group there are further, morphological, restrictions upon the forms of the verbs that can be used. The most stringent restrictions are found in connection with the verb *idti*. It was noted in the

[60] The *Source group* is discussed largely on a contrastive basis in comparison with the closely related *Spatial group*. A full list of the spatial examples may be found on pages 132–133.

TABLE 12

Transform Features of 'N^1 V ot N^2' Units of the Source Group

	N^1	V	*ot*	N^2	T1: → N^1 V *ot* N^2 *k* N^3	T2: → N^1, A^V *ot* N^2	T3: → N^1 *ot* N^2	T4: → N^2 V_t N^1
1.	par 'steam	šel wafted	ot from	vodoroslej the water plants'	+	–	+	–
2.	svežest' 'freshness	šla wafted	ot from	iskusstva the art'	+	–	+	–
3.	dym 'smoke	šel wafted	ot from	zemljanok the mud huts'	+	–	+	–
4.	čad 'fumes	šel wafted	ot from	kuči the heap'	+	–	+	–
5.	zapax 'an odor	šel wafted	ot from	kos the tresses'	+	–	+	–
6.	zapax 'an odor	šel wafted	ot from	češui the scales'	+	–	+	–
7.	aromat 'an aroma	šel wafted	ot from	cvetov the flowers'	+	–	+	–
8.	teplo 'warmth	idet wafts	ot from	peči the stove'	+	–	+	–
9.	blesk 'luster	isxodil issued	ot from	volos the hair'	+	–	+	–
10.	zapax 'an odor	isxodil issued	ot from	pana the Pan'	+	–	+	–
11.	vozdux 'air	isxodil issued	ot from	korpusa the building'	+	–	+	–
12.	teplo 'warmth	isxodilo issued	ot from	zipunov homespun coats'	+	–	+	–
13.	sila 'strength	isxodila issued	ot from	menja me'	+	–	+	–
14.	zvon 'a peal	isxodil issued	ot from	oružija the weaponry'	+	–	+	–
15.	svet 'light	isxodil issued	ot from	dymki the haze'	+	–	+	–
16.	iskry 'sparks	leteli flew	ot from	saxara the sugar'	+	–	+	–
17.	pux 'down	letit flies	ot from	ust the lips'	+	–	+	–
18.	veter 'the wind	dul blew	ot from	morja the sea'	+	–	+	–
19.	krov' 'blood	otlivaet pours out	ot of	golovy the head'	+	–	+	–
20.	volny 'waves	otlivajut pour out	ot from	mola the breakwater'	+	–	+	–

preceding section on N^1 V *ot* N^2 *k* N^3 units that ordinarily the unprefixed forms of *idti* with a following *ot* N were complemented by a second prepositional phrase *(k, do, v* + N^3). It was further observed that there was one prominent exception to this rule. That exception was the use of *idti* to indicate source. This usage is largely restricted to the present and past tense of the third person of the determined imperfective.[61] Forms of *xodit'* 'to walk' were not encountered in this meaning. A similar, but less constrained, set of restrictions applies to the remaining verbs of the *Source group*. All are in the third person and, to all appearances, are mandatorily imperfective. The perfective form of *isxodil, izojti* is not used in CSR in the sense of source.[62]

The pattern of verbal prefixation also opposes the *Source group* to the *Spatial group*. The dual prepositional spatial units *(ljudi perebegali ot dereva k derevu* 'the people ran across from tree to tree') either had a zero prefix or one of what might be termed the 'proximity' suffixes: *pri-*, *pro-*, *pod-*, and *pere-*. The single prepositional spatial type *(čelovek ušel ot tovariščej* 'the man walked away from [his] comrades') typically displays one of the ablative prefixes *u-*, *ot-*, *iz-*, or *s-*. Examples of the *Source group*, on the other hand, are either prefixless *(idti* 'to go', *letet'* 'to fly', *dut'* 'to blow') or use the prefixes *iz- (isxodit'* 'to issue') and *ot- (otlivat'* 'to pour out').

The nouns of the *Source group* also differ from those of the other groups. The subject noun of the former group of examples is inanimate, whereas it is animate for the latter. The nouns directly subordinate to *ot* are similar for both types and refer to concrete objects with no restrictions on animacy. From the derivational point of view, the nouns are not closely related to other parts of speech.

The semantic unity of the group is connected with the morphological feature of inanimacy of the head noun. In the *Source group* all of the examples refer to natural phenomena and their source. Thus, the group is fully parallel to the N *ot* N group with the identical meaning.[63] An interesting comparison with this semantic type is offered by the expressions *dožd'* 'rain' and *sneg* 'snow' + *idet* 'goes', *i.e.*, 'it's raining, it's snowing'. The contrast is twofold in that they are both nouns referring to natural phenomena and that they occur with *idti* 'to walk' under exactly the same restrictions as do nouns of the *Source group* —

[61] Although the basic corpus does not contain examples of *pojti* in this usage, it is possible. The *Slovar' sovremennogo russkogo literaturnogo jazyka* (henceforth cited as the *Academy Dictionary)* gives the following example: *Pojavilsja . . . grafin s vodkoj, ot kotoroj . . . pošel dux apel'sinnoj korki* 'there appeared . . . a carafe with vodka, from which . . . wafted the fragrance of orange peel', *X*, col. 819.

[62] No examples were found either in the basic corpus or in the *Academy Dictionary*, *V*, col. 232.

[63] See pages 50–55 for a discussion of the nominal group.

i.e., neither the non-determined form *xodit'* 'to walk' nor the perfective *pojti* 'to start to walk' is possible.[64]

TABLE 13

Transform Features of 'N^1 V ot N^2' Units of the Spatial Group

	N^1	V	*ot*	N^2	T1: $\rightarrow N^1$ V *ot* N^2 + *k* N^3	T2: $\rightarrow N^1, A^V$ *ot* N^2	T3: $\rightarrow N^1$ *ot* N^2	T4: $\rightarrow N^2 V_t N^1$
1.	žena	ušla	ot	Čerpunova	+	−	−	
	'the wife	went away	from	Čerpunov'				
2.	mal'čik	ušel	ot	njan'ki	+	−	−	−
	'the boy	went away	from	[his] nanny'				
3.	čelovek	ušel	ot	tovariščej	+	−	−	−
	'the man	went away	from	[his] comrades'				
4.	ty	ujdeš'	ot	vojny	+	−	−	−
	'you	will leave	—	the war'				
5.	—	ujti	ot	(besprijutnoj) noči	+	−	−	−
	'—	to go away	from	the (shelterless) night'				
6.	Pol'ša	uxodila	ot	vojny	+	−	−	−
	'Poland	was leaving	—	the war'				
7.	ty	uxodiš'	ot	žizni	+	−	−	−
	'you	are leaving	—	life'				
8.	damy	otošli	ot	kolodca	+	−	−	−
	'the ladies	walked away	from	the well'				
9.	my	otošli	ot	vokzala	+	−	−	−
	'we	walked away	from	the station'				
10.	poezd	otošel	ot	stancii	+	−	−	−
	'the train	moved away	from	the station'				
11.	doroga	otxodila	ot	obryva	+	−	−	−
	'the road	led away	from	the precipice'				
12.	baba	otxodila	ot	paravoza	+	−	−	−
	'an old woman	walked away	from	the locomotive'				
13.	Manjuška	otxodila	ot	Kati	+	−	−	−
	'Manjuška	walked away	from	Katy'				

[64] Both can occur with the perfective form *pojti*, but the meaning is no longer parallel to that of the non-prefixed imperfective form. The addition of the *po-*, in addition to making the verb perfective, introduces an inceptive meaning. Thus, *dožd' pošel* does not mean 'it rained', but 'it started to rain'.

TABLE 13 (*cont.*)

	N^1	V	*ot*	N^2	T1: → N^1 V *ot* N^2 + *k* N^3	T2: → N^1, A^V *ot* N^2	T3: → N^1 *ot* N^2	T4: → N^2 V_t N^1
14.	lodka	otošla	ot	berega	+	–	–	–
	'the boat	moved away	from	the shore'				
15.	polki	podxodjat	ot	Nežina	+	–	–	–
	'the regiments	are approaching	from	the Nežin'				
16.	načal'nik	podošel	ot	baraka	+	–	–	–
	'the chief	approached	from	the barracks'				
17.	ja	pojdu	ot	senej	+	–	–	–
	'I	shall set out	from	the entryway'				
18.	ja	poexal	ot	mogily	+	–	–	–
	'I	set out	from	the grave'				
19.	ja	ot"exal	ot	mestečka	+	–	–	–
	'I	went away	from	the village'				
20.	ja	ot"ezžal	ot	goroda	+	–	–	–
	'I	was going away	from	the city'				
21.	Torelli	s"exal	ot	nas	+	–	–	–
	'Torelli	moved away	from	us'				
22.	(on)	uezžaet	ot	mamy	+	–	–	–
	'(he)	moved away	from	mamma'				
23.	–	bežat'	ot	(ètix) mest	+	–	–	–
	'–	to run	from	(these) parts'				
24.	on	otbežal	ot	nas	+	–	–	–
	'he	ran away	from	us'				
25.	on	ubegal	ot	njani	+	–	–	–
	'he	ran away	from	[his] nanny'				
26.	gimnazisti	otletali	ot	nego	+	–	–	–
	'the gymnasiasts	flew away	from	him'				
27.	razvedčiki	otpolzli	ot	polja	+	–	–	–
	'the scouts	crawled away	from	the field'				
28.	on	otskočil	ot	menja	+	–	–	–
	'he	leaped away	from	me'				

4.3.2.2. *Spatial Group*

The sole transform positively characterizing this group is T1, which demonstrates the possibility of adding *k* + N to the N^1 V *ot* N^2 unit. This transformation is basic to the formal identification of the spatial examples and is common to all three types of verb heads.

In their expanded form, the spatial examples have the same outer form (N^1 Vø *ot* N^2 *k* N^3) as do the dual prepositional examples. The mono-prepositional examples are not, however, fully parallel to the dual forms. The dual prepositional units, it will be recalled, do not admit the dropping of the second PN. This is clearly not the case for the expanded spatial units since the deletion simply restores them to their original form. Since the list of verbal roots is largely the same for the two groups, what feature underlies this difference in transformational behavior? The major opposition between the verbs of the single and dual prepositional *Spatial groups* lies in their prefixation patterns. The dual prepositional group typically displays either no prefix or one of the prefixes *pod-*, *pri-*, *pro-*, *pere-* + V + *ot* + N plus non-deletable *k* + N. The single prepositional group normally displays one of the ablative prefixes *ot-*, *u-*, *s-* + V plus *ot* + N and can optionally be supplemented by *k* + N.

There are exceptions to these two general patterns. In Table 13 we find two verbs (examples 15 and 16) with the prefix *pod-*. The above noted pattern indicates that such verb types are typically found only in the dual prepositional spatial type. An examination of the context of usage of these examples explains, at least in part, this seeming anomaly. The sentence from which the first of these examples is extracted reads as follows: "*Strel'ba delalas' vse slyšnee, i gorod uznal, čto ot Nežina bystro podxodjat s bojami sovetskie polki* 'The shooting became continually more audible, and the town learned, that Soviet regiments were rapidly advancing from the Nežin by combat'." The expected *k* + N, although not stated, is strongly implied, *i.e.*, *podxodjat* K GORODU 'they are approaching the city'. The second example is a similar case. Other atypical cases include two examples wherein the prefix *po-* occurs (examples 17 and 18) and one (23) where no prefix is used. An examination of the context again shows intruding factors. In the case of examples 17 and 18, we find the verbs are semantically reinforced by the words *podal'še* 'farther away' and *proč'* 'away, off' respectively. These *direction indicators* assume the reinforcing role normally played by the auxillary *k* + N, for the non-prefixed verbs, or the ablative prefix commonly associated with the single preposition spatial type. The remaining exception (23) has an historical explanation. In Old Russian the verb *bežat'* 'to run' was usually followed by the genitive of the noun specifying the thing from which the subject of the verb was fleeing. In the course of time, this construction was gradually supplanted by the V + *ot* + N_g construction.[65]

The nouns of the simple and dual prepositional *Spatial groups* do not appear to display any opposition comparable to that of the verbs. The head nouns are

[65] Lomtev, 266. At the present time the construction *bežat' ot čego-to* 'to run from something' might be described as transitional. Its relative rarity compared to *otbežat'* + or *ubežat'* + *ot* 'to run away + from' suggests that it is yielding to the dichotomous pattern outlined above, *i.e.*, *bežat' ot* N^1 *k* N^2 or *otbežat' ot* N^1.

in the great majority animate — a feature that opposes these two groups to the *Source group* with its inanimate head nouns. The nouns that serve as the objects of the preposition are not differentiated among the three groups and refer, in almost all cases, to concrete objects. Derivationally the head nouns of the non-source groups have only remote ties with verbs; head nouns of the *Source group* are somewhat more closely related to their verbal cognates.[66]

The above examination of the interrelation between various morphological and syntactic devices on the one hand and the expression of the concept of spatial motion on the other leads to an interesting observation. Couched negatively, it is that simple verbs of motion plus *ot* + N are not ordinarily used to express the idea of physical motion through space unless supplemented either by a) *k* + N or b) an ablative prefix.[67] To perform this function, they require the presence of either a morphological intensifying element *(i.e.,* a particular type of prefix) or a lexical intensifying element *(i.e.,* the supplementary P + N). This rather paradoxical conclusion is reinforced by the fact that the few cases of single prepositional spatial examples that do not have the ablative prefixes (PO*jdu ot senej* 'I shall set out from the entryway' and PO*exal ot mogily* 'I set out from the grave') require reinforcement by lexical means, *e.g., pojdu* PODAL'ŠE *ot senej* 'I shall set out *away* from the entryway' and *poexal* PROČ' *ot mogily* 'I set out *away* from the grave'.

4.3.2.3. *Ablative Group*

The *Ablative group* is comprised of a small number of intransitive verbs that do not systematically undergo transformation.

1. *ona otdyxala ot sutoloki*
   'she was resting from the commotion'
2. *gospoda otdoxnuli ot dorogi*
   'the gentlemen rested from the road'
3. *ja otstal ot konvoja*
   'I fell behind the convoy'
4. *my otvykli ot slov*
   'we had become unused to words'

66 See page 50*ff.* above for a discussion of the transformationally defined degree of verbality of the head nouns of N^1 *ot* N^2 groups relating to natural phenomena and their sources.

67 The validity of the argument that not *ja šel ot doma* 'I walked from the house', but only *ja otošel ot doma* 'I walked away from the house' is a usual sequence may well be restricted to written as opposed to spoken Russian. The *ja šel ot doma* unit means 'I was on the way somewhere at the given moment'. It seems likely that occasions to use this type of utterance in writing probably would be relatively rare, whereas in speech they are probably much more common.

5. *sčast'e zavisit ot prosveščenija*
   'happiness depends on enlightenment'
6. *pulja pomogaet ot ljubvi*
   'a bullet helps against love'
7. *korabl' otvalival ot Odessy*
   'the ship put out from Odessa'
8. *ja otčalil ot Čerepaxa*
   'I cast off from Čerepax'
9. *on uvilival ot objazatel'stva*
   'he was shirking [his] duty'

Although no single transformation will work for the majority of these examples (and hence serve to isolate and characterize the group), some of the examples will admit at least one. Transformationally the most significant statement that can be made about this group is that none of the examples admit the addition of $k + N^3$. This marks them as basically different from those of the *Spatial group*. The type of verb is also different. No verbs of motion (in the grammatical sense) are found in the *Ablative group*. On the other hand, some, but not all, of the examples display an obvious semantic similarity to examples of the *Spatial groups, e.g., ja otstal ot konvoja* (3), *korabl' otvalival ot Odessy* (7).

The second transform, which replaces the verb with a cognate adjective, is sporadically possible *(e.g., ja otstal ot konvoja* 'I fell behind the convoy' → *ja, otstalyj ot konvoja* 'I, lagging behind the convoy'; *sčast'e zavisit ot prosveščenija* 'happiness depends on enlightenment' → *sčast'e zavisimoe ot prosveščenija* 'happiness dependent on enlightenment'). In other cases this transformation is marginally possible *(my otvykli ot slov* 'we had become unused to words' → *my, otvyčnye ot slov* 'we, unused to words')[68] or possible for other forms of the same root, but not for the word in question: *ona otdoxnula ot sutoloki* 'she rested from the commotion' ↛ *ona, *otdoxlaja ot sutoloki* 'she, rested from the commotion', whereas *lošadi doxli ot raboty* 'the horses died from work' → *lošadi doxlye ot raboty* 'the horses, dead from work'.

Although the unity of this group of examples is not satisfactorily shown by transformational procedures, it is reflected in other formal and semi-formal features. The unity of the ablative examples (and their opposition to the remaining groups) may be described in terms of the *weak/strong government* opposition.[69] All of the examples cited on the preceding page are characterized

[68] The form *otvyčnyj* 'unused to' is listed in Dal', but not in the *Academy Dictionary*.

[69] A purely pragmatic definition of strong government has been set forth on page 114 above. The matter of degrees of government on a scale ranging from strong to weak is even less well understood than the phenomenon itself. It is generally agreed, however, that there are substantial differences in the strength of the relationship between a preposition and its governor. (Kenneth E. Harper, "The Position of Prepositional Phrases in Russian", *Mechanical Translation*, VIII, No. 1 [1964], 6.) For present purposes, the

by strong government. Although concrete statistical data are lacking, it can safely be asserted that the spatial examples display this feature to a lesser degree. Further, it seems likely that the dual and simple prepositional spatial categories also represent different degrees of strong government. Thus the three groups present the following picture in terms of strength of government.

1. Ablative group: *otvyknut' ot slov* 'to become unused to words'
2. Single prepositional spatial: OT*ojti* OT *doma*[70] 'to go away from the house'
3. Double prepositional spatial: *idti ot doma k škole*[71] 'to go from the house to school'

In all of the ablative examples the likelihood of a dependent *ot* phrase is quite high, although the odds vary from verb to verb. The verbs of the *Ablative group* display one further characteristic normally associated with strong government in that nouns and adjectives derived from them have the capability to duplicate the verbal construction.[72] For example, not only does the verb *otdyxat'* 'to rest' usually combine with *ot,* but so does the derived noun *otdyx* 'a rest' (+ *ot)* and the derived adjective — *otdoxnovennyj* 'restful' + *ot.* Similarly: *otstat'* 'to fall behind', *otstalyj* 'lagging', *otstalost'* 'backwardness' + *ot; otvykanie* 'disusage', *otvyčnyj* 'disuse' + *ot; zaviset'* 'to depend', *zavisimyj* 'dependent', *zavisimost'* 'dependence' + *ot; pomogat'* 'to aid', *pomoščnyj* 'auxillary', *pomoč'* 'aid' + *ot; otvalivat'* 'to put out [of a ship]', *otval* 'the putting out', *otval'nyj* 'putting out' [adj.] + *ot; uvilivat'* 'to shirk', *uvilivanie* 'the shirking' + *ot;* and *otčalit'* 'to cast off', *otčal* 'the casting off' + *ot.*

Thus, although not transformationally defined as a group, there are ample syntactic and derivational grounds to support the unification of the ablative examples into a group.

concept of strength of government will be defined in terms of the relative frequency with which a given word is followed by a dependent *ot*. The maximum in strong government would be represented by an example of the type *zaviset'* 'to depend on', since *zaviset'* rarely, if ever, occurs without *ot*. The opposite end of the strength of government spectrum might be illustrated by examples of the sort *priznat'* 'to acknowledge' where the likelihood of an ensuing *ot* is presumably quite remote. This is basically the view espoused by Apresjan in his article "O sil'nom i slabom upravlenii (opyt količestvennogo analiza)".

[70] See Peškovskij, 285 in regard to the role of the interrelation between verbal prefixes and dependent prepositions in strong government.

[71] This hierarchy of relative strength of government can be augmented by the addition of examples of the causal type *(dama pokrasnela ot styda* 'the lady reddened because of shame') where the relationship of the verb and the preposition is usually described as weak government.

[72] This characteristic of certain Russian words is treated at length by N. N. Prokopovič in his article "K voprosu o roli slovoobrazovatel'nyx svjazej častej reči v postroenii slovosočetanij", cited in footnote 27, page 115.

TABLE 14

Transform Features of 'N^1 V ot N^2' Units of the Causal Group

	N^1	V	*ot*	N^2	T1: → N^1 V *ot* N^2 + *k* N^3	T2: → N^1, A^V *ot* N^2	T3: → N^1 *ot* N^2	T4: → N^2 V_t N^1
1.	zemlja	pobelela	ot	snega	—	+	—	+
	'the earth	had become white	because of	the snow'				
2.	mostovaja	pobelela	ot	bumagi	—	+	—	+
	'the roadway	had become white	because of	the paper'				
3.	glaza	pobeleli	ot	zloby	—	+	—	+
	'the eyes	had become white	because of	spite'				
4.	sotrudniki	beleli	ot	zavisti	—	+	—	+
	'the collaborators	became white	because of	envy'				
5.	ona	poblednela	ot	smuščenija	—	+	—	+
	'she	had become pale	because of	embarrassment'				
6.	ja	poblednel	ot	obidy	—	+	—	+
	'I	had become pale	because of	the offense'				
7.	Sil'vio	poblednel	ot	zlosti	—	+	—	+
	'Sil'vio	had become pale	because of	malice'				
8.	starik	poblednel	ot	bešenstva	—	+	—	+
	'the old man	had become pale	because of	rage'				
9.	prožekter	razbogatel	ot	(odnoj) kuricy	—	+	—	+
	'the schemer	grew rich	because of	a (single) chicken'				
10.	ona	zabolela	ot	opečatki	—	+	—	—
	'she	fell ill	because of	a misprint'				
11.	starik	zabolel	ot	gorja	—	+	—	—
	'the old man	fell ill	because of	grief'				
12.	my	dureli	ot	zapaxa	—	+	—	+
	'we	were stupefied	because of	the smell'				
13.	intelligenty	poglupeli	ot	nedobroželatels'tva	—	+	—	+
	'the intelligencia	had become stupid	because of	ill-will'				
14.	vse	golubelo	ot	šineli	—	+	—	—
	'everything	became blue	because of	the overcoat'				
15.	pal'cy	ogrubeli	ot	zemli	—	+	—	+
	'fingers	had become coarse	because of	the earth'				
16.	devuška	krasnela	ot	stesnenija	—	+	—	+
	'the girl	reddened	because of	uneasiness'				
17.	oni	pokrasneli	ot	gneva	—	+	—	+
	'they	had reddened	because of	anger'				

TABLE 14 (*cont.*)

N^1	V	*ot*	N^2	T1: → N^1 V *ot* N^2 + *k* N^3	T2: → N^1, A^V *ot* N^2	T3: → N^1 *ot* N^2	T4: → N^2 V_t N^1
18. vse	mertveet	ot	mraka	–	+	–	+
'everything	grew numb	because of	the darkness'				
19. žena	mlela	ot	vosxiščenija	–	+	–	–
'the wife	was thrilled	because of	delight'				
20. načal'niki	razomleli	ot	žary	–	+	–	–
'the chiefs	grew languid	because of	the heat'				
21. babuška	pomolodela	ot	plat'ja	–	+	–	+
'grandma	grew younger	because of	the dress'				
22. ženščiny	onemeli	ot	izumlenija	–	+	–	–
'the women	became dumb	because of	amazement'				
23. on	op'janel	ot	gorja	–	+	–	+
'he	got drunk	because of	grief'				
24. ja	op'janel	ot	(odnoj) rjumki	–	+	–	+
'I	got drunk	because of	(one) wineglass'				
25. lico	porozovelo	ot	moroza	–	+	–	–
'the face	shown pink	because of	the frost'				
26. železo	ržaveet	ot	vody	–	+	–	+
'the iron	rusts	because of	the water'				
27. kinžal	zaržavel	ot	krovi	–	+	–	+
'the dagger	started to rust	because of	the blood'				
28. ja	posedel	ot	otčajanija	–	+	–	–
'I	turned gray	because of	despair'				
29. žerdi	posereli	ot	vetrov	–	+	–	–
'the poles	turned gray	because of	the winds'				
30. ja	stareju	ot	astmy	–	+	–	+
'I	am getting old	because of	asthma'				
31. les	otsyrel	ot	vetra	–	+	–	–
'the forest	became damp	because of	the wind'				
32. trava	otsyrela	ot	morja	–	+	–	–
'the grass	became damp	because of	the sea'				
33. zemlja	zatverdela	ot	šeluxi	–	+	–	+
'the ground	became hard	because of	the husks'				
34. glaza	potemneli	ot	gneva	–	+	–	+
'the eyes	darkened	because of	anger'				
35. my	otupeli	ot	goloda	–	+	–	+
'we	had become torpid	because of	hunger'				
36. ona	otupela	ot	sna	–	+	–	+
'she	had become torpid	because of	sleep'				

TABLE 14 (*cont.*)

	N^1	V	*ot*	N^2	T1: → N^1 V *ot* N^2 + *k* N^3	T2: → N^1, A^V *ot* N^2	T3: → N^1 *ot* N^2	T4: → N^2 V_t N^1
37.	fotografija	potusknela	ot	syrosti	−	+	−	+
	'the photo	had become dim	because of	the dampness'				
38.	nogi	otjaželeli	ot	grjazi	−	+	−	+
	'[his] feet	had become heavy	because of	the mud'				
39.	on	obezumel	ot	straxa	−	+	−	+
	'he	had gone mad	because of	terror'				
40.	koža	xolodela	ot	nix	−	+	−	+
	'the skin	grow cold	because of	them'				
41.	ona	poxudela	ot	zabot	−	+	−	−
	'she	grew thin	because of	worries'				
42.	ja	zdoroveju	ot	solnca	−	+	−	+
	'I	grow healthy	because of	the sun'				
43.	prilavok	pozelenel	ot	pyl'cy	−	+	−	+
	'the counter	turned green	because of	the pollen'				
44.	steny	pozeleneli	ot	syrosti	−	+	−	+
	'the walls	turned green	because of	the dampness'				
45.	knjaginja	pozelenela	ot	zlosti	−	+	−	+
	'the princess	turned green	because of	spite'				
46.	lico	počernelo	ot	slez	−	+	−	+
	'[his] face	blackened	because of	the tears'				
47.	korpusa	počerneli	ot	kopoti	−	+	−	+
	'the buildings	had become black	because of	the soot'				
48.	ksendzy	ošaleli	ot	(ee) prisutstvija	−	+	−	−
	'the priests	went crazy	because of	(her) presence'				
49.	gazety	ošaleli	ot	sluxov	−	+	−	−
	'the papers	went crazy	because of	the rumors'				
50.	trava	poželtela	ot	solnca	−	+	−	+
	'the grass	turned yellow	because of	the sun'				
51.	cvety	poželteli	ot	xoloda	−	+	−	+
	'the flowers	turned yellow	because of	the cold'				
52.	čerepa	poželteli	ot	grjazi	−	+	−	+
	'the skulls	turned yellow	because of	the mud'				
53.	vremja	ocepenelo	ot	stuži	−	+	−	−
	'time	had frozen	because of	the cold'				
54.	dveri	nabuxli	ot	syrosti	−	+	−	−
	'the doors	had swollen	because of	the dampness'				
55.	lošadi	doxnut	ot	raboty	−	+	−	+
	'the horses	are dying	because of	the work'				

TABLE 14 (*cont.*)

N^1	V	*ot*	N^2	T1: → N^1 V *ot* N^2 + *k* N^3	T2: → N^1, A^V *ot* N^2	T3: → N^1 *ot* N^2	T4: → N^2 V_t N^1
56. koptilki	gasli	ot	vzryvov	–	–	–	+
'the wick lamps	had gone out	because of	the explosions'				
57. vrag	pogibnet	ot	meča	–	–	–	+
'the enemy	will perish	because of	the sword'				
58. ja	oglox	ot	oščuščenija	–	+	–	+
'I	had become deaf	because of	the sensation'				
59. ja	oglox	ot	volnenija	–	+	–	+
'I	had become deaf	because of	the excitement'				
60. on	gloxnul	ot	pily	–	+	–	+
'he	became deaf	because of	the saw'				
61. ja	ogloxnul	ot	voplej	–	+	–	+
'I	had become deaf	because of	the wails'				
62. krov'	kisnet	ot	ètogo	–	+	–	–
'the blood	turns sour	because of	this'				
63. ravnina	raskisla	ot	doždej	–	+	–	–
'the plain	had become limp	because of	the rains'				
64. vse	pomerknet	ot	dyma	–	+	–	–
'everything	will grow dim	because of	the smoke'				
65. rukava	namokli	ot	krovi	–	+	–	+
'the sleeves	were soaked	because of	the blood'				
66. binty	promokli	ot	krovi	–	+	–	+
'the bandages	were soaked through	because of	the blood'				
67. bumaga	promokla	ot	kraski	–	+	–	+
'the paper	was soaked through	because of	the paint'				
68. list'ja	ponikli	ot	znoja	–	+	–	+
'the leaves	drooped	because of	the heat'				
69. trava	ponikla	ot	rosy	–	+	–	–
'the grass	drooped	because of	the dew'				
70. kolos'ja	ponikli	ot	buri	–	+	–	–
'the ears [of grain]	drooped	because of	the storm'				
71. vy	slepli	ot	slez	–	+	–	+
'you	became blind	because of	the tears'				
72. ja	oslep	ot	sveta	–	+	–	+
'I	became blind	because of	the light'				
73. –	oslepnut'	ot	čertežej	–	+	–	+
'–	to become blind	because of	draft plans'				

TABLE 14 (*cont.*)

	N^1	V	*ot*	N^2	T1: $\to N^1\ V\ ot\ N^2 + k\ N^3$	T2: $\to N^1, A^V\ ot\ N^2$	T3: $\to N^1\ ot\ N^2$	T4: $\to N^2\ V_t\ N^1$
74.	nogi	slabnut	ot	bolezni	−	+	−	+
	'the legs	become weak	because of	illness'				
75.	derev'ja	stynut	ot	zapaxa	−	+	−	+
	'the trees	become cool	because of	the smell'				
76.	bol'	utixla	ot	prikosnovenija	−	+	−	+
	'the pain	subsided	because of	the touch'				
77.	odyška	utixla	ot	ritma	−	+	−	+
	'[his] breathlessness	subsided	because of	the rhythm'				
78.	my	oxripli	ot	xoloda	−	+	−	−
	'we	grew hoarse	because of	the cold'				
79.	mir	pogibaet	ot	nenavisti	−	+	−	+
	'the world	perishes	because of	hatred'				
80.	on	razmjakal	ot	slez	−	+	−	+
	'he	softened	because of	the tears'				
81.	my	opuxali	ot	goloda	−	+	−	−
	'we	were bloated	because of	hunger'				
82.	opuxoli	isčezali	ot	ètogo	−	−	−	−
	'the swellings	disappeared	because of	this'				
83.	sestra	rydala	ot	smexa	−	−	−	−
	'the sister	sobbed	because of	laughter'				
84.	ja	stonal	ot	naprjaženija	−	−	−	−
	'I	groaned	because of	the effort'				
85.	damy	oxali	ot	užasa	−	−	−	−
	'the ladies	moaned	because of	terror'				
86.	mal'čik	tjavkaet	ot	toski	−	−	−	−
	'the boy	yelps	because of	anguish'				
87.	Jaša	kašljal	ot	smexa	−	−	−	−
	'Jaša	coughed	because of	laughter'				
88.	okno	xlopaet	ot	vetra	−	−	−	−
	'the window	bangs	because of	the wind'				
89.	stekla	zvjakali	ot	šagov	−	−	−	−
	'the window panes	tinkled	because of	the steps'				
90.	stekla	pozvjakivali	ot	marša	−	−	−	−
	'the window panes	tinkled a bit	because of	the marching'				

TABLE 14 (*cont.*)

	N^1	V	*ot*	N^2	T1: → N^1 V *ot* N^2 + *k* N^3	T2: → N^1, A^V *ot* N^2	T3: → N^1 *ot* N^2	T4: → N^2 V_t N^1
91.	kanarejka	popiskivaet	ot	skuki	–	+	–	–
	'the canary	is chirping	because of	boredom'				
92.	vyključateli	vzvizgivali	ot	ržavčiny	–	+	–	–
	'the switches	screeched	because of	the rust'				
93.	on	posapyvaet	ot	gneva	–	–	–	–
	'he	sniffled a bit	because of	anger'				
94.	sobaka	podvyvala	ot	vostorga	–	–	–	–
	'the dog	howled	because of	ecstasy'				
95.	ja	axnul	ot	izumlenija	–	–	–	–
	'I	exclaimed	because of	amazement'				
96.	on	krjaknul	ot	voprosa	–	–	–	–
	'he	groaned	because of	the question'				
97.	ja	vskriknul	ot	boli	–	–	–	–
	'I	screamed	because of	the pain'				
98.	Raxil'	vsplesnula	ot	radost'i	–	–	–	–
	'Raxil'	clapped [her hands]	because of	joy'				
99.	kot	zaurčal	ot	naslaždenija	–	–	–	–
	'the cat	began to rumble	because of	enjoyment'				
100.	doma	treščat	ot	napora	–	+	–	+
	'the houses	crackle	because of	the pressure'				
101.	xrustal'	drebezžal	ot	basa	–	–	–	–
	'the crystal	tinkled	because of	[his] bass'				
102.	ja	kriču	ot	boli	–	–	–	–
	'I	shout	because of	the pain'				
103.	kritiki	molčat	ot	neuverennosti	–	+	–	–
	'the critics	are silent	because of	lack of confidence'				
104.	derevo	xrustit	ot	listv	–	+	–	–
	'the tree	crackles	because of	the foliage'				
105.	trava	šelestit	ot	vetra	–	–	–	–
	'the grass	rustles	because of	the wind'				
106.	xarčevnja	gudela	ot	mux	–	–	–	–
	'the inn	hummed	because of	the flies'				
107.	vokzal	gudel	ot	topot	–	–	–	–
	'the station	hummed	because of	the clatter'				
108.	on	sopel	ot	natugi	–	–	–	–
	'he	wheezed	because of	strain'				

TABLE 14 (*cont.*)

	N^1	V	*ot*	N^2	T1: → N^1 V *ot* N^2 + *k* N^3	T2: → N^1, A^V *ot* N^2	T3: → N^1 *ot* N^2	T4: → N^2 V_t N^1
109.	bašnja	zvenit	ot	udarov	−	+	−	−
	'the tower	rings	because of	the blows'				
110.	berega	šumeli	ot	vetra	−	+	−	−
	'the shores	made a noise	because of	the wind'				
111.	krovat'	skripela	ot	dviženija	−	+	−	−
	'the bed	squeaked	because of	the movement'				
112.	syščik	xripel	ot	jarosti	−	+	−	−
	'the detective	wheezed	because of	rage'				
113.	sestra	xoxotala	ot	sčast'ja	−	−	−	−
	'the sister	laughed	because of	happiness'				
114.	lošadi	ržut	ot	udovol'stvija	−	−	−	−
	'the horses	neigh	because of	satisfaction'				
115.	vyveski	skrežeščut	ot	vetra	−	−	−	−
	'the signboards	make a grinding noise	because of	the wind'				
116.	my	plakali	ot	dyma	−	−	−	−
	'we	cried	because of	the smoke'				
117.	on	poet	ot	skuki	−	−	−	−
	'he	sings	because of	boredom'				
118.	my	vyli	ot	užasa	−	−	−	−
	'we	howled	because of	terror'				
119.	on (ne mog)	govorit	ot	volnenija	−	−	−	−
	'he (could not)	speak	because of	excitement'				
120.	on	vopil	ot	vostorga	−	−	−	−
	'(he)	howled	because of	rapture'				
121.	komnata	zamercala	ot	krasok	−	−	−	−
	'the room	shimmered	because of	the colors'				
122.	čelovek	sijaet	ot	blagodušija	−	+	−	+
	'the man	beams	because of	goodwill'				
123.	osen'	sijaet	ot	listva	−	+	−	−
	'the fall	beams	because of	the foliage'				
124.	ščeki	sverkali	ot	žira	−	−	−	−
	'[his] cheeks	shone	because of	the grease'				
125.	nos	blestel	ot	vodki	−	+	−	−
	'[his] nose	shone	because of	the vodka'				
126.	pidžak	blestel	ot	starosti	−	+	−	−
	'the jacket	shone	because of	age'				

TABLE 14 (*cont.*)

	N^1	V	*ot*	N^2	T1: → N^1 V *ot* N^2 + *k* N^3	T2: → N^1, A^V *ot* N^2	T3: → N^1 *ot* N^2	T4: → N^2 V_t N^1
127.	lico	gorelo	ot	solnca	−	+	−	−
	'[his] face	burned	because of	the sun'				
128.	uši	goreli	ot	ljubopystva	−	+	−	−
	'[his] ears	burned	because of	curiosity'				
129.	flag	vygorel	ot	solnca	−	+	−	−
	'the flag	faded	because of	the sun'				
130.	on	vspyxnul	ot	(ee) zamečanija	−	+	−	−
	'he	flared up	because of	(her) remark'				
131.	gul	voznikal	ot	šepota	−	−	−	−
	'the hum	arose	because of	the whispering'				
132.	my	umirali	ot	lixoradki	−	+	−	+
	'we	were dying	because of	the fever'				
133.	p'janica	umer	ot	vodki	−	+	−	+
	'the drunkard	died	because of	vodka'				
134.	ja	ustal	ot	raboty	−	+	−	−
	'I	grew tired	because of	the work'				
135.	učitel'	dremal	ot	čtenija	−	+	−	−
	'the teacher	dozed	because of	the reading'				
136.	krest'janki	stradajut	ot	goloda	−	−	−	−
	'the peasants	suffer	because of	hunger'				
137.	kaševary	stradajut	ot	buntov	−	−	−	−
	'the cooks	suffer	because of	revolts'				
138.	nevesta	trepeščet	ot	ispuga	−	+	−	−
	'the bride	trembles	because of	fright'				
139.	Babel'	zadrožal	ot	otvraščenija	−	−	−	−
	'Babel'	started to shake	because of	revulsion'				
140.	list'ja	drožali	ot	muzyki	−	−	−	−
	'the leaves	shook	because of	the music'				
141.	ruki	boleli	ot	vody	−	+	−	−
	'[his] hands	ached	because of	the water'				
142.	starik	potrjasal	ot	bešenstva	−	+	−	+
	'the old man	shook	because of	rage'				
143.	starik	prisel	ot	neožidannosti	−	−	−	−
	'the old man	cowered	because of	surprise'				
144.	on	prisedal	ot	ispuga	−	−	−	−
	'he	cowered	because of	fright'				
145.	bumaga	vycvela	ot	doždej	−	−	−	−
	'the paper	faded	because of	the rains'				

TABLE 14 (*cont.*)

	N^1	V	ot	N^2	T1: → N^1 V *ot* N^2 + *k* N^3	T2: → N^1, A^V *ot* N^2	T3: → N^1 *ot* N^2	T4: → N^2 V_t N^1
146.	junoši	rascvetali	ot	razgromov	—	—	—	—
	'the youths	flourished	because of	the havoc'				
147.	ja	vzdrognul	ot	volnenija	—	—	—	—
	'I	winced	because of	excitement'				
148.	xvost	vzdragival	ot	razdraženija	—	—	—	—
	'the tail	was shaking	because of	irritation'				
149.	on	dejstvoval	ot	toski	—	—	—	—
	'he	acted	because of	despair'				
150.	on	poexal	ot	zlosti	—	—	—	—
	'he	went	because of	spite'				
151.	temperatura	upala	ot	užasa	—	—	—	—
	'[his] temperature	fell	because of	terror'				

4.3.2.4. *Causal Group*

The largest of the semantic subgroups subsumed within the N Vø *ot* N constructional type is that expressing causal relations. In addition to being the largest in absolute terms, it is also by far the most variegated in terms of the number of verbal roots. It is perhaps this variety that makes it difficult, if not impossible, to find transformational procedures of sufficient generality to characterize all of the causal examples as a unified group. None of the causal examples admits T1, *i.e.*, $k + N^3$ cannot be added to causal N^1 V *ot* N^2 units, whereas this is possible for the *Spatial* and *Source groups*. T3, which involves deletion of the verb, is also uniformly negative for causal examples. However, since these two transformations are also negative for examples of the *Ablative group*, they cannot provide a unique negative set of transform specifications for the causal examples.

The *Causal group*, as noted above, also lacks any single transform that positively characterizes the group as a whole. About one-half of the different verb roots of the examples, however, do admit T2, which involves the conversion of the verb of N^1 V *ot* N^2 into an adjective, thus yielding a new phrase of the form N^1, A^V *ot* N^2, *e.g.*, T2: *ženščiny onemeli ot izumlenija* 'the women became dumb because of amazement' → *ženščiny, onemelye ot izumlenija* 'the women, dumb because of amazement' or *dveri nabuxli ot syrosti* 'the doors had swollen because of the dampness' → *dveri, nabuxlye ot syrosti* 'the doors, swollen because of dampness'. This transform demonstrates the most important single fact about the causal examples as opposed to the other semantic groups in the N^1 V *ot* N^2 format. This is that a large group of the causal examples duplicate a parallel adjective construction. This is not the case for any of the spatial or source examples and is only possible for occasional examples of the small *Ablative group, e.g., ja otstal ot konvoja* 'I fell behind the convoy' → *ja, otstalyj ot konvoja* 'I, lagging behind the convoy'.

About one-half of the verb roots displayed in causal examples admitting T2 also admit T4. This transform involves the conversion of an intransitive verb *(p'janet'* 'to get drunk') into a transitive one *(p'janit'* 'to make drunk') and may be symbolized as N^1 V *ot* N^2 → N^2 V_t N^1. For example, *starik op'janel ot gorja* 'the old man got drunk because of grief' → *gore op'janilo starika* 'grief made drunk the old man'. This transformation makes possible the formalization of the traditional description of this group as causal. The *Academy Grammar* classifies this type of example as causal because the dependent noun names the cause of the action of the verb.[73] T2 restates this grammatically by making the dependent noun the subject of a transitive verb that takes the former subject as its object. The transformation brings into play the fact that the language has a set of derived factitive verbs that parallel the above-mentioned set of adjective-related intransitive verbs. Unfortunately the parallel is not complete since only a portion of the intransitives have parallel factitive forms.

The remaining examples (about one-half of the total number) do not systematically admit any of the four transforms. The examples, in whole or in part, can undergo a number of other transformations, but the resulting transforms do not make interesting discriminations among different semantic groups. For example, almost any of the examples under discussion, *i.e.*, those numbered between 83 and 151, will undergo a transformation of the type N^1 V *ot* N^2 → N^1 V_{pap} *ot* N^2 *(sestra rydala ot smexa* 'the sister sobbed because of laughter' → *sestra, rydajuščaja ot smexa* 'the sister, sobbing because of laughter'). This type of transform is useless for analytic purposes, however, since almost any N^1 V *ot* N^2 with an imperfective verb may be similarly transformed regardless of the semantic type of the phrase. Note that a purely spatial example of the type *muž otbegal ot doma* 'the man ran away from the house' may also be transformed to *muž, otbegajuščij ot doma* 'the man, running away from the house', as can the ablative example *čelovek otdyxaet ot raboty* 'the man rests from the work' → *čelovek, otdyxajuščij ot raboty* 'the man, resting from the work'. Thus,

[73] *AG, II*, 1, 145.

over one-half of the causal examples lack any distinctive transformational characterization. This is not to say, however, that they lack features that unite them to the causal examples just described, and which separate them from the examples of the other semantic groups. It is rather that these features do not lend themselves to transformational specification — at least of the sort being used here.

The distinctive characteristics of the examples of the *Causal group* are, on the whole, somewhat more clear-cut on the morphological than on the syntactic or transformational level. There is also an unusually high degree of correlation between the formal morpho-syntactic properties of the verbs and the non-formal semantic categories expressed by them.

One aspect of this set of correlations is reflected by T2, which restates N^1 V *ot* N^2 as N^1, A^V *ot* N^2, *e.g.*, *nogi otjaželi ot grjazi* '[his] legs had become heavy because of the mud' → *nogi, tjaželye ot grjazi* '[his] legs, heavy because of the mud'. Syntactically, this illustrates that the verbal construction is parallel to an adjectival construction. On the morphological level we can go a step further and point out that the 35 verbs represented in examples 1–53 are derived from adjectives.[74] Furthermore, they all belong to the productive class of intransitive verbs in *-et'* *(tolstet', tolsteju, tolsteet* 'to get fat'). Although new members of this class are not formed from verbs, " . . . any descriptive adjective, and also a large number of nouns, can form verbs with the general meaning: 'to be, to become, or to seem to be such as that indicated in the corresponding noun,' *e.g.:* . . . *svetlyj* 'light' — *svetlet'* 'to get light' . . .; *kamen'* 'stone' — *kamenet'* 'to turn to stone', *sirota* 'orphan' — *sirotet'* 'to become an orphan'."[75]

Examples 54–82, which like the above were characterized transformationally by the admissability of T2, also form a sharply defined morphological set. All of these verbs belong to the non-productive group of intransitive verbs with the suffix *-nu-* in the infinitive and present stem formations, but dropping it in past stem formations, *e.g.*, *slepnut'* 'to become blind' in the infinitive, but *slep* in the masculine singular past tense. In their unprefixed form this class of verbs has the same generic meaning as those in *-et'*. They indicate either a state taking place in time *(merznut'* 'to freeze') or a gradual transition in

[74] This requires minor qualification. The verbs *mlet'* 'to be thrilled' and *razomlet'* 'to grow languid' have only the deverbative *obomlelyj* 'stupified' *(obomlet'* 'to be stupified') as a cognate adjective in CSR. *Ocepenet'* 'to become torpid' with its derivative adjective *ocepenelyj* 'benumbed' stems from the noun **cep'* 'fetter'. (M. Vasmer, *Russisches Etymologisches Wörterbuch, III* [Heidelberg, 1953], 289.) The verb *tusknet'* 'to grow dim' is apparently not adjectival in origin since the most closely related adjective *tusklyj* 'dim' is marked as a deverbative by its *-l-* suffix. *(AG, I,* 351.)

[75] *AG, I,* 538.

some sort of state *(soxnut'* 'to dry out', *moknut'* 'to become wet').[76] The semantic similarity of these verbs in *-nu-* to the above discussed group in *-et'* is formally reflected by the existence of a number of doublets such as *slabnut'/oslabnut'* and *slabet'/oslabet'* (both meaning 'to become weak'). Thus, in addition to their transformational and morphological characteristics, the above two groups share a common generic meaning.

It should be noted that in spite of the semantic homogeneity of these two verbal groups they have different derivational histories. Whereas the *-et'* group is derived from adjectives *(tverdet'* 'to harden' ← *tverdyj* 'hard'), the *-nu-* verbs have a less homogeneous derivational background. Unlike the productive *-et'* verbs, the non-productive *-nu-* verbs are not, as a group, formed from adjectives since in 8 of the 18 examples the corresponding adjectives are clearly derived from the verbs, thus reversing the pattern of the *-et'* group. Adjectives of the type *nabuxlyj* 'swollen', *doxlyj* 'dead', *giblyj* 'threatened with destruction', *kislyj* 'acid', *merklyj* 'dim', *niklyj* 'drooping', *xriplyj* 'hoarse', and *puxlyj* 'puffy' are derived only from verbs.[77]

The remaining groups of causal examples (83–151) do not display the same degree of morphological unity as the foregoing. Their distribution in terms of derivational classes and semantic classes is by no means random however. Examples 83–120 have the meaning 'to produce some sort of sound'. From the point of view of derivational classifications, several groups are represented.[78] Examples 83–94 contain verbs of Class I. Only 7 of the examples (83–89), however, are primary members of this class. It is of interest that all of these are atypical members of Class I in that they are defective in regard to aspect: *rydat'* 'to sob' and *stonat'* 'to groan' lack any perfective forms; *oxat'* 'to say oh', *tjavkat'* 'to yelp', *kašljat'* 'to cough', *xlopat'* 'to bang', *zvjakat'* 'to tinkle' lack paired perfectives and have only the semelfactive forms — *oxnut'*, *tjavknut'*, *kašljanut'*, *xlopnut'*, and *zvjaknut'*. The remaining examples of Class I (90–94) fall into this category as a result of secondary imperfectivization. That is, they are derived from other more basic verb forms, which belong to non-productive classes. *Pozvjakivat'* 'to tinkle from time to time' is a partial exception to this in that it is an iterative derivative of *zvjakat'* 'to tinkle'. The remaining examples, *popiskivat'* 'to chirp from time to time', *vzvizgivat'* 'to screech from time

[76] A. V. Isačenko, *Grammatičeskij stroj russkogo jazyka v sopostavlenii s slovackim: morfologija, II* (Bratislava, 1960), 81.

[77] *AG, I*, 351.

[78] For the sake of convenience, in the following discussion we shall use the system of verb classification proposed by Isačenko, *II*, 42–5. It is as follows: I. *-at'*, *-aju*, *-aet (čitat')*; II. *-et'*, *-eju*, *-eet (krasnet')*; III. *-ovat'*, *-uju*, *-uet (risovat')*; IV. *-nut'*, *-nu*, *-net (kriknut')*; V. *-it'*, *-ju*, *-it (stroit')*; VI. *-at'*, *-u*, *-et (pisat')*; VII. *-at'*, *-u*, *-it (ležat')*; VIII. *-et'*, *-u*, *-it (videt')*; IX. *-nut'*, *-nu*, *-net (merznut')*; and X. *-sti*, *-st'*, *-zt'* or *-č'*, *-u*, *-et (nesti)*. Only Classes I–V are productive in CSR.

to time', *posapyvat'* 'to sniffle from time to time', *podvyvat'* 'to howl from time to time', ultimately stem from the onomatopoeic layer of the lexicon. They also possess cognate forms that belong to the two verb classes that consist largely of verbs having to do with sounds: Class VII, *vizžat'* 'to screech', *piščat'* 'to chirp'; and Class VIII, *zvenet'* 'to clink', *sopet'* 'to sniffle'.

Examples 95–98 *(axnut'* 'to say ah', *krjaknut'* 'to groan', *vskriknut'* 'to scream', and *vsplesknut'* 'to clap') all share the semelfactive *-nu-* suffix. The two non-prefixed forms are derived from Class I verbs and are aspectually unpaired. The final two examples are Church Slavonic borrowings and have derived imperfectives belonging to Class I. Their native East Slavic forms belong to Classes VI *(pleskat', pleščn, pleščet* 'splash') and VII *(kričat', kriču, kričit* 'shout') and are aspectually unpaired. Thus, if we exclude those of the above that fall into Class I by virtue of secondary imperfectivization or through the formation of iteratives and via borrowing, we are left with the following list of verbs: *rydat'* 'to sob', *oxat'* 'to say oh', *axat'* 'to say ah', *tjavkat'* 'to yelp', *zvjakat'* 'to tinkle', *xlopat'* 'to bang', *krjakat'* 'to groan', and *stonat'* 'to groan'. The last example represents a recent migration from the non-productive Class VI. The other prefixed verbs in Class I are all derived from Classes VII, VIII, and IV.

Verb Classes VII and VIII consist in large part of verbs with the meaning 'to make various types of sounds'.[79] Historically, these two groups represent one derivational group, since they both utilize the formant *-ě-*.[80] Including the base forms from which the secondary members of Class I were derived, the two groups contain the following verbs: VII *určat'* 'to rumble', *treščat'* 'to crackle', *drebezžat'* 'to tinkle', *kričat'* 'to shout', *vizžat'* 'to screech', *piščat'* 'to chirp', and *molčat'* 'to be silent'; VIII *xrustet'* 'to crunch', *šelestet'* 'to rustle', *gudet'* 'to whistle, to ache', *sopet'* 'to sniffle', *zvenet'* 'to tinkle', *šumet'* 'to make noise', *skripet'* 'to scrape', and *xripet'* 'to wheeze'. Like the Class I verbs indicating sounds, these verbs do not enter into aspectual pairs.

The final derivational grouping of 'sound' verbs is represented by examples 113–118. The list of Class VI verbs, including those serving as base forms for Class I derivatives, includes: *xoxotat'* 'to laugh', *ržat'* 'to neigh', *skrežetat'* 'to

[79] Isačenko, *II*, 77 and 80.

[80] When this formant followed velars, the latter became sibilants. These, in turn, led to an alteration in the articulation (and ultimately the spelling) of *-ě-* to *-a-*. Hence, Class VII consists of stems ending in a sibilant plus *-a-* *(*krik + ě → krič + a)*, whereas verbs of Class VIII have *-e-*, the usual reflex of *-ě-* in Russian *(*zven + ě → zven + e)*.

For a demonstration of the equivalence of the *-a-* and the *-e-* of Class VII and VIII verbs on a purely synchronic level, see Morris Halle, "O pravilax russkogo sprjaženija (Predvaritel'noe soobščenie)", *American Contributions to the Fifth International Congress of Slavists*, I (The Hague, 1963), 126.

make a grinding sound', *plakat'* 'to cry', and marginally *pet'* 'to sing' and *vyt'* 'to howl'.

Thus the second of the large semantic groups of the causal category of N^1 V *ot* N^2 constructions displays several formal characteristics. From the purely morphological point of view, three derivational verb classes are involved. The largest is that utilizing the formant -*ě*- (Classes VII and VIII). This is of particular importance in defining the formal unity of the causal category since the largest single derivational group, which was made up of Class II deadjectivals, also utilized the -*ě*- formant, *i.e.*, *krasnet'* 'to redden' ← *krasnyj* 'red'. It must be noted, however, that the productive Class II verbs belong to the first conjugation, whereas those of Classes VII and VIII belong to the second conjugation. The interrelation of the Class II -*ě*- suffix and the Class IX -*nu*- suffix has already been mentioned. The other two verb classes that provide 'sound' verbs are VI and I.

There are two additional formal features that unite and characterize all of the verbs of the examples with the meaning 'to produce sound'. With very few exceptions, the verbs do not enter into imperfective-perfective aspect pairs. On the other hand, they very commonly have semelfactive variants. The final point opposing the 'sound' verbs to the 'becoming' verbs of the *Causal group* is that the former, with a handful of exceptions, are not prefixed. The causal deadjectival 'becoming' verbs are opposed to the verbs of the non-causal groups by the absence of the 'ablative' prefixes typical of the latter groups. The 'sound' verbs are, in turn, opposed to the 'becoming' verbs by their lack of any prefixes. This feature is probably correlated with the onomatopoeic origin of many of the verbs meaning 'to produce a given sort of sound'.

The above three groupings account for the great majority of the causal usages of *ot* with intransitive verbs and, as we have seen, have a number of formal correlates paralleling their semantic similarity. The remaining examples do not lend themselves to such systematic categorization. Roughly speaking, the remaining examples (121–151) fall into three semantic groupings. The verbs of examples 121–130 may be described as referring to the production of light and heat: *zamercat'* 'to shimmer', *sijat'* 'to beam', *sverkat'* 'to shine', *blestet'* 'to shine', *(vy)goret'* 'to burn up, to fade', and *vspyxnut'* 'to flare up'. These are semantically parallel to the above group of 'sound' verbs. Although the number of examples is small, it appears that the 'light and heat' verbs have the same sort of derivational structure as the 'sound' group.

The second small group (131–148) is somewhat more diverse in its make-up. Its verbs *(voznikat'* 'to arise', *umeret'* 'to die', *ustat'* 'to tire', *dremat'* 'to doze', *stradat'* 'to suffer', *trepetat'* 'to tremble', *[za]drožat'* 'to [start to] shake', *bolet'* 'to ache', *trjasat'* 'to shake', *prisedat'* 'to cower', *vzdragivat'* 'to shake', and *vy-/ras-cvetat'* 'to fade/to flourish') share a general meaning, which might be summarized as stadial. As in the preceding group, the morphological structure of the verbs is similar to that of the 'sound' group. Both the 'light' and 'stadial' groups seem to have a higher proportion of concrete dependent nouns than did the preceding groups.

The final group containing the verbs *dejstvovat'* 'to act', *poexat'* 'to go', and *upast'* 'to fall' is totally lacking in similarity to any of the earlier groups — either morphologically or semantically. It is opposed to the preceding 148 examples in that its verbs have the meaning of 'physical action'. This type is extremely rare in the expression of causality in the N V *ot* N constructional format. In common with Popova, we note that in those few cases where an 'action' verb is used the dependent noun refers to an emotion. This latter type is the most frequent and favorable for the expression of causality.[81]

With the exception of the last small group, the verbs expressing causal relations share one morphological feature that opposes them to the verbs of the non-causal groups. The great majority of the causal verbs are of non-verbal origin. They tend to be derived from nominal roots and from the onomatopoeic layer of the lexicon. It is this derivational history that underlies their general 'non-action' meaning and opposes them to the verbs of the *Spatial* and the *Source groups*.

4.3.3. *Analisis of* $N^1 V_{sja}$ *ot* N^2 *Units*

It has been noted that verbs serve as the grammatical heads of *ot* constructions in the great majority of cases. In a count of 1,100 running examples of *ot* constructions, it was found that verbs served as the head word in about 68 per cent of all occurrences.[82] Within this group, the verb was intransitive in 76 per cent of the cases. Of this latter number, slightly more than one-half (55 per cent) were unmarked intransitives (*e.g.*, *krasnet'* 'to redden'), whereas the remaining 45 per cent were marked by the *-sja* suffix.

There are at least two reasons why dependent *ot* constructions occur more frequently with intransitive verbs than with transitive ones.[83] The first of these is that the dependency of the *ot* phrase is often in doubt in transitive verb constructions. In an example of the type *On polučil pis'mo ot materi* 'He received a letter from [his] mother', the *ot materi* can equally well be assigned to the verb *polučil* or to the noun *pis'mo*. If the latter choice is made, this will reduce the number of examples of transitive verb usages with a dependent *ot* phrase. A second and more tenuous explanation for the relative infrequency of *ot*

[81] See page 121 above for a summary of Popova's findings in this connection.

[82] Paustovskij, *Povest' o žizni*.

[83] This discussion of the relative frequency of *ot* + N after intransitive versus transitive verbs of necessity overlooks one important point — that of the relative frequency of transitive and intransitive verbs in the language as a whole. Lacking this information, our discussion of the relative frequency of *ot* + N after these two types of verbs stands in need of further statistical verification.

phrases after transitive verbs may be put in the following terms: transitive verbs, by definition, have complementation in the form of a noun in the accusative case. Thus an *ot* phrase is, of necessity, a secondary and somewhat peripheral complementation for a transitive verb. Intransitive verbs also often require complementation of some type. Since direct objects are specifically excluded for this group, prepositional phrases are a primary means of providing this complementation. Indeed, such supplementation is either obligatory (*žena vozderžalas' ot ocenok* 'the wife refrained from evaluations') or strongly implied (*muž prjatalsja ot ženy* 'the husband hid from the wife') for many intransitive verbs. This is rarely the case for transitive verbs.

Verbs with the *-sja* suffix comprise by far the largest group of intransitive verbs since the *-sja* suffix can be added to virtually any Russian verb. The *-sja* suffix has a wide range of semantic meanings, but only one invariable morphological function. It makes any verb intransitive.[84] The general meaning of the *-sja* suffix and particularly its meanings in conjunction with various verb groups is much disputed. The *Academy Grammar* gives two general meanings of the suffix. With certain (but unspecified) kinds of verbs, it "... expresses the meaning of referral (*obraščennost'*) of the action to its own bearer — the subject; it points to the concentration, the retention of the action in the subject itself."[85] Added to certain other (but unspecified) kinds of verbs, the *-sja* suffix gives them a passive meaning.[86] These two meanings are respectively termed the *medio-passive* (*vozvratno-srednij*) and the *passive* voice and are both opposed to the active voice. No formal basis for the distinction is given.

A more inclusive definition is provided by Irina Lynch who notes that "The general effect of *-sja* on all verbs is that of elimination of a participant and of a stronger emphasis on the process itself."[87] Of the several meanings which the addition of *-sja* introduces into a verb (passivity, reflexivity, reciprocality, impersonal, *etc.*), passivity is formally isolated by the fact that the verb is generally imperfective and has an inanimate subject.[88]

The Soviet scholar N. A. Janko-Trinickaja has made a detailed and penetrating study of *-sja* verbs that sheds a great deal of light on the meaning(s) of the suffix and has considerable bearing on the resolution of syntactic homonyms of the form N^1 V_{sja} *ot* N^2. Janko-Trinickaja divides *-sja* verbs into two major groups — de-objectivals (*otob''ektnye*) and de-subjectivals (*otsubektnye*). The de-objectival group consists of those cases where the subject of the *-sja* verb

[84] Isačenko, *II*, 374.

[85] *AG*, *I*, 413.

[86] *AG*, *I*, 414.

[87] Irina Lynch, "Russian -sja Verbs, Impersonally Used Verbs, and Subject/Object Ambiguities", *1961 First International Conference on Machine Translation of Languages and Applied Language Analysis, II* (London, 1961), 477–502.

[88] Lynch, 470.

construction is equivalent to the grammatical object of the equivalent non-*sja* construction.[89] This relationship can be symbolized as follows: $N^2\ V_{sja}\ (N^1_i) \leftarrow N^1\ V_t\ N^2$, *e.g.*, *lico ukrašaetsja ulybkoj* 'a face is adorned with a smile' ← *ulybka ukrašaet lico* 'a smile adorns the face' or *ja terzalsja ot mysli* 'I was tormented by the thought' ← *mysl' terzala menja* 'the thought tormented me'. The second group, the de-subjectivals, includes those cases where the subject of the parallel *-sja* and non-*sja* constructions remains constant:[90] $N^1\ V_{sja} \leftarrow N^1\ V_t\ N^2$, *e.g.*, *Efimka soščurilsja ot solnca* 'Efimka squinted because of the sun' ← *Efimka soščuril glaza ot solnca* 'Efimka squinted [his] eyes because of the sun'. This second group is subdivided into three parts depending upon the degree of exclusion of the object replaced by *-sja*.[91] These include: 1) *-sja* equals inclusion of an object of a non-*sja* verb into a *-sja* verb — *nasupit'sja* 'to furrow [one's brows]' ← *nasupit' brovi* 'to furrow [one's] brows', 2) *-sja* equals a transferred object — *brosat'sja* 'to throw at something' ← *brosat' kamen'jami* 'to throw stones', and 3) *-sja* equals an excluded object and the verb has a new lexical meaning — *podnjat'sja* 'to rise' ← *podnjat'* 'to pick up'.[92] The analysis of Janko-Trinickaja is borne out, in part, by the results of the transform analysis of N V_{sja} *ot* N made below. The most striking point of convergence between the two is that of the importance of the de-objectival and de-subjectival opposition in characterizing different groups. Roughly speaking, the former constitutes a marked group expressing causal meaning (*duša istomilas' toskoj* 'a soul exhausted by anguish' ← *toska istomila dušu* 'anguish exhausted the soul'), whereas the latter non-marked group expresses a variety of non-causal meanings.

In the N V *ot* N constructions it was found that the great majority of cases involved verbs from certain restricted derivational classes (*-et'*, *-nut'*, *etc.*) and expressed particular types of meanings such as 'to assume a given quality' or 'to make a particular sound', *etc.* This does not appear to be the case for the N V_{sja} *ot* N verbs. It was noted that almost any Russian verb can add *-sja*. This is reflected in the fact that the variety (both derivational and semantic) of verbs used with dependent *ot* phrases is very great. It is presumably for

[89] N. A. Janko-Trinickaja, *Vozvratnye glagoly v sovremennom russkom jazyke* (Moscow, 1962), 79.

[90] *Ibid.*, 80.

[91] *Ibid.*, 171–2.

[92] *Ibid.*, 171–212. The first of these subgroups contains further subdivisions based on the character of the included object. These included a division into *a reflexive object* (*izbavit'sja* 'to save [one's] self', *bereč'sja* 'to be on [one's] guard'), where *-sja* equals *sebja* 'one's self' (pp. 182–8), and a so-called *generalized object* (*brjakat'sja* 'to fall heavily', *kusat'sja* 'to bite'), where *-sja* serves to generalize the action of a transitive verb, *e.g.*, *sobaka kusaetsja* 'the dog bites' ← *sobaka kusaet mužika* 'the dog bites the peasant' (pp. 198–202).

these reasons that the results of the transformational analysis of the N V_{sja} *ot* N construction are not so informative as those of the N^1 V *ot* N^2 group.

The following transforms were utilized in the analysis of the N^1 V_{sja} *ot* N^2 construction.

T1:	N^1 V_{sja} ot N^2 *lentočki razvevalis' ot vetra* 'the ribbons waved because of the wind'	→	N^2 V_t N^1 *veter razveval lentočki* 'the wind waved the ribbons'
T2:	*Ivan vz''erošilsja ot zlosti* 'Ivan was dishevelled because of spite'	→	N^1, V_{ppp} N^2_i *Ivan, vz''erošennyj zlost'ju* 'Ivan, dishevelled by spite'
T3:	*Neva očistilas' oto l'da* 'the Neva was cleared of ice'	→	X V_t N^1 ot N^2 *X očistil Nevu oto l'da* 'X cleared the Neva of ice'
T4:	*vozdux podnimalsja ot pljažej* 'the air rose from the beaches'	→	N^1 ot N^2 *vozdux ot pljažej* 'the air from the beaches'
T5:	*student osvobodilsja ot služby* 'the student was freed from service'	→	N^1, A^v ot N^2 *student, svobodnyj ot služby* 'the student, free from service'
T6:	*sobaki rinulis' ot ognja* 'the dogs rushed from the fire'	→	N^1 V_{sja} ot N^2 k N^3 *sobaki rinulis' ot ognja k temnote* 'the dogs rushed from the fire toward the darkness'
T7:	*Karavaev otmaxivalsja ot Ivanova* 'Karavaev waved off Ivanov'	→	N^1 V_t N^2 *Karavaev otmaxival Ivanova* 'Karavaev waved off Ivanov'
T8:	*Ivan otreksja ot proekta* 'Ivan repudiated the project'	→	N^2, V_{ppp} N^1_i *proekt, otrečennyj Ivanom* 'the project, repudiated by Ivan'

Of the above transformations only T3 and T6 are of major importance in isolating the semantic groups subsumed within the N^1 V_{sja} *ot* N^2 structure. The primary line of demarcation within the V_{sja} group is provided by T3, which opposes the causal examples to the spatial and ablative units. The latter are in turn broken down by the operation of T6, which separates the spatial

TABLE 15

Transform Features of 'N^1 V_{sja} *ot* N^2' (+ *do* N^3) *Units of the Spatial Group*

	N^1	V_{sja}	*ot*	N^2	*do*	N^3	T1: → $N^2 V_t N^1$	T2: → N^1, $V_{ppp} N^2_i$	T3: → $X V_t N^1$ *ot* N^2	T4: → N^1 *ot* N^2	T5: → N^1, A^v *ot* N^2	T6: → $N^1 V_{sja}$ *ot* N^2 *k* N^3	T7: → $N^1 V_t N^2$	T8: → N^2, $V_{ppp} N^1_i$
1.	poezd	taščilsja	ot	Kieva	do	Moskvy	–	–	+	+	–	0	–	–
	'the train	dragged along	from	Kiev	to	Moscow'								
2.	(voennye) časti	vystroilis'	ot	porta	do	toržišča	–	–	+	+	–	0	–	–
	'the (military) units	lined up	from	the port	to	the market'								
3.	set'	raskinetsja	ot	lesov	do	morja	–	–	+	+	–	0	–	–
	'the net	will be spread	from	the forests	to	the sea'								
4.	toržišče	raskinulos'	ot	Samoteki	do	vorot	–	–	+	+	–	0	–	–
	'the market	spread	from	Samoteka	to	the gates'								
5.	okopy	tjanulis'	ot	dorogi	do	gorizonta	–	–	+	+	–	0	–	–
	'the trenches	stretched	from	the road	to	the horizon'								
6.	vzor	nosilsja	ot	lip	do	bašen	–	–	+	+	–	0	–	–
	'[his] gaze	was borne	from	the lindens	to	towers'								
7.	teni	potjanulis'	ot	lesa	po	polju	–	–	+	+	–	0	–	–
	'the shadows	stretched	from	the forest	along	the field'								
8.	rugan'	dokatyvalas'	ot	vagona	ko	mne	–	–	+	+	–	0	–	–
	'the swearing	rolled	from	the railroad car	to	me'								
9.	gudok	unosilsja	ot	dorogi	v	storožku	–	–	+	+	–	0	–	–
	'the whistle	was carried	from	the road	to	the guardhouse'								
10.	dym	podnimalas'	ot	cigarok	v	potolok	–	–	+	+	–	0	–	–
	'smoke	rose	from	the cigars	to	the ceiling'								
11.	par	podnimalsja	ot	lošadej			–	–	+	+	–	+	–	–
	'steam	rose	from	the horses'										

12. vozdux	podnimalsja	ot pljažej	–	–	+	+	–	+	–	–
'air	rose	from the beaches'								
13. pyl'	podnimalas'	ot devuški	–	–	+	+	–	+	–	–
'dust	rose	from the girl'								
14. pesnja	neslas'	ot vorot	–	–	+	+	–	+	–	–
'the song	carried	from the gates'								
15. zvon	polučilsja	ot oskolkov	–	–	+	+	–	+	–	–
'a ringing	came	from the [shell] fragments'								
16. par	klubilsja	ot polov	–	–	+	+	–	+	–	–
'steam	swirled	from the floors'								
17. zapax	razletalsja	ot usov	–	–	+	+	–	+	–	–
'the smell	flew off	from [his] mustache'								
18. listok	otorvalsja	ot vetki	–	–	+	+	–	+	–	–
'the leaf	was torn off	from the branch'								
19. korabl'	udalilsja	ot gavani	–	–	+	+	–	+	–	–
'the ship	moved away	from the harbor'								
20. mal'čik	otorvalsja	ot okna	–	–	+	–	–	+	–	–
'the boy	tore [himself] away	from the window'								
21. my	vozvraščalis'	ot stancii	–	–	+	–	–	+	–	–
'we	were returning	from the station'								
22. on	vorotilsja	ot kapitana	–	–	+	–	–	+	–	–
'he	turned	from the captain'								
23. Klarissa	vernulas'	ot bat'ki	–	–	+	–	–	+	–	–
'Klarissa	returned	from [her] father'								
24. Izja	otvernulsja	ot menja	–	–	+	–	–	+	–	–
'Izja	turned away	from me'								
25. ja	otšatnulsja	ot dveri	–	–	+	–	–	+	–	–
'I	reeled back	from the door'								
26. ona	popjatilas'	ot Nikitina	–	–	+	–	–	+	–	–
'she	moved back	from Nikitin'								
27. ljudi	šaraxalis'	ot domov	–	–	–	–	–	+	–	–
'the people	bolted	from the houses'								
28. sobaki	rinulis'	ot ognja	–	–	–	–	–	+	–	–
'the dogs	rushed	from the fire'								
29. ona	spuskalas'	ot deda	–	–	–	–	–	+	–	–
'she	came down	from grandfather'								

examples from those of the *Ablative group*. The remaining transformations provide a more detailed specification of one of the above groups or of some part of one of these groups.

The examples of the structural type N^1 V_{sja} *ot* N^2 fall into three major groups in terms of their responses to the above-listed transformations. One of the groups has three subgroups. The groups and their specifying transforms are as follows:[93]

	T1	T2	T3	T4	T5	T6	T7	T8
Spatial	−	−	+	+	−	+	−	−
Causal	+	+	−	−	−	−	−	−
Ablative	−	−	+	−	−	−	−	−
a) Pseudo-reflexive	−	−	+	−	−	−	+	+
b) Rejection	−	−	+	−	−	−	−	+
c) Adjectival	−	−	+	−	+	−	−	−

A detailed listing of the examples of each semantic group together with their transformational responses is given at the beginning of each of the three following sections.

4.3.3.1. *Spatial Group*

The N^1 V_{sja} *ot* N^2 spatial units, like those of the non-*sja* intransitives and the transitive verb types, occur both in an expanded form (examples 1–10)[94] and in a non-expanded form (examples 11–29). The fact that the latter admit this type of expansion (T6: *pesnja neslas' ot vorot* 'the song carried from the gates' → *pesnja neslas' ot vorot k nam* 'the song carried from the gates to us') is the identifying feature of the spatial units of all of the verbal structural types. It is only for the *-sja* verbs, however, that T3 is possible, *e.g.*, T3: → X V_t N^1 *ot* N^2, *pyl' podnimaetsja ot devuški* 'dust rises from the girl' → *X podnimaet pyl' ot devuški* 'X raises dust from the girl'. This transform is characteristic of all the non-causal examples of the N^1 V_{sja} *ot* N^2 structural type and illustrates the previously noted distinction of de-objectival and de-subjectival constructions. It shows that the grammatical subject of the *-sja* verb is the object of the non-*sja* form of the verb. Since the *-sja* suffix is a relatively late development in East Slavic, the latter form must be assumed to be basic.[95]

[93] The written-out forms of the transformations for examples of the different semantic groups may be seen in the list given on 155.

[94] The irrelevance of T6 for these units, which already have the requisite prepositional complementation, is indicated in Table 15 by a 0.

[95] S. P. Obnorskij, *Očerki po morfologii russkogo glagola* (Moscow, 1953), 59.

Within the *Spatial group* as defined by the above two transformations, there are three small subdivisions. The first is largely coterminous with the dual prepositional units embracing the examples from 1–8. These examples are united by a deletion transformation calling for the dropping of the second preposition and its object.[96] The inadmissibility or very marginal admissibility of such deletions separates these examples from the remaining units, which can add and delete PN^3 without restriction. The marginal role of the verb is indicated by the positive response of the examples to T4, which deletes the verb. The examples of this subgroup display a spatial range function.

The second subgroup (9–17), like the first, is characterized by its capability to delete the verb *(par podnimaetsja ot lošadej* 'steam rises from the horses' → *par ot lošadej* 'steam from the horses'). This transformation opposes the first two subgroups to the third (20–29) where it yields only nonsensical word-combinations *(sobaki rinulis' ot ognja* 'the dogs rushed from the fire' ↛ **sobaki ot ognja* 'the dogs from the fire'). In general, the results of this transformation coincide with the animacy/non-animacy of the subject. Those examples for which the deletion is possible tend to have inanimate subjects. Counter-examples can be found, however: *parom dvigalsja ot berega* 'the raft moved from the shore', where *parom ot berega* 'raft from the shore' is not possible. It would appear that there is a tendency for dual prepositional examples of *-sja* verbs not to have animate subjects, although it is possible, *e.g.*, *ja doberus' ot Baxčisaraja do Sevastopolja* 'I shall get from Baxčisaraj to Sevastopol'.

It is this animacy/inanimacy opposition that underlies the difference in the verbs of the first two subgroups in contrast to the third. The inanimate group is also subdivided in terms of a second feature. Examples 1–5 have concrete nouns as subjects — *poezd* 'train', *okopy* 'trenches', *set'* 'net', *etc.* The remaining inanimate examples contain nouns referring largely to natural phenomena *(ten'* 'shadow', *par* 'steam', *dym* 'smoke', *zapax* 'odor', *vozdux* 'air') and sounds *(rugan'* 'swearing', *gudok* 'whistle', *pesnja* 'song'). In respect to both the nouns and the verbs represented, this group has much in common with the *Source groups,* which have been previously specified in the N *ot* N (pp. 50—55) and the N V *ot* N (pp. 130—133) constructional types.

The examples of the third and final subgroup, which is formally opposed to the preceding by its inability to delete the verb and the animacy of its subjects, express physical motion. The last three examples of this group (27–29) do not admit T3 *(ljudi šaraxalis' ot domov* 'the people bolted from the houses' ↛ **X šaraxal ljudej ot domov)* because the transitive forms of the verb have

[96] This transformation (N^1 V_{sja} *ot* N^2 *do* N^3 → N^1 V_{sja} *ot* N^2) is not indicated in Table 15 since it is only of peripheral importance in defining one spatial subgroup, whereas the eight transformations specified constitute a uniform set applying to all N^1 V_{sja} *ot* N^2 units.

TABLE 16

Transform Features of 'N^1 V_{sja} *ot* N^2' *Units of the Causal Group*

	N^1	V_{sja}	*ot*	N^2	T1: → $N^2 V_t N^1$	T2: → N^1, $V_{ppp} N^2_i$	T3: → X V_t N^1 *ot* N^2	T4: → N^1 *ot* N^2	T5: → N^1, A^v *ot* N^2	T6: → N^1 V_{sja} *ot* N^2 *k* N^3	T7: → $N^1 V_t N^2$	T8: → N^2, V_{ppp} N^1
1.	reka	razlilas'	ot	doždja	+	+	–	–	–	–	–	–
	'the river	overflowed	because of	the rain'								
2.	muzej	lomilsja	ot	publiki	+	+	–	–	–	–	–	–
	'the museum	was crammed	because of	the public'								
3.	dom	obrušilsja	ot	vzryvov	+	+	–	–	–	–	–	–
	'the house	collapsed	because of	the explosions'								
4.	transporty	vzryvalis'	ot	bomb	+	+	–	–	–	–	–	–
	'the transports	were blown up	because of	the bombs'								
5.	jad	rastopilsja	ot	znoja	+	+	–	–	–	–	–	–
	'the poison	melted	because of	the heat'								
6.	zemlja	spečetsja	ot	znoja	+	+	–	–	–	–	–	–
	'the earth	will cake	because of	the heat'								
7.	inej	osypalsja	ot	udarov	+	+	–	–	–	–	–	–
	'the frost	scattered	because of	the blows'								
8.	dno	izmenjaetsja	ot	napora	+	+	–	–	–	–	–	–
	'the bottom	changes	because of	the pressure'								
9.	gimnasterka	natjanulas'	ot	dviženija	+	+	–	–	–	–	–	–
	'the gym suit	stretched	because of	the movement'								
10.	bakeny	sbilis'	ot	starosti	+	+	–	–	–	–	–	–
	'[his] sideburns	had clumped										
		together	because of	age'								
11.	vse	sdvinulos'	ot	udara	+	+	–	–	–	–	–	–
	'everything	swayed	because of	the blow'								
12.	borodka	trjaslas'	ot	negodovanija	+	+	–	–	–	–	–	–
	'[his] beard	shook	because of	indignation'								
13.	ona	sodrogalas'	ot	slez	+	+	–	–	–	–	–	–
	'she	shuddered	because of	the tears'								
14.	listočki	ševelilis'	ot	vetra	+	+	–	–	–	–	–	–
	'the leaves	trembled	because of	the wind'								
15.	koški	šatalis'	ot	goloda	+	+	–	–	–	–	–	–
	'the cats	staggered	because of	hunger'								
16.	pensnè	kačalos'	ot	dyxanija	+	+	–	–	–	–	–	–
	'[his] pince-nez	jiggled	because of	[his] breathing'								
17.	ten'	kolebletsja	ot	vetra	+	+	–	–	–	–	–	–
	'the shadow	vacillates	because of	the wind'								
18.	lentočki	razvevalis'	ot	vetra	+	+	–	–	–	–	–	–
	'the ribbons	waved	because of	the wind'								

TABLE 16 (*cont.*)

	N^1	V_{sja}	*ot*	N^2	T1: → $N^2 V_t N^1$	T2: → $N^1, V_{ppp} N^2_i$	T3: → $X V_t N^1$ *ot* N^2	T4: → N^1 *ot* N^2	T5: → N^1, A^v *ot* N^2	T6: → $N^1 V_{sja}$ *ot* N^2 *k* N^3	T7: → $N^1 V_t N^2$	T8: → $N^2, V_{ppp} N^1_i$
19.	banty	motalis'	ot	vetra	+	+	–	–	–	–	–	–
	'the bows	dangled	because of	the wind'								
20.	kryl'ja	vertelis'	ot	briza	+	+	–	–	–	–	–	–
	'the wings	revolved	because of	the breeze'								
21.	lesa	raskololis'	ot	groma	+	+	–	–	–	–	–	–
	'the forests	split	because of	the thunder'								
22.	serdce	zakolotilos'	ot	mysli	+	+	–	–	–	–	–	–
	'[his] heart	began to thump	because of	the idea'								
23.	xoxolok	podnjalsja	ot	gneva	+	+	–	–	–	–	–	–
	'the tuft of hair	raised	because of	[his] anger'								
24.	čelovek	sžimalsja	ot	odinočestva	+	+	–	–	–	–	–	–
	'the man	was racked	because of	[his] solitude'								
25.	serdce	sžalos'	ot	slov	+	+	–	–	–	–	–	–
	'[his] heart	wrenched	because of	the words'								
26.	serdce	zabilos'	ot	mysli	+	+	–	–	–	–	–	–
	'[his] heart	began to beat	because of	the idea'								
27.	serdce	ostanovilos'	ot	straxa	+	+	–	–	–	–	–	–
	'[his] heart	stopped short	because of	terror'								
28.	Dorofeja	ostanovilas'	ot	neožidannosti	+	+	–	–	–	–	–	–
	'Dorofeja	stopped short	because of	surprise'								
29.	Izja	zadoxsja	ot	volnenija	+	+	–	–	–	–	–	–
	'Izja	choked	because of	excitement'								
30.	my	zadyxalis'	ot	pyli	+	+	–	–	–	–	–	–
	'we	choked	because of	the dust'								
31.	vzor	somknulsja	ot	bleska	+	+	–	–	–	–	–	–
	'[his] gaze	narrowed	because of	the glare'								
32.	golova	kružilas'	ot	myslej	+	+	–	–	–	–	–	–
	'[his] head	spun	because of	the ideas'								
33.	golova	kružilas'	ot	oblačkov	+	+	–	–	–	–	–	–
	'[his] head	spun	because of	the clouds'								
34.	čeljust'	otvalilas'	ot	izumlenija	+	+	–	–	–	–	–	–
	'[his] jaw	dropped	because of	amazement'								
35.	vse	povalilis'	ot	xoxota	+	+	–	–	–	–	–	–
	'everybody	fell down	because of	laughter'								
36.	ščeka	peredergivalas'	ot	tika	+	+	–	–	–	–	–	–
	'[his] cheek	twitched	because of	the tic'								
37.	lico	peredergivalos'	ot	žadnosti	+	+	–	–	–	–	–	–
	'[his] face	twitched	because of	greed'								

TABLE 16 (*cont.*)

	N^1	V_{sja}	*ot*	N^2	T1: → $N^2 V_t N^1$	T2: → N^1, $V_{ppp} N^2_i$	T3: → $X V_t N^1$ *ot* N^2	T4: → N^1 *ot* N^2	T5: → N^1, A^V *ot* N^2	T6: → $N^1 V_{sja}$ *ot* N^2 *k* N^3	T7: → $N^1 V_t N^2$	T8: → N^2, $V_{ppp} N^1_i$
38.	golos	preryvalsja	ot	volnenija	+	+	–	–	–	–	–	–
	'[his] voice	broke	because of	the excitement'								
39.	guby	skleilis'	ot	molčanija	+	+	–	–	–	–	–	–
	'[his] lips	stuck together	because of	the silence'								
40.	ja	smuščalsja	ot	ètogo	+	+	–	–	+	–	–	–
	'I	was embarrassed	because of	this'								
41.	ja	volnovalsja	ot	soznanija	+	+	–	–	+	–	–	–
	'I	was excited	because of	the awareness'								
42.	mysli	putalis'	ot	ustalosti	+	+	–	–	+	–	–	–
	'[his] thoughts	got muddled	because of	tiredness'								
43.	Ivan	vstrepenulsja	ot	neožidannosti	+	+	–	–	+	–	–	–
	'Ivan	started	because of	the unexpectedness'								
44.	zemlja	prostudilas'	ot	vozduxa	+	+	–	–	+	–	–	–
	'the earth	got cold	because of	the air'								
45.	lico	raskrasnelos'	ot	bega	+	+	–	–	+	–	–	–
	'[his] face	flushed	because of	the running'								
46.	inspektor	krasilsja	ot	styda	+	+	–	–	+	–	–	–
	'the inspector	colored	because of	shame'								
47.	stepi	svetilis'	ot	solnca	+	+	–	–	+	–	–	–
	'the steppes	shone	because of	the sun'								
48.	Moskva	dymilas'	ot	stuži	+	+	–	–	+	–	–	–
	'Moscow	fumed	because of	the cold'								
49.	pidžak	losnilsja	ot	starosti	+	+	–	–	+	–	–	–
	'the jacket	shone	because of	age'								
50.	oščuščenie	usilivalos'	ot	belizny	+	+	–	–	+	–	–	–
	'the sensation	was strengthened	because of	the whiteness'								
51.	ona	krepilas'	ot	samoljubija	+	+	–	–	+	–	–	–
	'she	took heart	because of	[her] self-respect'								
52.	solnce	umen'šilos'	ot	oseni	+	+	–	–	+	–	–	–
	'the sun	grew smaller	because of	fall'								
53.	ona	rasterjalas'	ot	roskoši	–	–	–	–	+	–	–	–
	'she	was rattled	because of	the luxury'								
54.	Martynenko	napilsja	ot	ščekotlivosti	–	–	–	–	+	–	–	–
	'Martynenko	got drunk	because of	delicacy'								
55.	kartina	potreskalas'	ot	vremeni	–	–	–	–	+	–	–	–
	'the picture	had cracked	because of	time'								
56.	on	morščilsja	ot	dyma	–	+	–	–	–	–	–	–
	'he	squinted	because of	the smoke'								

TABLE 16 (*cont.*)

	N^1	V_{sja}	*ot*	N^2	T1: → $N^2\,V_t\,N^1$	T2: → N^1, $V_{ppp}\,N^2_i$	T3: → $X\,V_t\,N^1$ *ot* N^2	T4: → N^1 *ot* N^2	T5: → N^1, A^V *ot* N^2	T6: → $N^1\,V_{sja}$ *ot* N^2 *k* N^3	T7: → $N^1\,V_t\,N^2$	T8: → N^2, $V_{ppp}\,N^1_i$
57.	mičman	soščurilsja	ot	dyma	–	–	–	–	–	–	–	–
	'the warrant officer	squinted	because of	the smoke'								
58.	kazak	nasupilsja	ot	gorja	–	–	–	–	–	–	–	–
	'the Cossack	scowled	because of	grief'								
59.	Ivan	vz"erošilsja	ot	zlosti	–	–	–	–	–	–	–	–
	'Ivan	became angry	because of	spite'								
60.	polja	poeživalis'	ot	vospominanija	–	–	–	–	–	–	–	–
	'the fields	shivered	because of	the memory'								
61.	my	prosnulis'	ot	strel'by	–	–	–	–	–	–	–	–
	'we	woke up	because of	the shooting'								
62.	Nataša	očnulas'	ot	tolčka	–	–	–	–	–	–	–	–
	'Nataša	came to	because of	the jolt'								
63.	ja	zaikalsja	ot	vozbuždenija	–	–	–	–	–	–	–	–
	'I	stammered	because of	excitement'								
64.	redaktor	zakašlalsja	ot	smexa	–	–	–	–	–	–	–	–
	'the editor	started to cough	because of	laughter'								
65.	ja	zasmejalsja	ot	naslaždenija	+	+	–	–	–	–	–	–
	'I	started to laugh	because of	enjoyment'								
66.	Vera	zajdetsja	ot	zavisti	–	–	–	–	–	–	–	–
	'Vera	will become numb	because of	envy'								
67.	nervoznost'	razygrivaetsja	ot	ètogo	–	–	–	–	–	–	–	–
	'nervousness	flares	because of	this'								
68.	golova	razbalivalas'	ot	cvetov	–	–	–	–	–	–	–	–
	'[his] head	ached	because of	the flowers'								
69.	on	uxmyl'nulsja	ot	vosxiščenija	–	–	–	–	–	–	–	–
	'he	smirked	because of	delight'								
70.	xoxolox	zagorelsja	ot	luča	–	–	–	–	–	–	–	–
	'the crest	shone	because of	the ray'								
71.	èto	slučilos'	ot	ustalosti	–	–	–	–	–	–	–	–
	'this	happened	because of	tiredness'								

radically different meanings from the *-sja* forms. In the case cited, *šaraxat'sja* means 'to bolt', whereas the non-*sja* form means 'to hit something hard'.

The structure of the *-sja* verbs of the *Spatial group* taken as a whole differs markedly from those of the non-*sja* intransitives. In the latter only a small number of very frequent verbs of motion were found. These were normally prefixed with *ot-* or *u-*. In the V_{sja} *Spatial group* the total number of occurrences is much smaller, but the degree of lexical and morphological diversity is considerably larger and the ablative prefixes occur only sporadically — mostly in conjunction with the animate subjects.

4.3.3.2. *Causal Group*

The *Causal group* is negatively opposed to all of the other N^1 V_{sja} *ot* N^2 units by T3. It is impossible to transform examples of the type *inej osypaetsja ot udarov* 'the frost scatters because of the blows' to **X osypaet inej ot udarov* 'X scatters the frost because of the blows', whereas this is possible for all other semantic groups within the N^1 V_{sja} *ot* N^2 construction. The examples of the *Causal group* are characterized positively by T1 and T2. The first transform reverses the position of the two nouns and makes the second the object of the transitive verb. To illustrate: N^1 V_{sja} *ot* $N^2 \rightarrow N^2\ V_t\ N^1$, *inej osypaetsja ot udarov* 'the frost scatters because of the blows' → *udary osypajut inej* 'the blows scatter the frost'. This rearrangement shows both why T3 does not work for this type of example and why the underlying basis of the identification of the group is causal. T3 is impossible because it attempts to introduce a superfluous subject into the sentence. N^2 is the subject of the verb in the kernel form of the utterance. This group corresponds to Janko-Trinickaja's de-objectival classification.

T2 is dependent upon the result of T1. That is, if T1 (T: $\rightarrow N^2\ V_t\ N^1$) is not possible, then T2 (T: $\rightarrow N^1,\ V_{ppp}\ N^2_i$) is automatically excluded. T2 operates as follows: *jad rastopilsja ot znoja* 'the poison melted because of the heat' → *znoj rastopil jad* 'the heat melted the poison'. This transformation again demonstrates the close relationship between passive constructions and the causal use of *ot*, which has been pointed out at several points in our study.[97] Russian has two constructions for the expression of the passive voice. The first and older involves the passive participle system *(jad, rastoplennyj znojem* 'poison, melted by the heat') while the second and more recent utilizes the *-sja* suffix *(jad rastopilsja ot znoja* 'the poison melted because of the heat'). Both derive from the kernel sentence — *znoj rastopil jad* 'the heat melted the poison'. The particular point of interest here is the device used to indicate the agent in the two passive constructions. In CSR both the passive participle and the *-sja* verb constructions can use a noun in the instrumental case to express agent, *e.g.*, *dom postrojen arxitektorom* 'the house is being built by the architect' and *dom stroitsja (arxitektorom)* 'the house is being built (by the archi-

[97] See pages 64–65, 97, and 147.

tect)'.[98] The former is usual for perfective verbs and the latter for imperfectives. In Old Russian, however, the agent of the participial construction could also be indicated by *ot* + N_g, *e.g.*, *ubit" ot" Jaropolka* 'killed by Jaropolk'. This is no longer possible in CSR. In contrast to this, the use of *ot* N to indicate agent in the *-sja* passive construction is quite frequent in the modern language. Furthermore, it does not seem to share the aspect restriction typical of the N^1 V_{sja} N^2_i form. Thus the periphrastic N^1 V_{sja} *ot* N^2, with its freedom from aspectual restriction, is, in some measure, supplanting the older participial construction.[99]

Both T1 and T2 have a number of exceptions. There are several reasons for the atypical cases. Examples 56–60 fail to undergo the transforms because of their highly restricted degree of transitivity. The non-*sja* forms of these verbs, *soščurit'* 'to squint', *morščit'* 'to wrinkle', and *nasupit'* 'to furrow', are transitive, but are limited to one or at the most two or three possible objects. That is, one can *morščit lico* 'to wrinkle [one's] face' or *lob* 'forehead' *soščurit glaza* 'to squint [one's] eyes' and *nasupit' brovi* 'to furrow [one's] brows', but these verbs cannot meaningfully have an animate noun for an object. In other cases such as *ona rasterjalas ot roskoši* 'she got rattled because of the luxury', the *-sja* form of the verb has a different meaning from the non-*sja* source form. In this case the transform *roskoš' rasterjaet ee* means not 'the luxury rattled her', but 'the luxury loses her bit by bit'. The most common single reason underlying negative responses to T1 and T2 is that the non-*sja* source verbs were themselves intransitive, *e.g.*, *prosnut'sja* 'to wake up', *očnut'sja* 'to regain consciousness', *razbalivat'sja* 'to ache', *uxmyt'sja* 'to smirk', *etc.* A few are *reflexiva tantum* — *zasmejat'sja* 'to start to laugh', *zaikat'sja* 'to stammer'. It is interesting to note that these and *zakašljat'sja* 'to start to cough' are the only verbs in this group denoting sounds and that the former two would be found in the 'sound' category of the N V *ot* N group were it not for the obligatory nature of their *-sja* suffix. *Zakašljat'(sja)* does, in fact, occur in this category.

A number of causal examples also admit T5, which converts the verb into an adjective: T: → N^1, A^V *ot* N^2, *stepi svetilis' ot solnca* 'the steppes shone because of the sun' → *stepi, svetlye ot solnca* 'the steppes, alight because of the sun'. This is not surprising in view of the close relationship between adjectives and the expression of causal meaning shown in the analysis of the N, A *ot* N construction and again in the demonstration of the de-adjectival derivation of many of the verbs in the N V *ot* N causal units *(e.g., derevo tjaželeet ot*

[98] In the *-sja* form the agent is not usually indicated by an instrumental noun.

[99] The tension between these competing forms of the passive is probably not very intense since they only marginally share domains of occurrence. The participial forms, apart from the predicative short form of the past passive participle, are common only in literary and learned prose, whereas the *-sja* forms are more frequent in other usages.

plodov 'the tree grows heavy because of the fruits' ← *derevo, tjaželoe ot plodov* 'the tree, heavy because of fruits'). The adjectives in the present case are of two sorts. First, those formed from participles but having achieved independent adjectival status *(vzvolnovannyj* 'agitated', *smuščennyj* 'embarrassed', *etc.)*, and second, those of non-verbal provenience *(dymnyj* 'smoky', *krepkij* 'strong', *etc.)*.

Morphologically these verbs display little of the unity that characterized the causal non-*sja* intransitives. The most noteworthy generalization that can be made about the verbs as a whole is that their distribution in terms of the derivational classes listed on page 149 above is very different from that of the non-*sja* causal intransitives. The latter fall into four such classes: II *(krasnet'* 'to redden'), IX *(čaxnut'* 'to wither'), VII (*kričat'* 'to shout') and VIII *(vizžat'* 'to screech'). The causal *-sja* intransitives occur in these classes only rarely, whereas a very sizeable per cent of them fall into Class V *(obrušit'sja* 'to collapse'), whose members are usually transitive in their non-*sja* forms. The basis of this opposition of derivational classes between the *-sja* and the non-*sja* intransitives lies in the correlation of these verb classes with the categories of transitivity and intransitivity. The verbs of Classes II and IX are almost entirely intransitive and those of VII and VIII very largely so. The *-sja* suffix may be added to most of these verbs but does not, of course, affect their (in)-transitivity. Since there is a close connection between intransitivity and the expression of causal meaning in verbal *ot* constructions, verbs of the above classes only rarely make use of the *-sja* suffix. In contrast, verbs of Class V, which predominate in the *-sja* verb *Causal group*, are, for the most part, transitive in their non-*sja* form and hence must add the transitivity neutralizing *-sja* suffix in order to express causal meaning in conjunction with *ot* N.

The verbs of the *Causal* N V_{sja} *ot* N *group* share with the *Causal* N V *ot* N *group* the fact that ablative prefixes are entirely lacking. There does not appear to be any class restrictions on the character of the nouns, although the dependent noun is non-concrete more of the time than not. Semantically the verbs might be loosely characterized as sharing the meaning of 'non-directional activity'. There is one type of causal example that, while rather common, does not share the transform pattern displayed by most of the causal examples. Examples of the type *opuxoli pojavilis' ot nedoedanija* 'swellings appeared because of starvation' admit only T4, which deletes the verb. This amounts to a formal demonstration of the purely copulative functions of the verb in examples of this type.[100]

[100] Another and very frequent type of copulative verb construction with *ot* is represented by the examples *tabak ostalsja ot otca* 'the tobacco remained from father' or *bol' ostalas' ot ljubvi* 'the pain remained from love'. These also admit deletion of the verb, but do not undergo other transformations. Semantically they do not seem to be closely akin to any of the three V_{sja} groups — *Spatial, Causal,* or *Ablative.*

TABLE 17

Transform Features of 'N¹ V_{sja} *ot* N²' *Units of the Ablative Group*

	N¹	V_{sja}	*ot*	N²	T1: → $N^2 V_t N^1$	T2: → $N^1, V_{ppp} N^2_i$	T3: → $X V_t N^1$ *ot* N^2	T4: → N^1 *ot* N^2	T5: → N^1, A^v *ot* N^2	T6: → $N^1 V_{sja}$ *ot* N^2 *k* N^3	T7: → $N^1 V_t N^2$	T8: → $N^2, V_{ppp} N^1_i$
1.	sapery	otbilis'	ot	kazakov	−	−	+	−	−	−	+	+
	'the sappers	beat off	—	the Cossacks'								
2.	on	otstranilsja	ot	redaktury	−	−	+	−	−	−	+	+
	'he	kept aloof	from	the editorship'								
3.	Karavaev	otmaxivalsja	ot	Ivanova	−	−	+	−	−	−	+	+
	'Karavaev	waved off	—	Ivanov'								
4.	Karavaev	otmaxivalsja	ot	kašlja	−	−	+	−	−	−	+	+
	'Karavaev	waved off	—	the coughing'								
5.	ja	uklonjalsja	ot	raboty	−	−	+	−	−	−	+	+
	'I	shunned	—	work'								
6.	ja	otložilsja	ot	mira	−	−	+	−	−	−	+	+
	'I	detached [myself]	from	the world'								
7.	park	otrjaxivalsja	ot	doždej	−	−	+	−	−	−	+	+
	'the park	shook off	—	the rain'								
8.	čelovek	otkazyvaetsja	ot	prošlogo	−	−	+	−	−	−	−	+
	'man	is repudiating	—	the past'								
9.	ja	otkazalsja	ot	česti	−	−	+	−	−	−	−	+
	'I	refused	—	the honor'								
10.	Ivan	otreksja	ot	proekta	−	−	+	−	−	−	−	+
	'Ivan	repudiated	—	the project'								
11.	Nikolaj	otreksja	ot	prestola	−	−	+	−	−	−	−	+
	'Nikolaj	abdicated	—	the throne'								
12.	ja	uderžalsja	ot	smexa	−	−	+	−	−	−	−	+
	'I	refrained	from	laughter'								
13.	izdatel'stva	vožderzalis'	ot	pečatanija	−	−	+	−	−	−	−	+
	'the publishers	abstained	from	printing'								
14.	čelovek	otličaetsja	ot	životnogo	−	−	+	−	+	−	−	−
	'man	differs	from	animals'								
15.	žizn'	otličaetsja	ot	groteska	−	−	+	−	+	−	−	−
	'life	differs	from	the grotesque'								
16.	sluga	raznilsja	ot	nix	−	−	+	−	+	−	−	−
	'the servant	differs	from	them'								
17.	student	osvobodilsja	ot	služby	−	−	+	−	+	−	−	−
	'a student	was freed	from	service'								
18.	Neva	očistilas'	ot	l'da	−	−	+	−	+	−	−	−
	'the Neva	was cleared	of	ice'								

TABLE 17 (*cont.*)

	N^1	V_{sja}	*ot*	N^2	T1: → $N^2 V_t N^1$	T2: → N^1, $V_{ppp} N^2_i$	T3: → $X V_t N^1$ *ot* N^2	T4: → N^1 *ot* N^2	T5: → N^1, A^V *ot* N^2	T6: → $N^1 V_{sja}$ *ot* N^2 *k* N^3	T7: → $N^1 V_t N^2$	T8: → N^2, $V_{ppp} N^1_i$
19.	oficer	otdelilsja	ot	junkerov	−	−	+	−	+	−	−	−
	'an officer	was detached	from	the Junkers'								
20.	oblast'	obosobljalas'	ot	drugix	−	−	+	−	+	−	−	−
	'an area	was isolated	from	the others'								
21.	kamni	obnažatsja	ot	vody	−	−	+	−	+	−	−	−
	'the stones	are bared	from	the water'								
22.	ded	prjačetsja	ot	ženy	−	−	+	−	−	−	−	−
	'grandfather	hides	from	[his] wife'								
23.	on	sprjatalsja	ot	solnca	−	−	+	−	−	−	−	−
	'he	hid	from	the sun'								
24.	evrej	prikryvalsja	ot	snega	−	−	+	−	−	−	−	−
	'the Jew	covered himself	from	the snow'								
25.	my	ukrylis'	ot	doždja	−	−	+	−	−	−	−	−
	'we	sheltered ourselves	from	the rain'								
26.	ja	skrylsja	ot	nego	−	−	+	−	−	−	−	−
	'I	hid	from	him'								
27.	on	otsiživalsja	ot	babki	−	−	+	−	−	−	−	−
	'he	hid	from	grandmother'								
28.	on	smylsja	ot	nas	−	−	+	−	−	−	−	−
	'he	disappeared	from	us'								
29.	my	spasalis'	ot	tarakanov	−	−	+	−	−	−	−	−
	'we	escaped	—	the cockroaches'								
30.	my	izbavilis'	ot	opasnosti	−	−	+	−	−	−	−	−
	'we	were saved	from	danger'								
31.	my	izbavilis'	ot	banditov	−	−	+	−	−	−	−	−
	'we	were saved	from	bandits'								
32.	čelovek	oberegalsja	ot	pyli	−	−	+	−	−	−	−	−
	'the man	protected himself	from	the dust'								
33.	ty	ogradilsja	ot	nas	−	−	+	−	−	−	−	−
	'you	guarded yourself	from	us'								
34.	vy	otkupilis'	ot	tjurmy	−	−	+	−	−	−	−	−
	'you	were ransomed	from	prison'								
35.	Liza	opravilas'	ot	ispuga	−	−	+	−	−	−	−	−
	'Liza	recovered	from	the fright'								

TABLE 17 (*cont.*)

N^1	V_{sja}	*ot*	N^2	T1: → $N^2 V_t N^1$	T2: → N^1, $V_{ppp} N^2_i$	T3: → X $V_t N^1$ *ot* N^2	T4: → N^1 *ot* N^2	T5: → N^1, A^v *ot* N^2	T6: → $N^1 V_{sja}$ *ot* N^2 *k* N^3	T7: → $N^1 V_t N^2$	T8: → N^2, $V_{ppp} N^1_i$
36. Kleopatra	probuždaetsja	ot	zadumčivosti	–	–	+	–	–	–	–	–
'Cleopatra	awakes	from	[her] pensiveness'								
37. Ivan	prosnulsja	ot	sna	–	–	+	–	–	–	–	–
'Ivan	awoke	from	sleep'								
38. on	očnulsja	ot	dremy	–	–	+	–	–	–	–	–
'he	came to	from	the doze'								

4.3.3.3. *Ablative Group*

The *Ablative group* is not a single transformationally defined group, but rather a loosely united collection of small subgroups and isolated examples. As a unifying feature, they share only a positive response to T3. That is, they all undergo a transformation of the type N^1 V_{sja} *ot* N^2 → X V_t N^1 *ot* N^2: *my ukrylis' ot doždja* 'we were sheltered from the rain' → *X ukryl nas ot doždja* 'X sheltered us from the rain'. This feature classes the type as a variety of Janko-Trinickaja's de-objectival category. It does not distinctively characterize the *Ablative group*, however, since the spatial examples also undergo T3.[101] The *Ablative group* breaks down into three small subgroups that have distinctive transformational characteristics and into several smaller non-formal semantic groups.

The first of the small formal subgroups, which will be termed the *pseudo-reflexive*, is represented by examples 1–7 in Table 17. Transformationally these examples are characterized by T7 and T8. T7 restates the N^1 V_{sja} *ot* N^2 unit as N^1 V_t N^2: *sapery otbilis' ot kazakov* 'the sappers beat off the Cossacks' → *sapery otbili kazakov* 'the sappers beat off the Cossacks'. T8 recasts the source phrase into the form N^2, V_{ppp} N^1_i: *kazaki, otbitie saperami* 'the Cossacks, beaten off by the sappers'.

It is to be noted that this *Ablative subgroup* is diametrically opposed to the homomorphic *-sja* causal units in its transformational reflexes. Compare the following pairs:

[101] The *Spatial group* is formally opposed to the *Ablative group* by the fact it can be expanded by *k* N, whereas the latter cannot.

1. Causal: T1.

$N^1\ V_{sja}$ ot N^2	$\rightarrow$	$N^2\ V_t\ N^1$
dom obrušilsja ot vzryvov		*vzryvi obrušili dom*
'the house collapsed because of the explosions'		'the explosions destroyed the house'

2. Pseudo-Reflexive: T7.

$N^1\ V_{sja}$ ot N^2	$\rightarrow$	$N^1\ V_t\ N^2$
park otrjaxivalsja ot doždja		*park otrjaxival dožd'*
'the park shook off the rain'		'the park shook off the rain'

3. Causal: T2.

$N^1\ V_{sja}$ ot N^2	$\rightarrow$	N^1, $V_{ppp}\ N^2$
jad rastopilsja ot znoja		*jad, rastoplennyj znojem*
'the poison melted because of the heat'		'the poison, melted by the heat'

4. Pseudo-Reflexive: T8.

$N^1\ V_{sja}$ ot N^2	$\rightarrow$	N^2, $V_{ppp}\ N^1_i$
ja uklonjalsja ot raboty		*rabota, uklonennaja mnoj*
'I shunned work'		'the work, shunned by me'

These contrasting sets provide a striking example of the degree of syntactic homonymy present in the $N^1\ V_{sja}$ *ot* N^2 framework. Examples of a single constructional pattern may be resolved into two kernels in which the subject and object roles are diametrically opposed. Within this particular subgroup the meaning of the phrase remains substantially the same with or without the *-sja* + *ot* complex. Another variant transformation, which these examples can undergo, involves rewriting the *-sja ot* + N^3 complex as N^3 *ot sebja* 'from oneself': *e.g.*, *on otstranilsja ot redaktury* 'he kept away from the editorship' → *on otstranil redakturu ot sebja* 'he kept the editorship away from himself'.

From the derivational point of view, the only common feature of the verbs of this group is the presence of the ablative *ot-/u-* prefixes. Additionally, these verbs, like the great majority of verbs in the *Ablative group*, are characterized by the property of strong government. In token of this, they are often listed in dictionaries with an accompanying *ot* to indicate that in one or more of their meanings they obligatorily occur in combination with the preposition (or better post-position) *ot*.

The second of the formal subgroups (examples 8–13) is similar to the group just discussed in that its members admit T8, *e.g.*, *ja otkazalsja ot česti* 'I refused the honor' → *čest'*, *otkazannaja mnoj* 'the honor, refused by me'. It does not admit T7, however (T: $\not\rightarrow$ **ja otkazal čest'* 'I refused the honor'). The existence of the past passive participle forms *(otkazannyj* 'refused', *otrečennyj* 'repudiated'), however, indicates that at one time the non-*sja* forms of these verbs were transitives. Now, like the pseudo-reflexive units, they constitute fixed phrases characterized by strong government. All four examples have the general meaning of 'rejection'.

The last of the formally characterized *Ablative subgroups* is that transformationally characterized by its derivational relationship to parallel adjectival constructions (examples 14–21). This is shown by T5: $N^1\ V_{sja}$ *ot* $N^2 \rightarrow N^1$, A^V *ot* N^2 *(oblast' obosobljalas' ot drugix* 'the area stood apart from the others' → *oblast'*, *obosoblennaja ot drugix* 'an area, detached from others'). The unity of this subgroup is further indicated by the fact that the examples all permit complementation by an instrumental noun, *e.g.*, *čelovek otličaetsja ot životnogo umom* 'man differs from the animal by [his] mind' or *student osvobodilsja ot služby bolezn'ju* 'the student was freed from the service by illness'. Of the several roots represented, only two use the ablative prefixes typical of strong government. The prefix *ob-* occurs four times in connection with the seven roots listed.

Most of the remaining examples fall into several small semantic categories. Transformationally, they are characterized only by the possibility of $N^1\ V_{sja}$ *ot* $N^2 \rightarrow X\ V_t\ N^1$ *ot* N^2 (T3). Examples 22–27 have the meaning 'to hide from'. Numbers 29–33 mean 'to save from' or 'to guard against'. The ablative prefixes are not typical of these verbs, although all of them occur very frequently with *ot* phrases and hence are characterized by strong government.

The final three examples with the verbs *probuždat'sja* 'to awake', *prosnut'sja* 'to awake', and *očnut'sja* 'to regain consciousness' share a degree of semantic similarity. They have the meaning 'to (re)gain consciousness'. The dependent nouns indicate the prior state of the subject. Only the verb *probuždat'sja* has a transitive form and undergoes T3 (T: → *X probuždaet Kleopatru ot zadumčivosti* 'X awakens Cleopatra from [her] pensiveness'). No other transformation is admitted by any of the three examples, although they do share another common semantic feature. In the examples cited where N^2 designates a state or condition of the subject, the meaning is clearly ablative. In cases where the role of N^2 is played by a less abstract noun, the meaning of all three shifts radically and they express causal relations. Compare the following three examples with those in Table 17: 1) *Kleopatra probuždaetsja ot groma* 'Cleopatra awakens because of the thunder', 2) *Ivan prosnulsja ot strel'by* 'Ivan awoke because of the shooting', and 3) *on očnulsja ot tolčka* 'he came to because of the jolt'. This stands in sharp contrast to most of the verbs of this group, which retain their 'ablative' meaning regardless of the following noun, *e.g.*, *my izbavilis' ot banditov* 'we were saved from bandits', *ot ljubvi* 'from love', *ot raboty* 'from work', *ot begstva* 'from flight', *etc.*

Thus the members of the *Ablative group* taken as a whole tend to have three features in common: 1) they admit T3 *(kamni obnažilis' ot vody* 'the rocks were bared from the water' → *X obnažit kamni ot vody* 'X bares the rocks from the water'); 2) with the aforementioned exceptions, they display the ablative prefixes *ot-/u-;* 3) they generally are characterized by a high degree of strong government.

The use of transforms (and also of derivational data) in the analysis of N V_{sja} *ot* N units, although illuminating in certain spots, proves to be markedly less effective than in the case of N^1 V *ot* N^2 units. Some possible reasons for this were touched upon in the foregoing analysis. In the broadest sense, the problem is connected with the nature of *-sja* verbs in Russian. Every major Russian grammar book attempts to make a description of the different meanings of *-sja* and to categorize the verbs accordingly. It is highly significant that each grammar has a somewhat different list of categories and that in no case are the groups based on formal criteria.

The problem underlying all of these classificatory attempts has been succinctly pointed out by A. V. Isačenko, who notes that these semantic groups are "... not so much a matter of the ambiguity of the affix *-sja/-s'* as of the lexical meaning of the verbs, which constitute these groups."[102] Since almost any Russian verb can take the *-sja* suffix, Isačenko's observation has one extremely important consequence. The resolution of the multiple ambiguity of *sja*-verb constructions is not a matter of the *-sja* suffix, but of the entire semantic spectrum of the Russian verb. Even taken within the restricted context of N V_{sja} *ot* N, the variety of verbs represented is very great.

4.3.4. *Analysis of* N^1 V_t N^2 *ot* N^3' *Units*

The occurrence of dependent *ot* phrases in constructions with transitive verbs is much less frequent than in such constructions involving intransitive verbs. In the material examined, structures of the type N^1 V_t N^2 *ot* N^3 accounted for less than one-quarter of *ot* N occurrences in conjunction with verbs.[103] In general, the transitive verb group resembles the intransitive *-sja* verb group in the particular root morphemes and the types of transformationally defined semantic groupings. They are both opposed to the sharply defined unmarked (non-*sja)* intransitive verbal constructions by their relative lack of formal and/or semantic unity. The similarity of the *-sja* intransitive and the transitive verbs is not surprising since the former, in their great majority, consist of transitive verbs to which the *-sja* suffix has been added.

The general pattern, as defined by the transforms, consists of a *Spatial*

[102] Isačenko, *II*, 382.

[103] Some possible reasons for this have been mentioned above. See pages 152–153.

group, a *Causal group*, a *Source group*, and an *Ablative group*. With the exception of the *Source group*, this is the same set of categories as was found for the *-sja* units. As was the case for the *-sja* constructions, the spatial and causal examples present a fairly high degree of internal unity, whereas the large *Ablative group* includes a rather diverse collection of examples, which are united primarily by their non-membership in the *Spatial*, *Source*, or *Causal groups*. The basis of the transformational characterization of the ablative examples is their inability to undergo any of the requisite transforms.

The following transformations are utilized in the analysis of N^1 V_t N^2 *ot* N^3 units:

T1:	N^1 V_t N^2 ot N^3 *žena otvela gromil ot doma* 'the wife led the pogromists away from the house'	→	N^1 V N^2 ot N^3 k N^4 *žena otvela gromil ot doma k cerkvi* 'the wife led the pogromists away from the house to the church'
T2:	*načal'nik zabral vas ot dobroty* 'the chief took you because of kindness'	→	A^{n3} N^1 V N^2 *dobryj načal'nik zabral vas* 'the kind chief took you'
T3:	*Aleksej terjaet soznanie ot ustalosti* 'Aleksej loses consciousness because of tiredness'	→	N^1 $V^{n3}_{(sja)}$ *Aleksej ustal* 'Aleksej got tired'
T4:	*oni otkryli rty ot izumlenija* 'they opened [their] mouths because of amazement'	→	X V^{n3} N^1 *X izumljaet ix* 'X amazes them'
T5:	*čitatel' polučil svedenie ot knigi* 'the reader got the information from a book'	→	N^3 V^{n2} (N^1) *kniga osvedomljaet čitatelja* 'the book informs the reader'
T6:	*ja slyšal slovo ot otca* 'I heard the word from [my] father'	→	N^1 V_t A^{n3} N^2 *ja slyšal otcovo slovo* 'I heard the paternal word'
T7:	*on ostereg ee ot ošibok* 'he forewarned her against errors'	→	N^2 $V^{n3}_{(sja)}$ *ona ošibaetsja* 'she errs'

The examples of the N^1 V_t N^2 *ot* N^3 group fall into the following four groups in terms of their reactions to the above transformations.

GROUP	T1	T2	T3	T4	T5	T6	T7
Spatial	+	—	—	—	—	—	—
Causal	—	+	+	+	—	—	—
Source	—	—	—	—	+	+	—
Ablative	—	—	—	—	—	—	—

We will now turn to a more detailed examination of each of these groups.

4.3.4.1. *Spatial Group*

The spatial examples of the N^1 V_t N^2 *ot* N^3 construction are transformationally distinguished by the fact that they can be expanded by the addition of *k* N, *e.g., ja otvel glaza ot ugla* + *k dveri* 'I directed [my] eyes away from the corner to the door'. The spatial examples do not systematically undergo any of the other listed transformations. The spatial examples of the N^1 V_t N^2 *ot* N^3 construction differ structurally from those of the other verbal constructions only in one respect. The spatial examples of the two verbal groups examined earlier commonly occur with either single prepositional complementation *(ja otošel ot doma* 'I went away from the house') or with dual prepositional complementation *(poezd taščilsja ot Kieva do Odessy* 'the train dragged along from Kiev to Odessa'). The identifying characteristic of spatial examples is that the former type can always be expanded to form the latter. For the unmarked intransitive verbs and for the intransitive verbs marked by *-sja,* the dual prepositional form occurs comparatively frequently.[104] For spatial examples of the transitive verb construction, however, the dual prepositional construction, while possible in principle, seems to appear only rarely. None of the examples collected is of the structural type N^1 V_t N^2 *ot* N^3 *k/do* N^4, although informants do not reject *de novo* examples.

Two factors may be relevant to this situation. First, spatial examples are relatively rare in the constructional type under discussion. Second, there is probably a tendency to limit the number of dependent modifiers of a verb. In constructions of the type N^1 V_t N^2 *ot* N^3, the verb already has two dependent elements (N^2 and *ot* N^3). It may be that there is a tendency to avoid overloading the verb with still another dependent element. In the case of intransitive verbal constructions where the direct object is automatically excluded, the dual prepositional complementation represents a lighter dependency load for the verb.

[104] See Tables 11 and 15.

TABLE 18

Transform Features of 'N^1 V_t N^2 ot N^3' Units of the Spatial Group

	N^1	V_t	N^2	*ot*	N^3	T1: → $N^1 V N^2$ *ot* N^3 *k* N^4	T2: → $A^{n3} N^1 V N^2$	T3: → $N^1 V^{n3}_{(sja)}$	T4: → $X V^{n3} N^1$	T5: → $N^3 V^{n2} (N^1)$	T6: → $N^1 V_t A^{n3} N^2$	T7: → $N^2 V^{n3}_{(sja)}$
1.	on	uvel	menja	ot	ljudej	+	–	–	–	–	–	–
	'he	led away	me	from	the people'							
2.	popytka	uvodit	issledovatelja	ot	materiala	+	–	–	–	–	–	–
	'the attempt	leads away	the investigator	from	the material'							
3.	ja	otvel	glaza	ot	ugla	+	–	–	–	–	–	–
	'I	directed away	[my] eyes	from	the corner'							
4.	žena	otvela	gromil	ot	doma	+	–	–	–	–	–	–
	'the wife	led away	the pogromists	from	the house'							
5.	zanjatija	otveli	Rajskogo	ot	predanij	+	–	–	–	–	–	–
	'[his] studies	led away	Rajskij	from	traditions'							
6.	paroxod	unosil	menja	ot	berega	+	–	–	–	–	–	–
	'the ship	carried away	me	from	the shore'							
7.	Lena	ottaščila	menja	ot	kraja	+	–	–	–	–	–	–
	'Lena	dragged away	me	from	the edge'							
8.	letčiki	ottjanuli	ix	ot	aèrodroma	+	–	–	–	–	–	–
	'the fliers	drew off	them	from	the airfield'							
9.	on	otobral	stul	ot	steny	+	–	–	–	–	–	–
	'he	took away	the chair	from	the wall'							
10.	my	otbrosili	ee	ot	goroda	+	–	–	–	–	–	–
	'we	threw back	them	from	the town'							
11.	voiska	otžali	denikincev	ot	Orla	+	–	–	–	–	–	–
	'the troops	pressed back	the Denikinites	from	Orlov'							
12.	policija	otžimali	tolpu	ot	sten	+	–	–	–	–	–	–
	'the police	pressed back	the crowd	from	the walls'							
13.	on	otgreb	sneg	ot	sten	+	–	–	–	–	–	–
	'he	raked away	the snow	from	the walls'							
14.	ona	otxidyvala	lokony	ot	lica	+	–	–	–	–	+	–
	'she	brushed away	the curls	from	[her] face'							
15.	–	otženi	smert'	ot	bat'ki	+	–	–	–	–	+	–
	'–	drive away	death	from	father'							
16.	ja	gnal	mysl'	ot	sebja	+	–	–	–	–	–	–
	'I	drove away	the idea	from	myself'							
17.	on	podnimal	golovu	ot	zapisej	+	–	+	–	–	–	–
	'he	lifted	[his] head	from	the records'							
18.	tetja	otšvyrivala	ix	ot	sebja	+	–	–	–	–	–	–
	'[his] aunt	flung away	them	from	herself'							

TABLE 19

Transform Features of 'N^1 V_t N^2 ot N^3' Units of the Causal Group

	N^1	V_t	N^2	*ot*	N^3	T1: → N^1 V N^2 *ot* N^3 *k* N^4	T2: → A^{n3} N^1 V N^2	T3: → N^1 $V^{n3}_{(sja)}$	T4: → X V^{n3} N^1	T5: → N^3 V^{n2} (N^1)	T6: → N^1 V_t A^{n3} N^2	T7: → N^2 $V^{n3}_{(sja)}$
1.	satana	gložet	kosti	ot	zlosti	−	+	+	+	−	−	−
	'Satan	gnaws	the bones	because of	spite'							
2.	komandir	kusal	zemlju	ot	dosady	−	+	+	+	−	−	−
	'the commander	bit	the earth	because of	vexation'							
3.	vrač	soščuril	glaza	ot	zlosti	−	+	+	+	−	−	−
	'the doctor	squinted	[his] eyes	because of	spite'							
4.	on	pozabyl	imena	ot	starosti	−	+	+	+	−	−	−
	'he	forgot	the names	because of	age'							
5.	on	vyryval	volosy	ot	zlosti	−	+	+	+	−	−	−
	'he	tore out	[his] hair	because of	spite'							
6.	Izja	bil	stenu	ot	dosady	−	+	+	+	−	−	−
	'Izja	beat	the wall	because of	vexation'							
7.	oni	otkryli	rty	ot	izumlenija	−	+	+	+	−	−	−
	'they	opened	[their] mouths	because of	amazement'							
8.	načal'nik	zakryl	glaza	ot	udovol'stvija	−	+	+	+	−	−	−
	'the chief	closed	[his] eyes	because of	satisfaction'							
9.	čelovek	priotkrivaet	rot	ot	udivlenija	−	+	+	+	−	+	−
	'the man	half-opened	[his] mouth	because of	amazement'							
10.	Sidorkin	prikryl	glaza	ot	sčast'ja	−	+	+	+	−	+	−
	'Sidorkin	closed	[his] eyes	because of	happiness'							
11.	Petr	gryzet	zausenicy	ot	neterpenija	−	+	+	−	−	+	−
	'Petr	gnaws	[his] hangnails	because of	impatience'							
12.	Aleksej	terjaet	soznanie	ot	ustalosti	−	+	+	−	−	+	−
	'Aleksej	loses	consciousness	because of	tiredness'							
13.	načal'nik	zabral	vas	ot	dobroty	−	+	+	−	−	−	−
	'the chief	took	you	because of	kindness'							
14.	soldaty	izževajut	okurki	ot	boli	−	+	+	−	−	−	−
	'the soldiers	chew	the butts	because of	the pain'							
15.	ja	tolkal	ego	ot	negodovanija	−	+	+	−	−	−	−
	'I	shoved	him	because of	indignation'							
16.	ja	podnjal	glaza	ot	okrika	−	+	+	+	−	−	−
	'I	lifted	[my] eyes	because of	the shout'							

The great majority of the verbs of the *Spatial group* contain one of the ablative prefixes *ot-* or *u-*. The only unprefixed verb, *gnat'*, is paralleled by an example where the same root is prefixed by *ot-*. Lexically the verbs are very similar to those of the *Spatial group* of the intransitive *-sja* group.

4.3.4.2. *Causal Group*

Causal examples of the $N^1 V_t N^2$ *ot* N^3 construction are proportionately much less common than in the intransitive constructional types. Furthermore, the examples tend to be of a stereotyped nature. The key transformation in the characterization of the causal units is T3: $N^1 V_t N^2$ *ot* $N^3 \rightarrow N^1 V^{n3}_{(sja)}$ *(satana gložet kosti ot zlosti* 'Satan gnaws the bones because of spite' → *satana zlitsja* 'Satan becomes angry').[105] This transformation, which all of the causal examples undergo, demonstrates that the dependent noun can be restated as a verb which serves as a predicate for the subject noun N^1. N^3 does not relate to either the original verb or its object. The transformational demonstration of this relationship is carried a step further by T2, which recasts N^3 as an adjective modifying the subject; *e.g., zlostnyj satana gložet kosti* 'malicious Satan gnaws the bones'. This transform shows N^3 to be an attribute of N^1.

In some cases N^3 (examples 1–10) may be viewed as an action affecting the subject. This is illustrated by T4, which restates N^3 as a transitive verb with N^1 as its object; *e.g., vrač soščuril glaza ot zlosti* 'the doctor squinted [his] eyes because of spite' → *X zlil vrača* 'X angered the doctor' (and *vrač soščuril glaza* 'the doctor squinted [his] eyes'). Finally a small group of examples (7–10), all involving forms of the verb root $\sqrt{kry}$, admit T5, which transforms N^3 into an adjectival modifier of N^2; *e.g., Sidorkin prikryl glaza ot sčast'ja* 'Sidorkin closed [his] eyes because of happiness' → *Sidorkin prikryl sčastlivye glaza* 'Sidorkin closed [his] happy eyes'. These constitute synechdochical restatements of T2, *i.e., sčastlivyj Sidorkin prikryl glaza* 'the happy Sidorkin closed [his] eyes'.

Apart from their transformational reflexes, the examples in Table 19 display several points of interest. All of the subject nouns refer to persons and the lexical range of N^3 is very limited. The great majority of causal examples of this structural type have one of a very small number of abstract nouns. The units *ot zlosti* 'spite', *ot ustalosti* 'tiredness', and *ot boli* 'pain' are so frequent as to approach adverbial status. The verbs and their objects also represent a restricted lexical cass. No less than six of the sixteen examples (1, 2, 7, 9, and 11 and 14) involve the mouth while four concern motion of the eyes (3, 8, 10, 16) and one the hair (5). Thus it becomes evident that the expression of causal meaning in $N^1 V_t N^2$ *ot* N^3 units is a rather marginal phenomenon and in large measure involves various combinations of a small number of lexical items.

[105] If so desired, the $N^1 V_t N^2$ *ot* N^3 construction may be viewed as the result of an embedding transformation: $N^1 V_{(sja)} + N^1 V_t N^2 \rightarrow N^1 V_t N^2$ *ot* $N_i V_{sja}$.

TABLE 20

Transform Features of 'N^1 V_t N^2 *ot* N^3' *Units of the Source Group*

	N^1	Vt	N^2	*ot*	N^3	T1: → N^1 V N^2 *ot* N^3 *k* N^4	T2: → A^{n3} N^1 V N^2	T3: → N^1 $V^{n3}_{(sja)}$	T4: → X V^{n3} N^1	T5: → N^3 V^{n2} (N^1)	T6: → N^1 V_t A^{n3} N^2	T7: → N^2 V^{n3}
1.	ja	slyšal	slovo	ot	otca	−	−	−	−	−	+	−
	'I	heard	the word	from	father'							
2.	ja	slyšal	sravnenie	ot	Babelja	−	−	−	−	+	+	−
	'I	heard	the comparision	from	Babel' '							
3.	ja	slyšal	kličku	ot	brata	−	−	−	−	+	+	−
	'I	heard the	the nick-name	from	[my] brother'							
4.	my	uznali	izvestie	ot	voznicy	−	−	−	−	+	+	−
	'we	learned	the news	from	the driver'							
5.	my	uznali	rasskaz	ot	Babelja	−	−	−	−	+	+	−
	'we	learned	the tale	from	Babel' '							
6.	on	vyvedal	istoriju	ot	navodčika	−	−	−	−	−	−	−
	'he	found out	the story	from	the gun-layer'							
7.	on	zaslužil	uprek	ot	sestry	−	−	−	−	+	+	−
	'he	merited	the reproach	from	[his] sister'							
8.	čitatel'	polučil	svedenie	ot	knigi	−	−	−	−	+	+	−
	'the reader	got	the information	from	a book'							
9.	Nadja	polučila	telegrammu	ot	podrugi	−	−	−	−	+	+	−
	'Nadja	got	a telegram	from	[her] friend'							
10.	ja	polučila	den'gi	ot	otca	−	−	−	−	−	+	−
	'I	got	the money	from	father'							
11.	on	polučil	raznos	ot	direktora	−	−	−	−	+	+	−
	'he	got	a dressing down	from	the director'							
12.	redakcija	polučila	zapros	ot	komissara	−	−	−	−	+	+	−
	'the editorship	got	an inquiry	from	the commissar'							
13.	my	ždali	milostej	ot	prirody	−	−	−	−	+	+	−
	'we	expected	kindness	from	nature'							
14.	on	treboval	poznanij	ot	nas	−	−	−	−	+	+	−
	'he	demanded	knowledge	from	us'							
15.	oni	xoteli	otvetov	ot	soldat	−	−	−	−	+	+	−
	'they	wanted	answers	from	the soldiers'							
16.	ja	unasledoval	počtenie	to	otca	−	−	−	−	+	+	−
	'I	inherited	the respect	from	[my] father'							

4.3.4.3. *Source Group*

The *Source group* is defined by two transformations. The first of these, T5, involves the restatement of N^3 as the subject of a verb derived from N^2: $N^1 V_t N^2$ *ot* $N^3 \rightarrow N^3 V^{n2}$ *(ja slyšal sravnenie ot Babelja* 'I heard the comparison from Babel' → *Babel' sravnivaet* 'Babel' compares'). In the examples admitting T5, N^3 indicates the source of some type of communication. The accusative noun (N^2) and the noun that serves as the object of *ot* combine in this type to indicate the source and the communication received by the subject of the verb. The attributive nature of the N^2 *ot* N^3 unit is indicated by T6, which recasts N^3 as an adjective modifying N^2: $N^1 V_t N^2$ *ot* $N^3 \rightarrow N^1 V_t A^{n2} N^2$ *(on polučil raznos ot direktora* 'he got a dressing down from the director' → *on polučil direktorskij raznos* 'he got the director's dressing down'). Both of these transforms demonstrate that the unique factor in this type, in contrast to the spatial or causal types, is that N^3 relates to N^2 and not to the verb or to the subject as in the types just mentioned.

Three of the verbs represented in this group *(ždat'* 'to wait', *trebovat'* 'to require', and *xotet'* 'to wish') have the property of taking their object in the genitive case. Derivationally, the verbs of the *Source group* are opposed to those of the *Ablative group* by the relative rarity of the prefixes *ot-* and *u-*. Although *u-* occurs as the prefix of three of the ten verbs listed, it serves to form the perfective aspect in two cases *(u-slyšat'* 'to hear' and *u-nasledovat'* 'to inherit') and occurs in both aspect forms of only one *(uznat'/uznavat'* 'to find out').[106] As a whole this group is parallel to the *Communication-Originator group* discussed in that part of the chapter on nominal constructions.[107]

4.3.4.4. *Ablative Group*

The *Ablative group* of the $N^1 V_t N^2$ *ot* N^3 construction very closely resembles that of the $N^1 V_{sja} N^2$ *ot* N^3 constructional type. Consequently, little new can be said about it. Like their *-sja* counterparts, the ablative transitive verb *ot* constructions do not form a single unified group. The ablative examples which constitute the largest class of $N^1 V_t N^2$ *ot* N^3 constructions, are formally classed together because they do not systematically undergo any of the transformations that specified the spatial, source, or causal examples.

The majority of the ablative examples (1–23) admit none of the transforms. The remaining examples fall into three transformationally defined groups, although these groups do not appear to correspond to any intuitively apparent

[106] It might be argued that *u-* in contrast to *ot-* does not have inherent ablative meaning since in its prepositional use it often has a non-motion meaning, *e.g.*, *My stojali u kassy* 'We were standing by the box office'. The ablative meaning occurs only when it is used (either as a prefix or as a preposition) with verbs specifying motion.

[107] See pages 57–61.

TABLE 21

Transform Features of 'N^1 V_t N^2 ot N^3' Units of the Ablative Groups

	N^1	V_t	N^2	*ot*	N^3	T1: → N^1 V N^2 *ot* N^3 *k* N^4	T2: → A^{n3} N^1 V N^2	T3: → N^1 $V^{n3}_{(sja)}$	T4: → X V^{n3} N^1	T5: → N^3 V^{n2} (N^1)	T6: → N^1 V_t A^{n3} N^2	T7: → N^2 V^{n3}
1.	deva	izbavit	menja	ot	nix	—	—	—	—	—	—	—
	'the maid	will save	me	from	them'							
2.	luna	zagoraživaet	zvezdy	ot	nas	—	—	—	—	—	—	—
	'the moon	fenced off	the stars	from	us'							
3.	on	otkleil	meč	ot	ladony	—	—	—	—	—	—	—
	'he	unstuck	the sword	from	[his] palm'							
4.	Babel'	obereg	tajnu	ot	vsex	—	—	—	—	—	—	—
	'Babel'	guarded	the secret	from	everyone'							
5.	ja	oberegal	privjazannost'	ot	glaz	—	—	—	—	—	—	—
	'I	guarded	[her] affectionateness	from	[their] eyes'							
6.	Lenja	otnjal	ruku	ot	lica	—	—	—	—	—	—	—
	'Lenja	removed	[her] hand	from	[my] face'							
7.	on	otličil	plač	ot	smexa	—	—	—	—	—	—	—
	'he	differentiated	the wailing	from	the laughter'							
8.	sud	otdelil	zoloto	ot	primesi	—	—	—	—	—	—	—
	'the court	separated	the gold	from	the mixture'							
9.	tolpa	otdelila	nas	ot	Suboča	—	—	—	—	—	—	—
	'the crowd	separated	us	from	Suboč'							

10.	on	otdiraet	doski	ot	kryl'ca	–	–	–	–	–	+	–
	'he	rips off	the boards	from	the wing'							
11.	ona	prikryla	golovu	ot	snega	–	–	–	–	–	–	–
	'he	covered	[his] head	from	the snow'							
12.	Svita	zakryla	Nikolaja	ot	nas	–	–	–	–	–	–	–
	'Svita	hid	Nikolaj	from	us'							
13.	gory	ukryvajut	Tiflis	ot	vetrov	–	–	–	–	–	–	–
	'the mountains	shelter	Tiflis	from	the winds'							
14.	otec	skryval	dolgi	ot	mamy	–	–	–	–	–	–	–
	'father	concealed	the debts	from	mamma'							
15.	on	prjačet	niščenstvo	ot	Tamary	–	–	–	–	–	–	–
	'he	hides	the poverty	from	Tamara'							
16.	on	otpugnul	klientov	ot	portnogo	–	–	–	–	–	–	–
	'he	frightened off	the clients	from	the tailor'							
17.	žavoronki	spasut	nas	ot	vojny	–	–	–	–	–	–	+
	'the larks	will save	us	from	war'							
18.	my	taili	smert'	ot	grafini	–	–	–	–	–	–	–
	'we	concealed	the death	from	the countess'							
19.	Vdovuškin	obter	termometr	ot	rastvora	–	–	–	–	–	–	–
	'Vdovuškin	wiped [free]	the thermometer	of	the solution'							
20.	vojska	otrezali	gorodki	ot	Moskvy	–	–	–	–	–	–	–
	'the troops	cut off	the towns	from	Moscow'							
21.	ja	otorval	glaza	ot	knigi	–	–	–	–	–	–	–
	'I	tore away	[my] eyes	from	the book'							
22.	stena	zaščiščaet	gavan'	ot	morja	–	–	–	–	–	–	–
	'the wall	protects	the harbor	from	the sea'							
23.	my	očiščali	belyx	ot	mesta	–	–	–	–	–	–	–
	'we	cleared	the Whites	from	the place'							
24.	ja	ubereg	tebja	ot	niščety	–	–	–	–	–	+	+
	'I	guarded	you	from	poverty'							
25.	mama	vylečila	menja	ot	uvlečenija	–	–	–	–	–	–	+
	'mamma	cured	me	of	[my] passion'							

TABLE 21 (*cont.*)

	N^1	V_t	N^2	*ot*	N^3	T1: → N^1 V N^2 *ot* N^3 *k* N^4	T2: → A^{n3} N^1 V N^2	T3: → N^1 $V^{n3}_{(sja)}$	T4: → X V^{n3} N^1	T5: → N^3 V^{n2} (N^1)	T6: → N^1 Vt A^{n3} N^2	T7: → N^2 V^{n3}
26.	Galja	otgovarivala	ee	ot	želanija	–	–	–	–	–	–	+
	'Galja	dissuaded	her	from	the desire'							
27.	on	otvratil	Akulinu	ot	namerenija	–	–	–	–	–	–	+
	'he	turned away	Akulina	from	the intention'							
28.	on	očistil	žizn'	ot	grjazi	–	–	–	–	–	–	+
	'he	purified	life	of	[its] filth'							
29.	ženščiny	otščipyvali	kusočki	ot	vatina	–	–	–	–	–	+	–
	'the women	pinched off	bits	from	the wadding'							
30.	oni	otcepili	teplušku	ot	poezda	–	–	–	–	–	+	–
	'they	uncoupled	the heated car	from	the train'							
31.	on	otbil	kusok	ot	jakorka	–	–	–	–	–	+	–
	'he	knocked off	a piece	from	the anchor'							
32.	stul'ja	otgoraživajut	zonu	ot	zony	–	–	–	–	–	+	–
	'the chairs	fenced off	zone	from	zone'							
33.	on	otkleil	listok	ot	steny	–	–	–	–	–	+	–
	'he	unstuck	the list	from	the wall'							
34.	my	otkololi	povjazki	ot	šineli	–	–	–	–	–	+	–
	'we	unpinned	the bands	from	the coat'							
35.	on	otlomil	končik	ot	karandaša	–	–	–	–	–	+	–
	'he	broke off	the point	from	the pencil'							

36.	oni	vylomali	ramu	ot	dveri	–	–	–	–	–	+	–
	'they	broke off	the frame	from	the door'							
37.	oni	otlučili	verootstupnika	ot	cerkvi	–	–	–	–	–	+	–
	'they	excommunicated	the apostate	from	the church'							
38.	on	otpajaet	nosik	ot	apparata	–	–	–	–	–	+	–
	'he	unsolders	the spout	from	the apparatus'							
39.	ja	otdelil	pisatelja	ot	napisannogo	–	–	–	–	–	–	+
	'I	separated	the writer	from	that which is written'							
40.	on	ostereg	ee	ot	ošibok	–	–	–	–	–	+	+
	'he	warned	her	against	mistakes'							
41.	on	spas	ee	ot	smerti	–	–	–	–	–	–	+
	'he	saved	her	from	death'							
42.	sovet	osvobodil	brata	ot	uplaty	–	–	–	–	–	–	+
	'the council	freed	[his] brother	from	fees'							
43.	on	otučil	menja	ot	privyčki	–	–	–	–	–	–	+
	'he	broke	me	of	the habit'							

semantic or derivational groups and are consequently of little interest. The transforms concerned are T6 ($N^1 V_t N^2$ *ot* $N^3 \rightarrow N^1 V_t A^{n3} N^2$: *oni otcepili teplušku ot poezda* 'they uncoupled the heated car from the train' → *oni otcepili poezdnuju teplušku* 'they uncoupled the train's heated car') and T7 ($N^1 V_t N^2$ *ot* $N^3 \rightarrow N^2 V^{n3}$: *on očistil žizn' ot grjazi* 'he purified life of [its] filth' → *žizn' grjaznilas'* 'life became soiled').

The list of verbs in these examples appears to be very similar, if not identical, to that found in the ablative $N^1 V_{sja}$ *ot* N^2 units. Apart from two features, the verbs are notable only for their lexical and morphological diversity. The first of these unifying features is the high frequency of the *ot-* and *u-* prefixes that yield the typical ablative prefix + verb + *ot* pattern. The second feature is the tendency of verbs to possess the property of *strong government.*[108]

These two related features are reflections of the dependency pattern that opposes the ablative examples to those of the *Causal* and *Source groups*. In the causal examples, it was demonstrated that the dependency of N^3 was on the subject noun, *(e.g., satana gložet kosti ot zlosti* 'Satan gnaws the bones because of spite' → *zlostnyj satana* 'spiteful Satan'). For the *Source group*, N^3 shared the closest syntactic linkage with N^2 as reflected in the possible rearrangements: *on zaslužil uprek ot sestry* 'he merited the reproach from [his] sister' → *sestrin uprek* 'the sister's reproach' or *sestra uprekaet* 'the sister reproaches'. For the *Ablative* (and the *Spatial) group*, the primary syntactic dependency of N^3 is on the *prefixed* verb. Transformationally this is demonstrated only negatively in that, for ablative examples, N^3 cannot be shown to be syntactically dependent upon either the subject noun (N^1) or the object noun (N^3) as can be shown for the other two groups. This leaves the verb as the only possible head for *ot* N^3. From the traditional point of view, this syntactic relationship is not morphologically expressed. This is not entirely accurate, however, since the relationship is not only formally expressed but expressed in a very striking way. The verbs of the *Ablative group* typically utilize the device of reduplication to mark the relationship between themselves and *ot* N^2. The internal structure of the ablative N^1 V (N^2) *ot* N^3 units is not V + *ot* N, but OT-*V*-OT → N.[109] The second *ot* is not a *pre*-position of N, but a *post*-position of V, which serves to link N^3 to the verb.

4.4. CONCLUDING REMARKS

The purpose of the foregoing analysis has been the resolution of syntactically ambiguous homomorphs of the general structure N V (N) *ot* N and, more specifically, to isolate and formally characterize each of the semantic groups subsumed within the three constructional types. In other words, the study

[108] See pages 114 and 136–137 above for a discussion of this syntactic property.
[109] The OT- symbolizes all of the prefixes that are used in the *Ablative* sense.

attempts to ascertain what formal features are correlated with various intuitively identified semantic groups contained in the construction in question. The primary analytic technique has been transform analysis, although other procedures have been utilized where they provided results not attainable within the limits of the kinds of transformations used herein.

The present study differs from previous ones in that it utilizes various formal features that have been drawn upon only marginally in earlier analyses. On the syntactic level, these features include:[110] 1) co-occurrence privileges, 2) the category of transitivity, and 3) the strong/weak government opposition. The morphological features fall into two groups. The first, that of inflectional morphology, is only of marginal interest and is largely dependent on the above-mentioned syntactic features. The second, and more important group of features, is that under the heading of derivational morphology. These features can be divided into three subdivisions: 1) root structure, *i.e.*, whether a verb is of nominal or of verbal origin; 2) suffixation patterns, particularly those pertaining to verb classes; and 3) prefixation patterns — ablative versus all other types including the prefixless. Transformations utilize all of these features in an integrated fashion, although some features lend themselves to transformational manipulation more easily than others. For example, transformational procedures are particularly convenient and effective for the determination of co-occurrence privileges, but much less so for handling prefix patterns.

By the use of transformations and supplementary morphological data, the following three major semantic classes within the N V *ot* N structures were isolated:[111] 1) spatial, 2) ablative, and 3) causal. The association of each of these semantic groups with one or more formal features was demonstrated. This linkage is not on an absolute basis, but in terms of the relative frequency with which certain formal features were associated with certain semantic groups.

The spatial examples of the three structural types were all isolated and characterized by the admissability of supplementary prepositional complementation. Spatial examples are relatively much more frequent within the N^1 Vø *ot* N^2 constructional type than in the remaining two constructional patterns. In all types the verbs of the *Spatial group* are distinguished by the rarity of ablative prefixes.

The *Ablative group* is generally characterized among all three structural types by its low susceptibility to transformation. Its salient features are those of strong government and the ablative prefix pattern. Examples of these types

[110] It is not meant to suggest that these features are independent of each other. Their interrelations and interdependencies are many and complex.

[111] The *Source group* is small and its nature differs considerably among the three structural types. It will not be included in the following comments.

are the most frequent among examples of the transitive verb construction. It is infrequent among examples of the unmarked intransitive verb construction.

The causal examples form the most strongly marked group in terms of several types of criteria. They constitute the majority type for both of the intransitive verbal constructions, whereas they are a peripheral type for the transitive verbs. This group is the one most successfully characterized by the transformations and is also the one most sharply defined in terms of derivational criteria. It is opposed to the *Ablative group* in its possession of the following three characteristics: 1) intransitivity, 2) predominance of non-verbal roots, and 3) weak government.

The *Academy Grammar* sets forth roughly the same three major categories.[112] Thus from the point of view of the number of classes, the present analysis cannot claim superiority over the system of the *Academy Grammar*. The superiority of the system offered above is that it provides a formal definition of semantic classes in terms of rigorous assignment procedures for the classifying of examples. There are a large number of cases for which the transformations do not make such assignments, but a considerable portion of these may be handled on the basis of other formal and semi-formal criteria. Unfortunately, there still remains a sizable residue of cases where purely semantic criteria offer the only apparent solution to the resolution of constructional verbal homomorphs. The transformations also offer a degree of insight into the basis of some of the categories and the examples. The results for the *Causal group* are the most satisfactory on this count.

Our investigation does provide an answer to the question about which word in the N V *ot* N unit is the key to the generic meaning of the phrase. The systems of Šaxmatov, Peškovskij, and the *Academy Grammar* agree in assigning this role to the dependent noun. The above investigation shows that almost all formal features that oppose homomorphic examples of different semantic types reside in the head word — that is, in the verb. This conforms to our findings for the nominal and adjectival constructions.

It will be noted that the analysis of the verbal constructions is somewhat less effective than that of the nominal units in isolating semantic subgroups and providing them with formal specifications. The reasons for this are not altogether clear but would appear to include at least two general factors. Our investigation has shown that transformation analysis is intimately connected with derivational morphology. It is equally clear that the nominal elements

[112] The *Academy Grammar* also establishes temporal categories and an attributive-circumstantial category. No examples were found in our corpus outside of the examples in the *AG*. Both groups are simply small sets of fixed word-combinations (*e.g.*, *bolet' ot kolybeli* 'to be ill from the cradle' or *skazat' ot vsej duši* 'to say from the soul') and hence were not included in our analysis.

of Russian morphology are much more easily categorized derivationally than the verbal elements. Hence, it is not surprising that transform analysis is less effective with verbal constructions than with nominal ones. A second and closely correlated reason for weaker performance of the technique on verbal units lies in the fact that the grammatical and semantic structure of the Russian verb is much more complex and much more poorly understood than that of the noun. A more satisfactory analysis of the N V *ot* N unit, and of homomorphic verbal constructions generally, must await the attainment of a much deeper understanding of the Russian verb.

A SELECTED BIBLIOGRAPHY

Akademija Nauk SSSR, Institut jazykoznanija, *Grammatika russkogo jazyka*. 2 vols. (Moscow, 1954), 2nd ed. 1960

— —, *Osnovnye napravlenija strukturalizma*, eds. M. M. Guxman, V. N. Jarceva (Moscow, 1964)

Apresjan, Ju. D., "K voprosu o strukturnoj leksikologii", *Voprosy jazykoznanija*, XI (1962), 38–46

— —, "O sil'nom i slabom upravlenii (opyt količestvennogo analiza)", *Voprosy jazykoznanija*, III (1964), 32–49

— —, "Sovremennye metody izučenija značenij i nekotorye problemy strukturnoj lingvistiki", *Problemy strukturnoj lingvistiki*, ed. S. K. Šaumjan (Moscow, 1963), 102–50

Axmanova, O. S., *Očerki po obščej i russkoj leksikologii* (Moscow, 1957)

— —, "Slovosočetanie", *Voprosy grammatičeskogo stroja* (Moscow, 1955), 452–60

Babkin, A. M., "Predlogi kak ob"ekt leksikografii", *Leksikografičeskij sbornik*, III (1958), 69–76

Bach, Emmon, *An Introduction to Transformational Grammars* (New York, 1964)

Bielfeldt, Hans Holm, *Rückläufiges Wörterbuch der russischen Sprache der Gegenwart* (Berlin, 1958)

Bloomfield, Leonard, *Language* (New York, 1933)

Bondarenko, V. S., *Predlogi v sovremennom russkom jazyke* (Moscow, 1961)

Bukatevič, N. N., *Opyt istoričeskogo izučenija predlogov i predložnyx sočetanij v russkom literaturnom jazyke*. 2 vols. (Odessa, 1957, 1958)

Čerkasova, E. T., "K izučeniju obrazovanija russkix otymennyx predlogov", *Issledovanija po grammatike russkogo literaturnogo jazyka: sbornik statej*, eds. N. S. Pospelov, N. Ju. Švedova (Moscow, 1955), 73–139

— —, "K voprosu ob obrazovanii otglagol'nyx predlogov", *Issledovanija po sintaksisu russkogo literaturnogo jazyka* (Moscow, 1956), 131–76

Chomsky, Noam, "Current Issues in Linguistic Theory", *The Structure of Language*, eds. Jerry A. Fodor, Jerrold J. Katz (Englewood Cliffs, New Jersey, 1964), 50–118

— —, "Degrees of Grammaticalness", *The Structure of Language*, eds. Jerry A. Fodor, Jerrold J. Katz (Englewood Cliffs, New Jersey, 1964), 384–9

— —, "On the Notion 'Rule of Grammar' ", *Proceedings of the Twelfth Symposium in Applied Mathematics*, XII (1961), 6–24; also in *The Structure of Language*, eds. Jerry A. Fodor, Jerrold J. Katz (Englewood Cliffs, New Jersey, 1964), 119–51

— —, *Syntactic Structures* (The Hague, 1957)

— —, "A Transformational Approach to Syntax", *The Structure of Language*, eds.

Jerry A. Fodor, Jerrold J. Katz (Englewood Cliffs, New Jersey, 1964), 211-45
Daum, E., W. Schenk, *Die russischen Verben* (Leipzig, 1954)
Finkel', A. M., *Proizvodnye pričinnye predlogi v sovremennom russkom literaturnom jazyke* (Kharkov, 1962)
Galkina-Fedoruk, E. M., K. V. Gorškova, N. M. Šanskij, *Sovremennyj russkij jazyk: sintaksis* (Moscow, 1958)
Gleason, H. A., Jr., *An Introduction to Descriptive Linguistics*. Rev. ed. (New York, 1961)
Gvozdev, A. N., *Sovremennyj russkij literaturnyj jazyk, II: Sintaksis* (Moscow, 1961)
Halle, Morris, "O pravilax russkogo sprjaženija (Predvaritel'noe soobščenie)", *American Contributions to the Fifth International Congress of Slavists, I* (The Hague, 1963), 113–32
Harper, Kenneth E., *Machine Translation of Russian Prepositions* (= No. *P-1941*, May, 1960) (Mathematics Division, The Rand Corporation, Santa Monica, California)
— —, "The Position of Prepositional Phrases in Russian", *Mechanical Translation*, VIII (August, 1964), 5–10
— —, *Prepositional Phrases and Automatic Parsing (= Memorandum RM-4383-PR*, February, 1965). (The Rand Corporation, Santa Monica, California)
Harris, Zellig S., "Co-occurrence and Transformation in Linguistic Structure", *Language*, XXXIII (1957), 283–340; *The Structure of Language*, eds. Jerry A. Fodor, Jerrold J. Katz (Englewood Cliffs, New Jersey, 1964), 155–210
— —, "Discourse Analysis", *The Structure of Language*, eds. Jerry A. Fodor, Jerrold J. Katz (Englewood Cliffs, New Jersey, 1964), 355–83
Herodes, St., "Staroslavjanskie predlogi", *Issledovanija po sintaksisu staroslavjanskogo jazyka: sbornik statej*, ed. J. Kurz (Prague, 1963), 313–68
Iordanskaja, L. N., *Dva operatora dlja obrabotki slovosočetanij s "sil'nym upravleniem" (dlja avtomatičeskogo sintaksičeskogo analiza)* (Moscow, 1961)
Isačenko, A. V., *Die Russische Sprache der Gegenwart, 1, Formenlehre* (Halle, 1962)
— —, *Grammatičeskij stroj russkogo jazyka v sopostavlenii s slovackim: morfologija.* 2 vols. (Bratislava, 1954, 1960)
— —, "Transformacionnyj analiz kratkix i polnyx prilagatel'nyx", *Issledovanija po strukturnoj tipologii*, ed. T. N. Mološnaja (Moscow, 1963), 61–93
Ivič, M., "Jedan problem slovenske sintagmatike osvetljen transformacionim metodom (grammatička uloga morfeme *se* u serbskoxrvatskom jeziku)", *Južnoslovenski filolog*, XXV (1961/62), 137–51
Jakobson, Roman O., "Beitrag zur allgemeinen Kasuslehre: Gesamtbedeutungen der russischen Kasus", *Travaux du Cercle Linguistique du Prague*, VI (1936), 240–88
— —, "The Relationship between the Genitive and the Plural", *Scando-Slavica*, III (1957), 181–6
Janko-Trinickaja, N. A., *Vozvratnye glagoly v sovremennom russkom jazyke* (Moscow, 1962)
Josselson, Harry, H., *The Russian Word Count* (Detroit, Michigan, 1953)
Kačalina, N. S., "Struktura substantivnyx predložnyx slovosočetanij s zavisimym suščestvitel'nym v roditel'nom padeže (na materiale sovremennogo russkogo literaturnogo jazyka)". Avtoreferat kandidatskoj dissertatii (Moscow, 1963)
Kalabina, S. I., "Ispol'zovanie metoda transformacionnogo analiza pri issledovanii semantičeskix svojstv slovosočetanij", *Naučnye doklady vyšsej školy (= Filologičeskie nauki)*, 3 (1962), 63–72
Kalnberzin', R. Ja., "Vyraženie pričinnyx otnošenij slovosočetanijami s predlogom 'ot' i roditel'nym padežom suščestvitel'nogo v sovremennom russkom jazyke (na

materiale polnogo sobranija sočinenij A. M. Gor'kogo)", *Latvijas PSR, Zmanu Akademijas, Vestis*, XI (1956), 49–56

Kolesnikov, N. P., "O sintaksičeskoj omonimii v russkom jazyke", *Russkij jazyk v škole*, III (1960), 20–2

Kovtunova, I. I., "O sintaksičeskoj sinonimike", *Voprosy kultury reči*, I (1955), 115–42

Kuryłowicz, J., "Dérivation lexicale et dérivation syntaxique (contribution à la théorie des parties du discours)", *Bulletin de la Société de Linguistique de Paris*, XXXVII (1936), 79–92

Kuznecova, O. D., "O dvux značenijax glagolov zvučanija v tolkovom slovare russkogo jazyka", *Leksikografičeskij sbornik*, III (1958), 97–102

Lees, Robert B., "Čto takoe transformacija?", *Voprosy jazykoznanija*, X (1961), 69–77

— —, *The Grammar of English Nominalizations* (Bloomington, Indiana, Research Center in Anthropology, Folklore, and Linguistics, 1960)

— —, "O pereformulirovanii transformacionnyx grammatik", *Voprosy jazykoznanija*, X (1961), 41–50

— —, Review of Noam Chomsky, *Syntactic Structures* (The Hague, 1957), *Language*, XXXIII (1957), 375–408

Lomtev, T. P., *Očerki po istoričeskomu sintaksisu russkogo jazyka* (Moscow, 1956)

— —, *Osnovy sintaksisa sovremennogo russkogo jazyka* (Moscow, 1958)

Lynch, Irina, "Russian -sja Verbs, Impersonally Used Verbs, and Subject/Object Ambiguities", *1961 International Conference on Machine Translation of Languages and Applied Language Analysis, II* (London, 1961), 477–502

Manolova, V. P., *Transformation of Russian Syntagms of the Type $S + S$, $S + P$, $V + S$, $V + P + S$* (Moscow, 1962) English translation published by the U. S. Joint Publications Research Service, Washington, D. C. *(= JPRS*, 19.053, 6 May 1963), 28–71

Meščaninov, I. I., *Členy predloženija i časti reči* (Moscow, 1945)

Nazikova, E. A., "Vyraženie pričinnyx otnošenij v sovremennom russkom literaturnom jazyke". Unpublished candidate's dissertation (Leningrad, 1952)

Neuhauser (Worth), Gerta, "Les locutions calques dans le Russe moderne". Unpublished.

Nikolaeva, T. M., "Čto takoe transformacionnyj analiz?", *Voprosy jazykoznanija*, IX (1960), 111–5

— —, "Transformacionnyj analiz sočetanij s prilagatel'nym — upravljajuščim slovom", *Transformacionnyj metod v strukturnoj lingvistike*, ed. S. K. Šaumjan (Moscow, 1964), 142–68

Obnorskij, S. P., *Očerki po morfologii russkogo glagola* (Moscow, 1953)

Padučeva, E. V., A. L. Šumilina, "Opisanie sintagm russkogo jazyka (V svjazi s postroeniem algoritma mašinnogo perevoda)", *Voprosy jazykoznanija*, X (1961), 105–15

Palevskaja, M. F., "Omonimija kak sledstvie leksikalizacii otdel'nyx grammatičeskix form i perexoda slov iz odnoj časti reči v druguju", *Russkij jazyk v škole*, III (1960), 15–9

Papp, Ferenc, "Transformacionnyj analiz russkix prisubstantivnyx konstrukcij s zavisimoj čast'ju — suščestvitel'nym", *Slavica*, I (Debrecen, 1961), 55–83

— —, "Transformacionnyj analiz russkix prisubstantnnyx konstrukcij s zavisimoj čast'ju — suščestvitel'nym v roditel'nom padeže", *Studia slavica Academiae scientiarum Hungaricae*, VII (1961), 195–206

Paustovskij, K., *Povest' o žizni*. 2 vols. (Moscow, 1962)

Peškovskij, A. M., *Russkij sintaksis v naučnom osveščenii*. 7th ed. (Moscow, 1956)

Pittman, R. S., "Nuclear Structures in Linguistics", *Readings in Linguistics*, ed. M. Joos (New York, 1958), 375–8

Popova, L. N., "O značenii predloga v sovremennom russkom jazyke (Predlog ot +

roditel'nyj padež v značenii pričiny)", *Učenye zapiski Leningradskogo gosudarstvennogo universiteta*, 235 (= *Serija filologičeskix nauk*, 38) (1958), 190–208
— —, "Pričinnye ottenki nekotoryx predlogov v russkom jazyke", *Naučnye doklady vysšej školy (= Filologičeskie nauki)*, 3 (1958), 32–42
Potebnja, A. A., *Iz zapisok po russkoj grammatike* (Moscow, 1958)
Prokopovič, N. N., "K voprosu o prostyx i složnyx slovosočetanijax", *Voprosy jazykoznanija*, VIII (1959), 21–31
— —, "K voprosu o roli slovoobrazovatel'nyx svjazej častej reči v postroenii slovosočetanij", *Issledovanija po grammatike russkogo literaturnogo jazyka: sbornik statej*, eds. N. S. Pospelov, N. Ju. Švedova (Moscow, 1955), 140–58
— —, "O vlijanii slovoobrazovatel'nyx svjazej častej reči na postroenie slovosočetanij", *Voprosy jazykoznanija*, II (1953), 37–52
Revzin, I. I., *Modeli jazyka* (Moscow, 1962)
— —, V. Ju. Rozencvejg, *Osnovy obščego i mašinnogo perevoda* (Moscow, 1964)
Rixter, G. I., "Sintaksičeskaja sinonimika v sovremennom russkom jazyke", *Russkij jazyk v škole*, 3 (1937), 14–33
Rudnev, A. G., *Sintaksis sovremennogo russkogo jazyka* (Moscow, 1963)
Ružička, R., "O transformacionnom opisanii tak nazyvaemyx bezličnyx predloženij v sovremennom russkom literaturnom jazyke", *Voprosy jazykoznanija* (1963), 22–31
Samarina, E. S., "Slovosočetanija s predlogom 'ot' v russkom jazyke", *Trudy Tbiliskogo pedagogičeskogo instituta*, XV (1960), 229–36
Šanskij, N. M., "O proisxoždenii i produktivnosti suffiksa *-ost'* v russkom jazyke", *Voprosy istorii russkogo jazyka* (Moscow, 1959), 104–31
Šaumjan, S. K., "Teoretičeskie osnovy transformacionnoj grammatiki", *Novoe v lingvistike, II* (Moscow, 1962), 391–411
— —, P. A. Soboleva, *Applikativnaja poroždajuščaja model' i isčislenie transformacij v russkom jazyke* (Moscow, 1963)
Šaxmatov, A. A., *Sintaksis russkogo jazyka*. 2nd ed. (Leningrad, 1941). Photomechanic reprint (The Hague, 1963)
— —, *Sintaksis russkogo jazyka: učenie o predloženii i o slovosočetanijax*. Vypusk pervyj (Leningrad, 1925)
Šmelev, D. N., "O 'svjazannyx' sintaksičeskix konstrukcijax v russkom jazyke", *Voprosy jazykoznanija*, IX (1960), 47–60
Štejnfel'dt, È. A., *Častotnyj slovar' sovremennogo russkogo literaturnogo jazyka* (Tallin, 1963)
Šumilina, A. L., "Sinonimika v krugu glagol'no-imennyx prostranstvennyx slovosočetanij s predlogami *u, pri, pod, okolo, podle, bliz, vblizi*", *Russkij jazyk v škole*, 6 (1961), 25–30
Slovar' russkogo jazyka, comp. S. I. Ožegov (Moscow, 1960)
Slovar' sovremennogo russkogo literaturnogo jazyka, 17 vols., Akademija Nauk SSSR, Institut russkogo jazyka (Moscow–Leningrad, 1950/65)
Sørenson, H. C., *Studies on Case in Russian* (Copenhagen, 1957)
Sovremennyj russkij jazyk: morfologija, sintaksis, ed. E. M. Galkina-Fedoruk (Moscow, 1964)
Sovremennyj russkij jazyk: sintaksis, ed. E. M. Galkina-Fedoruk (Moscow, 1957)
Sovremennyj russkij jazyk, II, Sintaksis, ed. E. M. Galkina-Fedoruk (Moscow, 1958)
The Structure of Language: Readings in the Philosophy of Language, eds. Jerry A. Fodor, Jerrold J. Katz (Englewood Cliffs, New Jersey, 1964)
Suxotin, V. P., "Iz materialov po sintaksičeskoj sinonimike v russkom jazyke", *Issledovanija po sintaksisu* (Moscow, 1956), 5–47

— —, "Problema slovosočetanija v sovremennom russkom jazyke", *Voprosy sintaksisa sovremennogo russkogo jazyka*, ed. V. V. Vinogradov (Moscow, 1950), 127–82
— —, *Sintaksičeskaja sinonimika v sovremennom russkom literaturnom jazyke: glagol'nye slovosočetanija* (Moscow, 1960)
Tesnière, Lucien, *Éléments de syntaxe structurale* (Paris, 1959)
— —, *Esquisse d'une syntaxe structurale* (Paris, 1953)
Toporov, V. N., "O transformacionnom metode", *Transformacionnyj metod v strukturnoj lingvistike*, ed. S. K. Šaumjan (Moscow, 1964), 74–87
Vaillant, André, *Grammaire comparée des langues slaves: Morphologie, I*, Part 1, *Flexion nominale* (Paris, 1958)
Valgina, N. O., D. È. Rozental', M. I. Fomina, V. V. Capukevič, *Sovremennyj russijk jazyk*. 2nd ed., rev. (Moscow, 1964)
Vasmer, M., *Russisches Etymologisches Wörterbuch*. 3 vols. (Heidelberg, 1953)
Veselitskij, V. V., "Podača sostavnyx predlogov i sojuzov v slovare", *Leksikografičeskij sbornik*, III (1958), 77–83
Vinogradov, V. V., *Iz istorii izučenija russkogo sintaksisa* (Moscow, 1958)
— —, "Ponjatie sintagmy v sintaksise russkogo jazyka (kritičeskij obzor teorii i zadači sintagmatičeskogo izučenija russkogo jazyka)", *Voprosy sintaksisa sovremennogo russkogo jazyka*, ed. V. V. Vinogradov (Moscow, 1950), 183–256
— —, *Russkij jazyk: grammatičeskoe učenie o slove* (Moscow–Leningrad, 1947)
— —, ed., *Sovremennyj russkij jazyk: morfologija* (Moscow, 1952)
— —, "Voprosy izučenija slovosočetanija (Na materiale russkogo jazyka)", *Voprosy jazykoznanija*, III (1954), 3–24
Volockaja, Z. M., "Ustanovlenie otnošenija proizvodnosti meždu slovami (Opyt primenenija transformacionnogo metoda)", *Voprosy jazykoznanija*, IX (1960), 100–7
Walter, H., "Die Struktur der Reflexiven Verben in der modernen bulgarischen Literatursprache", *Zeitschrift für Slawistik*, VIII (1963), 793–806
White, James H., "The Methodology of Sememic Analysis with Special Application to the English Preposition", *Mechanical Translation*, VIII (August, 1964), 15–31
Worth, Dean S., "Ob otobraženii linejnyx otnošenij v poroždajuščix modeljax jazyka", *Voprosy jazykoznanija* (1964), 46–58
— —, "The Role of Transformations in the Definition of Syntagmas in Russian and Other Slavic Languages", *American Contributions to the Fifth International Congress of Slavists, Sofia, 1963*, 361–83
— —, "The Suffix -AGA in Russian", *Scando-Slavica*, X (1964), 174–93
— —, "Transform Analysis of Russian Instrumental Constructions", *Word*, XIV (1958), 247–90
— —, "Transformation Criteria for the Classification of Predicative Genitive Constructions in Russian", *1961 International Conference on Machine Translation of Languages and Applied Language Analysis, II* (London, 1961), 725–35
Worth, Gerta Hüttl, *Foreign Words in Russian: A Historical Sketch, 1550–1800* (= *University of California Publications in Linguistics*, XXVIII) (Berkeley–Los Angeles, 1963)
Zasorina, L. N., "Opyt sistemnogo analiza predlogov sovremennogo russkogo jazyka (Predlogi so značeniem pričiny)", *Učenye zapiski Leningradskogo gosudarstvennogo universiteta*, 301 (1961) (= *Serija filologičeskix nauk*, 60), 64–81
— —, "Transformacija kak metod lingvističeskogo èksperimenta v sintaksise", *Transformacionnyj metod v strukturnoj lingvistike*, ed. S. K. Šaumjan (Moscow, 1964), 99–113

INDEX OF AUTHORS

20. ROBERT T. OLIPHANT: The Harley Latin-Old English Glossary, edited from British Museum, MS Harley, 3376. 1966. 223 pp. Gld. 48.—
21. ERICA REINER: A linguistic Analysis of Akkadian. 1966. 155 pp., graph. Gld. 36.—
22. M. J. HARDMAN: Jaqaru: Outline of Phonological and Morphological Structure. 1966. 131 pp., 2 figs., map, 20 tables Gld. 30.—
23. MARVIN K. MAYERS: (ed.), Languages of Guatemala. 1966. 318. pp. Gld. 48.—
24. ROBERT LIVINGSTON ALLEN: The Verb System of Present-Day American English. 1966. 303 pp., 7 tables, 24 figs. Gld. 46.—
26. ANDREW MCLEISH: The Middle English Subject. Verb Cluster. 1969. 276 pp. Gld. 70.—
27. EMMA GREGORES and JORGE A. SUÁREZ: A Description of Colloquial Guarani. 1967. 248 pp. Gld. 54.—
29. HOWARD W. LAW: The Obligatory Constructions of Isthmus Nahuat Grammar. 1966. 73 pp., 21 tables Gld. 21.—
30. MARVIN H. FOLSOM: The Syntax of Substantive and Nonfinite Satellites to the Finite Verb in German. 1966. 96 pp. Gld. 21.—
31. DEBI PRASSANA PATTANAYAK: A Controlled Historical Reconstruction of Oriya, Assamese, Bengali and Hindi. 1966. 91 pp. Gld. 27.—
32. ABDELGHANY A. KHALAFALLAH: A Descriptive Grammar of Saεi:di Egyptian Colloquial Arabic. 1969. 124 pp. Gld. 36.—
33. H. M. ABOEL-FETOUH: A Morphological Study of Egyptian Colloquial Arabic. 1969. 150 pp. Gld. 42.—
34. SAUD M. GAMAL-ELDIN: A Syntactic Study of Egyptian Colloquial Arabic. 1967. 117 pp. Gld. 36.—
35. H. MARCOS HANNA: The Phrase Structure of Egyptian Colloquial Arabic. 1967. 58 pp. Gld. 21.—
36. IRMENGARD RAUCH: The Old High German Diphthongization: A Description of a Phonemic Change. 1967. 130 pp. Gld. 30.—
37. JOSEPH HAROLD FRIEND: The Development of American Lexicography, 1798-1864. 1967. 129 pp. 4 facs. Gld. 32.—
38. WILLIAM J. SAMARIN: A Grammar of Sango. 1967. 280 pp. Gld. 72.—
39. DEAN H. OBRECHT: Effects of the Second Formant on the Perception of Velarization Consonants in Arabic. 1968. 104 pp., 57 figs. Gld. 29.—
40. YOLANDA LASTRA: Cochobamba Quechua Syntax. 1968. 104 pp. Gld. 29.—
41. KAZUKO INOUE: A Study of Japanese Syntax. 1969. 160 pp. Gld. 36.—
42. R. S. P. BEEKES: The Development of the Proto-Indo-European Laryngeals in Greek. 1969. xxiv + 324 pp. Gld. 82.—
43. HARWOOD H. HESS: The Syntactic Structure of Mezquital Otomi. 1968. 159 pp. Gld. 40.—
44. PAUL W. PILLSBURY: Descriptive Analysis of Discoures in Late West Saxon Texts. 1967. 91 pp. Gld. 21.—
45. MADELINE ELIZABETH EHRMAN: The Meaning of the Modals in Present-Day American English. 1966. 106. pp. Gld. 21.—
46. VIKTOR KRUPA: Morpheme and Word in Maori. 1966. 83 pp., 26 tables, 1 fig. Gld. 24.—
47. JOHN C. FISHER: Linguistics in Remedial English. 1966. 71 pp., 4 tables Gld. 15.—